Navigating Business Information Sources

a practical guide for information managers

Maria E. Burke
Department of Information and Communications,
Manchester Metropolitan University

Hazel Hall
Department of Communication and Information Studies,
Queen Margaret College, Edinburgh

Library Association Publishing
London

Published by
Library Association Publishing
7 Ridgmount Street
London WC1E 7AE

Library Association Publishing is wholly owned by The Library Association.

First published 1998

British Library Cataloguing in Publication Data

A catalogue record for this book is available from the British Library.

⊤ ISBN 1-85604-258-8

Typeset in 101/13pt Century Schoolbook and Geometric 415 by Library Association Publishing.
Printed and made in Great Britain by Bookcraft (Bath) Ltd, Midsomer Norton, Somerset.

100174131

For our students: past, present and future

Contents

Foreword by David Kaye   ix
Preface   xi
Acknowledgments   xv
Introduction   xvii

Part 1 Defining business   1

1   The structure and growth of business   3
2   The legal status of businesses   24
3   Company finance   39
4   Investments and markets   66

Part 2 Defining information sources   85

5   Information in business   87
6   Information as a resource   97
7   Information formats   106

Part 3 Identifying business information sources   123

8   Company information sources   125
9   Marketing information sources   147
10   International trade information sources   162
11   Statistical information sources   177
12   Advertising and distribution information sources   189

**Part 4 Identifying business regulations and
          control   209**

13   Patents   211
14   Trade marks and related issues   233
15   Standards and regulations   243

Index   255

Foreword

My book *Information and business* appeared in 1991. A reading of this new work by Maria Burke and Hazel Hall demonstrates clearly how much change has taken place in only seven years in the business information world. It is a pleasure to see how effectively the authors have incorporated a mass of new material, particularly in online and Internet services, which have mushroomed in recent years. At the same time, it is gratifying to note that my original concept of marrying the study of business information sources to the understanding of business *per se* has worn well and underlies the new work. This book will appeal at once to its intended audience and I am delighted to commend it to all those with an interest in this fascinating and important sector of the information world.

David Kaye

Preface

In *Information and business*[1] David Kaye recognized the crucial importance of providing business information managers with an understanding of business *per se*, as well as the actual sources used in support of business. His work became the standard text for the teaching of several generations of business, information management and librarianship students, as well a reference source for practising business information managers. The compilation of this new textbook on business information sources, which results from a review of the business information landscape in the late 1990s, owes much to *Information and business* for its structure and content.

Since the preparation of *Information and business* a further decade of technical advances and deregulation (with regard to particular industries and national boundaries), combined with increased trade freedom in much of the world, have had a profound impact on the types and organization of business enterprise. Companies now take advantage of sophisticated global IT infrastructures for the purposes of the movement of resources such as capital and information. Car production, computer manufacturing and fashion have grown into truly international industries. Transitional ownership through mergers and acquisitions across diverse industries such as entertainment, food, media and publishing, pharmaceuticals and telecommunications is common.

To the average consumer of the 1980s, the manifestations of these changes, and their impact on everyday business transactions, would have been unimaginable: the electricity board has been transformed into a one-stop shop for the supply of electricity, gas, telecommunications and water; families save and pay for goods with international digital currencies (airmiles); football fans follow their team both in the league and on the London Stock Exchange; a business sneeze in the Far East carries economic influenza to the north-east of England, where employment opportunities rely on inward investment incentives.

The shift from product-to-service, or product-with-service, based industries continues to bear on how business enterprises handle their relationships with customers and employees. The use of IT in a global economy gives the impression that business interactions are 'closer'. With improved customer proximity competitive firms know that their products and services can easily be replicated by rivals, thus offering further choice to the fickle consumer. Accountability has therefore become a key differential. The focus falls on keenly gauging performance, benchmarking activity and looking for continuous improvement. There is the need to measure the productivity of employees, including information workers. New forms of work organization – right-sizing, job sharing, teleworking, hot-desking, outsourcing – have been tested to derive the highest return on investment from personnel.

In response to general developments in the business world, improvements are sought in the established business information sources, and new types of material acquire importance. Legislation to handle the pace of development in global, multi-functional, high technology companies has had an impact on the sources the business information specialist might consult in dealing with enquiries. Throughout this book can be found examples of established sources that have changed format due to legal requirements, for example European Directives aimed at standardization of the presentation of statistics across the Community. The transition from print to electronic media as the dominant format for information storage and retrieval, and the convergence of previously separate media such as text graphics and sound into multimedia resources, has not only widened the options for the delivery of information services, but also raised general awareness of the value of information.

The mainstream press is, at last, interested in information as a business resource, as demonstrated by its coverage of the Reuters reports on information as an asset[2] and information overload,[3] and features on topics such as knowledge management.[4] As recently as the early 1990s conversations would grind to a halt if a business information specialist started to explain to a generalist that part of routine enquiry work included the use of online sources. Now, with the term Internet in common usage, it has become so much easier to further the discussion, with the non-specialist having much to contribute.

This is not necessarily good news for those aiming to promote quality business information services. End-users of business information who work in well-resourced organizations now have a variety of options for the consumption of business information services, some of which seem not to require the involvement of business information specialists. The proliferation of cheap desk-top machines, running standardized software with common interfaces, sets the stage for the marketing of push technologies, which supply information according to predetermined criteria. These commercial information service providers work in alliance with technolo-

gy companies to deliver disintermediated online access to business information. Here lies a threat to effective business information provision,
where the assumption might be that since *sources* are so easily accessible
and convenient, centralized *services* are no longer necessary. A number of
commercial information units have fallen victim to attempts to 'redefine',
'reorganize' or 'transform' corporate information services provision, particularly in organisations on downsizing missions.[5]

Business information managers must therefore prove the worth of their
services in providing information that can, for example, lead to better
decision making (and the avoidance of poor decisions); move projects from
one stage to the next; facilitate improved relationships with clients; exploit
new business opportunities; save money and time. The business information
specialists' training in the discriminatory techniques of the selection,
acquisition, abstracting, cataloguing, classification, indexing and packaging
of information resources should be promoted. This can be achieved through
exercising the established basic principles of integrated information services
provision: offering expertise in the content and selection of the best available sources – be they print, online or even grapevine – and demonstrating
commitment to putting knowledge at work, linking information users to the
right resources at the right time. Strategies for achieving this – for example
liaising with commercial information service providers in taking sources to
the desk-top, playing an active role in combatting information overload,
demonstrating to colleagues the difference between sources (alone) and a
value-added service (sources plus) – are described in this book.

Kaye wrote in 1991 that there 'has never been a better time than now
for business information'. We believe this still to be the case for those who
can capitalize on the growing recognition of the contribution of efficient
information services provision to the balance sheet, and who can demonstrate their worth in providing integrated, tailored services to meet users'
needs.

Maria E. Burke and Hazel Hall

References

1 Kaye, D., *Information and business*, London, Library Association
   Publishing, 1991.
2 Reuters Business Information, *Information as an asset: the invisible
   goldmine,* London, Reuters, 1995.
3 Reuters Business Information, *Dying for information?*, London,
   Reuters, 1996.

4 *Financial Times information technology supplement*, 1 October 1997.
5 Matarazzo, J.E., 'Measuring the value of the corporate information resource', *Proceedings of the 21st International Online Meeting, London, 9–11 December 1997*, Oxford, Learned Information, 71–2.

Acknowledgments

Many people helped with the compilation of this book, to whom we owe our thanks. We would particularly like to note the support of Karen Blakeman, Owen Claxton, Dorothy Connor, Elisabeth Davenport, Jill Feldt, Tony Foster, Alyn Jones, David Kaye, Shaun Moores, Chris Preston, Stephen Ramsey, Tim Read, Jacqueline Stone, Kenny Walker, Steve Wallace, Sheila Webber and Hywel Williams, as well as colleagues in our respective departments.

A work such as this cannot be completed without guidance from practising information specialists. We would like to acknowledge the information services staff of Manchester Business Link, Manchester Business School, Manchester Chamber of Commerce, the Office for National Statistics, Queen Margaret College and the Scottish Business Information Service at the National Library of Scotland.

Introduction

The primary purpose of *Navigating business information sources: a practical guide for information managers* is to introduce readers to the business information landscape in the UK, with particular reference to the key print and electronic information sources. The material is organized into four parts. The first covers the context in which businesses operate; the second how information sources might be defined; the third the major business information sources; and the final part covers sources related to business regulations and control. The book has been designed for a variety of readers and requirements:

- Lecturers and students of business and information management can use the book as a course textbook for a series of linked modules.
- Practising information professionals with new responsibilities for business information services provision will find in Parts 1, 3 and 4 a grounding in the context of business information and the major sources.
- General business managers will find Parts 2, 3 and 4 useful in consolidating their interest in business information management.
- Established business information practitioners will find it useful to address an area outside their own expertise.

The pace of change in this area is such that it is inevitable that some detail in this book will be out of date before it reaches the hands of its intended readership: indeed, market meltdown in the Far East and the purchase of Knight Ridder by MAID in autumn 1997 necessitated the revision of chapters prepared only that summer. In addition, information that was unavailable when the book went to press will now be in the public domain. For these reasons readers are urged to follow up the advice on keeping up to date with business information issues, as outlined in Chapter 7 on information formats.

Armed with this guide to the major business information sources it is hoped that those concerned with business information services provision will be able to familiarize themselves with the business information landscape and thus effectively meet business information needs.

Part 1
Defining business

1 The structure and growth of business

1 Introduction

Every industry has its own particular structure. For example, motor-car manufacture is dominated by a handful of very large firms, while garment-making is characterized by hundreds of small ones. It is also instructive, indeed essential, to look at the structure of industry as a whole in the United Kingdom. Structural information on the national scale is perhaps more useful to the economist or to the government planner, while the structure of individual industries is more relevant to business. This chapter examines the ways in which industry structure can be studied, and introduces some key sources of information in this area. The structure of industry is not static of course, but changes as businesses grow, diversify and relocate. This chapter therefore also looks at some factors affecting company size and location and examines some commonly used concepts in business growth. It should be noted that the term 'industry' is used in this context to refer not merely to manufacturing and production industries in the narrow sense, but to all kinds of occupational activity. Thus the police, local government, the National Health Service and the armed forces, are all considered as industries, along with more obvious sectors such as catering or banking.

2 Structure of business

A natural first step is to divide industry by types, such as agricultural, extractive (mining, quarrying etc.), manufacturing, distribution (wholesaling, retailing, transport), personal services, and so on. This division is important, as we shall see. The main ways of classifying industrial activity are by:

- industry sector
- institutional classification (by ownership)
- geographical area
- size of firm.

Combinations of two or more of these are, of course, possible and often necessary.

2.1 Classification by industry sector

The official classification scheme for British industry is the *Standard industrial classification (SIC)*[1] produced by the Central Statistical Office in 1992. It was first issued in 1948 and revised in 1958, 1968, 1980 and 1992. The *SIC* provides a uniform framework for the collection, tabulation, presentation and analysis of data about economic activity. The 1980 revision applied the classification of the Statistical Office of the European Communities (Eurostat) to the structure of British industry. This European classification is known as *NACE*.[2] In 1990 *NACE* was revised and published as a regulation, so the UK was obliged to introduce *SIC(92)* (up until Spring 1998 the US Census Bureau used the US Standard Industrial Classification; this was replaced by the North American Industry Classification *(NAIC)*, details of which are available from the US Census Bureau web site.)

Table 1.1   *Sections of the Standard Industrial Classification (1992)*

A	Agriculture, hunting and forestry
B	Fishing
C	Mining and quarrying
D	Manufacturing
E	Electricity, gas and water supply
F	Construction
G	Wholesale and retail trade; repair of motor vehicles, motorcycles and personal and household goods
H	Hotels and restaurants
I	Transport, storage and communication
J	Financial intermediation
K	Real estate, renting and business activities
L	Public administration and defence; compulsory social security
M	Education
N	Health and social work
O	Other community, social and personal service activities
P	Private households with employed persons
Q	Extra-territorial organizations and bodies

In *SIC(92)* industry is first divided into Sections, some sections being sub-divided into Sub-sections. The Sections are in turn divided into divisions, the Divisions into Groups, the groups into Classes and the Classes into Sub-classes. Altogether there are 17 Sections, 14 Sub-sections, 60 Divisions, 222 Groups, 503 Classes and 142 Sub-classes. The Sections and Sub-sections are denoted by letters; digits are used to label all other subdivisions. Table 1.1 (page 4) shows the 17 Sections and Figure 1.1 gives an example of the hierarchy.

Section D Manufacturing
  Sub-section DM Manufacture of transport equipment
    Division 34 Manufacture of motor vehicles, trailers and semi-trailers
      Group 34.2 Manufacture of bodies (coachwork) for motor vehicles; manufacture of trailers and semi-trailers
        Class and Sub-class 34.20/3 Manufacture of caravans

Fig. 1.1   *Example of headings and sub-headings of SIC(92)*

The *SIC* and the two companion *Indexes*[3] are essential tools for the user of many official business statistics. One index lists each heading of the *SIC* numerically, followed by a list of characteristic activities included within the heading; the other index arranges the activities alphabetically and gives the numerical heading by which the activity is classified. (The classification for *SIC 1980* is also given.) For example, there are eleven entries for the word 'caravan' in the alphabetical index, as shown in Table 1.2.

Table 1.2   *Example of alphabetical index of SIC(92)*

SIC 1992	SIC 1980	Activity
55.22	6670	Caravan sites
34.20/3	3523	Caravan trailers, mfr.
34.20/3	3522	Caravan, chassis, mfr.
34.20/3	3523	Caravan, mfr.
34.20/3	3523	Caravan, repairing
50.10	6510	Caravan, retail dealing in
55.22	6670	Caravan, site operator/owner/proprietor, holiday caravans
70.20/2	8500	Caravan, site operator/owner/proprietor, residential caravans/mobile homes
50.10	6148	Caravans, wholesale dealing in
71.21/1	8480	Caravans, renting of
63.21	7610	Caravans, winter storage of

The *SIC* is used to classify many official statistics, including those pro-duced by the Business Statistics Group at the Office for National Statistics (ONS) in the publication of its annual sample enquiry into production and construction (*PRODCOM*).[4] The *Product sales and trade AR* series are the annual reports based on data collected from UK manufacturers by the ONS and HM Customs and Excise. The reports include data on UK pro-duction (manufacturer sales), exports, imports, the balance of trade and net supply to the UK market. *PRODCOM* covers around 4800 products from approximately 250 manufacturing industries. Information is pub-lished for each product and an aggregate for each industry. The 90 *AR* annual reports cover around 3400 products from 200 industries. The remaining 50 industries are surveyed quarterly and published separately.

Suppose we wish to identify a publication that would establish the value and volume of the UK sales of caravans. (This might be useful to a compa-ny to calculate its own share of UK exports; the net supply of caravans to the UK; the level of the import of caravans to the UK net supply and aver-age prices.) Report *AR75* on motor cycles, trailers and miscellaneous trans-port equipment covers Sub-class 34203 Caravans and report *AR90* on motor vehicles includes reference to the manufacture of motor vehicles in the product group 34100 – motor vehicles. It would therefore be useful to consult both of these reports.

As with all statistics of this kind, care must be taken when interpreting any data from sources such as the *PRODCOM* surveys: some data are aggregated; some are suppressed so that individual companies cannot be identified; some are rounded, therefore totals and other calculated values may not always agree with those calculated from the individual compo-nents shown in the tables; and some data are not available. The time of data collection and the limits of the group surveyed (smaller firms are not included) make a difference to statistics presented.

The caravan example above highlights the sources that use *SIC(92)* to establish the value to the UK economy of a given sector. More generally we could discover the numbers of enterprises over all appropriate Sections or Divisions of *SIC(92)*. Thus Table 5 of *Business monitor PA1002: manufac-turing summary volume*[5] shows that in 1994 1756 businesses were engaged in the manufacture of motor vehicles, trailers and semi-trailers, i.e. in the industry sector represented by Division 34 of *SIC(92)*.

Table 1.3   *Businesses engaged in the manufacture of motor vehicles, trailers and semi-trailers in 1994 (note that the totals are rounded)*

SIC(92)		Size group	Businesses	Employment		
				Total	Operatives	Administrative technical and clerical
				Thousand	Thousand	Thousand
34	Manufacture	1–9	711	3.1)		
	of motor	10–19	280	4.5)	23.5	7.6
	vehicles,	20–49	314	11.1)		
	trailers and	50–99	161	12.7)		
	semi-trailers	100–199	112	16.3	12.6	3.7
		200–299	52	13.3	10.1	3.1
		300–399	33	11.4	8.6	2.8
		400–499	20	8.8	6.8	2.0
		500–749	37	22.6	16.6	6.0
		750–999	15	12.6	8.7	3.8
		1000–1499	9	10.2	7.3	2.9
		1500–1999	3	5.0	4.0	1.0
		2000–2499	3	6.8	4.8	2.0
		2500–7499	3	14.6	10.4	4.2
		7500 and over	3	74.3	56.0	18.3
		Total	1756	227.2	169.5	57.5

Business Monitor PA1002: Table 5, Manufacturing summary volume, Office for National Statistics, Crown Copyright, 1997.

A much wider approach is to use *Business monitor PA1003: size and analysis of UK business*,[6] which analyses UK businesses by size. It covers legal units registered for VAT, whether or not their turnover is above or below the VAT threshold (in November 1996 the VAT threshold was set at £48,000). The VAT-exempt industries are excluded; i.e. betting, gambling and lotteries; burial and cremation; cultural services; education; finance; fund raising events by charities; health and welfare; insurance; land; postal services; sports; trade unions and professional bodies; art. The survey previously used the VAT Trade Classification and now provides figures according to *SIC(92)*.

Table 1.4 *Breakdown of VAT registered businesses in 1996*

Industry	VAT registered units
Agriculture	154,700
Production	156,950
Mining/quarrying	1,955
Manufacturing	154,990
Construction	175,080
Motor trades	70,615
Wholesale	113,980
Retail	215,170
Hotels and catering	102,725
Transport	65,085
Post and telecommunications	6,040
Finance	11,900
Property and business services	312,945
Education	5,895
Health	9,405
Public administration and other services	137,160

Business Monitor PA1003: Size and analysis of UK businesses, Office for National Statistics, Crown Copyright, 1996.

PA1003 is significant in covering businesses other than limited companies, and it gives analyses, similar to that shown in Table 1.4, separately for sole proprietors, partnerships, and government and non-profit making organizations. The introduction to *PA1003* notes that, excluding companies with a turnover of zero, in 1996 34% of all units were corporate businesses, 39% were sole proprietors, 25% partnerships and 2% government and non-profit making organizations. It is also interesting to note that property and business services was the largest sector, accounting for 20% of all units, followed by retail, with 14% and construction with 11%.

The British Chamber of Commerce's monthly *Business point*[7] provides a current awareness service on industry, employment, environment, taxation, transport, overseas trade, Europe, retail, health and safety, and education and training news. Major stories that relate to the structure of industry in the UK may be seen in *Business point* ahead of their publication in the official sources noted above.

2.2 Institutional classification (ownership)

A more general way of classifying businesses is to be found in the *Sector classification for the national accounts*[8] which has been used primarily for the annual ONS publication *United Kingdom national accounts*[9] (sometimes referred to as the *CSO blue book*). This scheme was devised for use with national economic measurements, such as the gross domestic product (GDP), and therefore encompasses households, local authorities and other economic units, as well as businesses as commonly understood. The broad outline of the scheme is as follows:

100	Personal sector
110	Individuals and households (including private trusts)
120	Unincorporated businesses
130	Private non-profit making bodies serving persons
140	Life assurance and pension funds (income and expenditure)
200	Corporate sector
210	Industrial and commercial companies
220	Financial companies and institutions
221	Banks
222	Building societies
223	Life assurance and pension funds (capital and financial accounts)
224	Other financial institutions
230	Public corporations
300	Central government
310	Central government
311	Trading
312	Non-trading
313	Social security funds
320	Local authorities
321	Trading
322	Non-trading
400	Overseas sector

Note that from 1998 the sector codes are changed. The new system uses the *Sector classification for the national accounts methodological guide*[10] which is compatible with the *European system of accounts classification: ESA 1995.*[11]

2.3 Geographical classification

It is instructive to study the geographical distribution of business and industry, which is important both for commercial reasons, for example in planning the location or relocation of businesses, and for purposes of government policy, for example in the distribution of economic assistance to deprived areas.

For over 30 years England was divided for statistical purposes into eight regions, and these together with Wales, Scotland and Northern Ireland were known as the Standard Statistical Regions: North; Yorkshire and Humberside; East Midlands; East Anglia; South East; South West; West Midlands; North West; Wales; Scotland; Northern Ireland. The use of these regions for *Regional trends*,[12] the comprehensive annual source of official statistics about regions of the UK, can be seen through the use of the CD-ROM compilation of 30 years of the publication.

During 1997, the primary classification of regional statistics in England changed so that it aligned with the Government Offices for the Regions. (Although Merseyside has a Government Office of its own, for statistical purposes it is not a region in its own right. Wherever possible in *Regional trends* figures for the North West and Merseyside regions are given separately.) The new English regions from 1997 became: North East; North West and Merseyside; Yorkshire and the Humber; East Midlands; West Midlands; Eastern; London, South East; South West. These, combined with Wales, Scotland and Northern Ireland make up the current regions for *Regional trends*. However, certain tables in *Regional trends* use other classifications, for example a few tables continue to be produced using the old Standard Statistical Regions, and some data are presented by Environment Agency regions, Regional Health Authority areas, Department of Trade and Industry regions and Tourist Board regions. This makes comparisons between regions on multiple commodity or service-fronts, and over time periods, extremely difficult. In June 1997 the ONS produced the *Gazetteer for the reorganised statistical regions and local authorities in the United Kingdom*[13] to help alleviate confusion in attempting to compare statistics based on the old and new geographies.

As an example of the use of the regions, *Regional trends*[14] *32* Table 5.8 could be consulted. This would show the industrial distribution at September 1995 of employees in employment. It gives a breakdown by gender, Government Office Regions and industry sectors according to *SIC(92)*. For example, in Scotland in September 1995 3.2% of male employees were working in agriculture, hunting, forestry and fishing, whereas in the London the figure was 0.1%.

2.4 Size of firm

The size distribution of businesses is very revealing. There is a very wide range of sizes, from the one-person owner-managed corner shop or plumbing business to the huge multinational, and all sizes are important to the economy in their own way. Size may of course be defined in different ways, for example by number of employees, nominal capital, turnover, market value, net worth, and so on. There are several directories that list firms in rank order which are useful for identifying the top companies, either generally or in a given sector. A prominent example in *The Times 1000 1996*[15] uses capital employed (i.e. shareholders' funds plus long-term debt, plus inter-group payables, plus deferred liabilities, minus technical reserves) as its main measure of size. Table 1.5 extracts from *The Times 1000* data for the 11 largest UK firms (showing their market capital, turnover and number of employees) in 1995. Between them ten of these firms employed over

Table 1.5 *The 11 largest UK firms, 1995*

Rank	Firm	Capital employed	Turnover	Employees
1	British Gas	24,639,000	9,698,000	69,971
2	British Petroleum Company	20,777,000	33,116,000	66,550
3	HSBC Holdings	20,637,000	13,975,000	106,861
4	Shell Transport and Trading Group	20,082,800	24,771,600	n/a
5	Abbey National	17,545,000	5,621,000	16,703
6	British Telecommunications	16,392,000	13,893,000	148,900
7	Hanson	14,832,000	11,199,000	74,000
8	National Westminster Bank	13,186,000	13,345,000	97,000
9	Barclays	11,562,000	13,429,000	95,700
10	Salomon Brothers Europe	11,086,900	2,406,300	1,024
11	Eurotunnel Group	9,604,644	30,598	2,302

The Times 1000 1996, Table I, The 1,000 largest industrial companies. Reproduced by kind permission of HarperCollins Publishers Ltd.

679,000 people (Shell Transport and Trading is excluded from this calculation since the number of employees is not stated). According to the *Monthly digest of statistics*,[16] the seasonally adjusted workforce (meaning the workforce in employment plus the unemployed claiming benefit) as at the year end of 1995 was 28,006,000. In short, ten of the 11 largest UK firms in 1995 employed between them about 4.1% of the total potential working population of the UK. (It must be borne in mind that this figure is arrived at by dividing two figures from different sources gathered at only approximately the same time.) This is a graphic reminder of the huge economic importance of some very large organizations. Little wonder, then, that the demise of such an organization can barely be contemplated by society, or that the takeover of one by a foreign firm or its privatization is so controversial.

Small firms, however, are also very important to the economy. It is often these that develop new technologies or products and are sometimes indeed founded to do just that. They may also provide a lot of support to large firms, selling them specialist components or services; for example the motor-car manufacturers are fed by a large number of ancillary firms supplying parts and materials. The smaller firms are also more flexible and can often switch production from one line to another much more quickly than larger firms. Taken collectively, small firms are also very significant in terms of employment. From Table 5 of *Business monitor PA1002*[17] (see Table 1.3 on page 7) for example, it can be calculated that in 1994 14% of employees engaged in the manufacture of motor vehicles, trailers and semi-trailers were employed in 1466 firms with fewer than 100 employees each, and 51% in 1735 firms with fewer than 1000 employees each.

3 Size, location and growth of business

3.1 Factors affecting size

The size and growth of firms are affected by a range of factors, which may encourage or inhibit growth. Some of the key factors are:

3.1.1 The availability of finance

In seeking money to expand, private companies are much more restricted than public ones (for the distinction between the two, see Chapter 2). Private firms may be able to borrow modestly from banks, persuade friendly individuals or organizations to invest privately, or simply plough back profits into the business. In addition to these means, public companies can raise capital by selling shares on the open market, and as some big flotations have shown in recent years, very large sums indeed can be raised in this way if the conditions are right. 'Going public' is often the key to real growth. The larger firms may also have long-established reputations which makes it easy for them to raise money. Thus the large get larger.

3.1.2 Changing technologies

New technologies render products obsolete and so firms overtaken in this way must adapt to change, develop new products and seek new markets. This may compel a firm to grow, by buying up other firms or by forms of diversification. Purchasing a going concern can be the quickest way to enter a new market.

3.1.3 Economies of scale

Operating on a large scale often reduces unit costs, because fixed costs and overheads are spread over more units of production. There may therefore be an incentive to install more capacity in order to achieve such economies of scale. Thus, automated production of motor-cars by robot assembly lines may offer labour savings and reduce unit costs, but must be done on a large scale, with big-volume markets, to make the investment pay off.

3.1.4 Changes in markets

Some markets are currently expanding all the time, for example holidays and leisure, food and drink; others, like the tobacco market, are shrinking. Changes of this kind are often linked to population trends and social changes. Expanding demand encourages existing firms to grow and new ones to enter the market. Contracting demand may have the opposite effect, though firms may respond by diversifying or changing the nature of their business.

3.1.5 Foreign competition

Foreign competition has proved to be a key factor in some trades, for example motor-car manufacture. The British Motor Corporation (as it once was), was originally formed, after several changes of fortune and with government help, by merging smaller firms like Austin, Morris and Rover. This was done partly because the original firms were too small to compete with the foreign giants such as General Motors. The strategy never really worked for various reasons, and the new group, although nominally a volume car producer, has never been in the same league as GM, Ford and the other big names. Although the Rover name lives on, ownership of the company in recent years has been with the Japanese company Honda and BMW of Germany.

3.1.6 'Empire building'

Some firms, especially those with charismatic leaders, seem to be driven by the desire simply to become bigger and own more. Richard Branson's Virgin empire is an example of this. The tendency also seems to run in the conglomerate type of firm such as Hanson.

The factors outlined above, and the concepts they introduce, are vital to an understanding of the dynamics of industrial structure. But we are interested also in sources, and statements like these should be substantiated. As an example, let us look at the evidence for some of the statements made in 3.1.4. Increased leisure time of individuals should lead to an expansion of the holiday market; thus, according to *Social trends*[18] British residents took 59 million holidays of four nights or more in 1995, an increase of 43% on the number taken in 1971. On the other hand, cigarette smoking by the population as a whole is on the decline; *Social trends* reports that in 1972/3 52% of men and 41% of women smoked, whereas in 1994/5 the figures were 28% and 26% respectively.

3.2 Factors affecting location

Why are businesses located where they are? There are several possible influences at work as follows:

3.2.1 Historical

In the 19th century coal and iron were often found and mined in close proximity, consequently steel and engineering industries grew up in these places because these essential raw materials were to hand and thus cheaper. Nowadays, even though all iron ore is imported and other fuels are available, firms may be committed to the same area because of heavy capital investment, the existence of a trained workforce and a traditional local culture of working in these trades, and the growth of supporting industries in the same area.

3.2.2 Tied industries

Coal mines, agriculture and quarrying are naturally sited where the minerals or the land happen to be located – obvious perhaps, but still worth stating.

3.2.3 Transport costs

Costs are incurred by moving raw materials on the one hand and finished goods on the other. A firm may choose to be located near the suppliers, near the market, or at some point in between. The nature of the product is important in this context. Thus, if a product loses weight in its manufacture, it may be best to be near the source of supply; for example canners of peas may well choose a location near the pea fields to avoid the cost of transporting the pods. If bulk or weight in respect of a given product is low in importance, then transport cost may not matter; for example, computer manufacture could be located almost without regard to transport, because the cost of moving the goods is very low compared with the high value of the finished product.

3.2.4 Labour

The existence of a pool of skilled and experienced labour, perhaps with a long tradition of the industry, could be a big influence on the choice of location.

3.2.5 Markets

The nature of the market will be a major consideration in some cases. Obviously, for example, businesses supplying personal services and retail outlets must be close to the customers. This will be an over-riding consideration for consumer retailing as distinct from business-to-business marketing.

3.2.6 The economics of concentration

If an industry has grown up in one place, other firms which supply it may choose to do likewise, so that their transport costs are minimized and they can more easily maintain contact with their customers and monitor activity in the trade. Thus, in the heyday of the Lancashire textile industry, manufacturers of textile dyes, weaving and spinning machinery, and so on, were also to be found in the same area, and many are still there, even though the cotton trade has been decimated since the Second World War.

3.2.7 Government policy

For political or economic reasons, governments of whatever colour have tried to encourage industry to develop in or relocate to certain areas, in order to offset unemployment, especially in those places where older industries like shipbuilding have declined. Various kinds of financial incentives have been employed since the 1940s, by both central and local government, and more recently by the European Union. Up to date information on grants available should be sought from Chambers of Commerce, Enterprise Trusts and the Business Link/Shop network.

3.2.8 Information technology

Recent developments in the convergence of computing and telecommunications technologies mean that some kinds of service businesses could be located almost anywhere, because both their raw materials and their products are simply forms of information which can be transferred great distances at low cost. Thus, investment services can be, and indeed often are, run in attractive off-shore locations, far from the big financial centres. Similarly teleworking has become a modern cottage industry.

3.3 Growth and diversification

Some factors affecting the size of firms have been outlined. It is also of interest to examine the patterns or modes of growth, because this introduces some commonly used concepts that aid our understanding of business strategy and the operation of markets. There are many discussions in the literature of the growth phenomenon; the following analysis is partly based on a book by Ansoff[19] to which the reader is directed for further discussion.

Product Mission*	Present	New
Present	Market penetration	Product development
New	Market development	Diversification

*or 'market'. Ansoff defines mission as 'an existing product need'.

Fig. 1.2   *The four main growth vectors*
(Reproduced by kind permission from Ansoff, H. I., *Corporate strategy*, London, Penguin Books, 1988, 109.)

The growth of a firm can be by a number of routes. Figure 1.2 illustrates the four main routes, or 'growth vectors', as he calls them. Broadly speaking, they consist of three kinds of expansion, and a fourth route, diversification, which may itself take different forms.

3.3.1 Market penetration

The firm continues to sell the same products to existing markets, but aims to obtain a greater share of the market. The goal is to increase the existing customers' rate of use, persuade competitors' customers to switch allegiance or attract non-users. This can be achieved by a variety of methods that may depend firstly on initiating a research campaign to increase the understanding of the potential market. Improved packaging and presentation, increased advertising expenditure, keener pricing and maximized distribution can be important in a campaign to increase market penetration.

3.3.2 Market development

The firm finds new markets for its existing products. To appeal to a new category of customer alternative media channels may be adopted for advertising, or previously untapped distribution channels may be used. It is also possible to use alternative promotional messages for an existing product to make it seem different: consider how Campbells has advertised its soup as a cooking ingredient.

3.3.3 Product development

The firm creates new products to replace the current ones, which may be becoming obsolete, or existing products are 'improved' by new features, types, sizes and ranges. The new products are still sold to the same markets. The car manufacturer which designs a new car that, unlike its previous model, can easily be converted to run on unleaded petrol, is putting product development into practice, as is the food manufacturer which brings out several ranges of the same basic product – such as coffee – and persuades the retailer to give over further shelf space to the line.

3.3.4 Diversification

In the fourth mode of growth, both the products and the markets are new to the firm. Diversification may take different forms. Figure 1.3, again reproduced from Ansoff, shows a possible breakdown. One very common form of diversification is vertical integration. In this mode of growth, a firm may diversify upwards, to secure its sources of supply, or downwards, to control outlets. For example, a manufacturer of aluminium sheets and billets could purchase a bauxite mine in the USA (upward integration) and a manufacturer of aluminium kitchenware (downward). Such a firm is said to be vertically integrated. In concentric diversification the growth pattern retains some common elements with the firm's present technology or types of customer, whereas in conglomerate diversification we are looking at completely unrelated technology and entirely new types of customer. A conglomerate is often a collection of unrelated subsidiaries acquired by a holding company purely as a financial investment, with no other common element of strategy. Diversification can be an extremely expensive option, but is often necessary if a company has a set target for growth that cannot be achieved otherwise.

Figure 1.4 shows how the diversification modes might be interpreted in a specific example, in this case a manufacturer of personal computers for home use and small business applications.

		New products	
	Products Customers	Related technology	Unrelated technology
New missions	Same type	Horizontal diversification	
	Firm its own customer	Vertical integration	
	Similar type	Concentric diversification	
	New type		Conglomerate diversification

Fig. 1.3 *Growth vectors in diversification*
(Reproduced by kind permission from Ansoff, H. I., *Corporate strategy*, 2nd rev. edn, London, Penguin books, 1977, 116.)

		New products	
	Products Customers	Related technology	Unrelated technology
New missions	Same type	modems, printers	electric cars
	Firm its own customer	silicon chips	paint, plastic housings
	Similar type	large mini-computers	office photocopiers
	New type	air-traffic control systems	bricks, tiles, building panels

Fig. 1.4 *Diversification modes for a manufacturer of personal computers*
(Adapted by kind permission from Ansoff, H. I., *Corporate strategy*, 2nd rev. edn, London, Penguin books, 1988, 158.)

It should be noted that the modes of expansion and diversification described above can take place in two ways: a firm may grow by increasing in size itself and developing its own activities; or it may grow by acquiring other existing businesses. The choice here is between 'make' and 'buy'. The latter option is often chosen because there might not be room in the market for another entrant, because it reduces competition, and because it is quicker and more convenient to purchase a going concern, with existing skills, goodwill and contacts, than to set up a new operation. Technically, acquisitions are made by purchasing some or all of the share capital of the target firm, either for cash, or by an offer of shares of the bidding company, or by a combination of both. Further discussion of such parents and subsidiaries will be found in Chapter 2.

Takeovers and mergers have become a very prominent feature of business in recent years, and some highly publicized cases have given the takeover a degree of notoriety. A development, imported from the USA where it is called the 'leverage buyout', enables smaller firms to take over much larger ones. This is done by borrowing money to finance the takeover, the money being raised by offering high-risk investments ('junk bonds' in US parlance). If the bid it successful, large parts of the target company will have to be sold off in order to pay the investors (asset stripping). The information industry has witnessed its own wave of takeovers and mergers in recent years and a number of concerns have been raised regarding their impact on customer services.[20]

Figures for the number and value of mergers are given in the quarterly dataset *Acquisitions and mergers within the UK*[21] published by the ONS. The most up-to-date official information is distributed at quarterly intervals in the series *First release: acquisitions and mergers involving UK companies*.[22] Its 13 May 1997 issue reported that in 1995 636 companies in the UK were acquired by overseas and UK companies. The figure for 1996 was 714.

Acquisitions and mergers may well be against the public interest of course, and the Monopolies and Mergers Commission (MMC) exists to enquire into and report on such matters as mergers, monopolies and anti-competitive practices. The MMC derives its powers from the Fair Trading Act 1973, the Competition Act 1980, the Deregulation and Contracting Out Act 1994 and a number of other acts related to specific industries such as utilities and broadcasting. Because of the privatization of nationalized industries the MMC has recently conducted fewer investigations into public sector bodies. It does not initiate investigations itself, and is permitted to enquire only into matters referred to it by another body or individual. Table 1.6 shows the sources of the MMC's work.

Table 1.6   *Sources of the MMC's work*

Type of inquiry	Governing legislation	Referral made by:
Monopoly	Fair Trading Act 1973	Director-General of Fair Trading, Secretary of State for Trade and Industry or certain Utility Regulators
Merger	Fair Trading Act 1973	Secretary of State
Newspaper merger	Fair Trading Act 1973	Secretary of State
Anti-competitive practices	Competition Act 1980	Director of Fair Trading or certain utility regulators
Public sector references	Competition Act 1980	Secretary of State
General references	Fair Trading Act 1973	Secretary of State
Restrictive labour practices	Fair Trading Act 1973	Secretary of State
Broadcasting	Broadcasting Act 1990	Independent Television Commission or holder of regional Channel 3 licence
Utility references		
Telecommunications	Telecommunications Act 1984	Director-General of Telecommunications
Gas	Gas Acts 1986 and 1995	Director-General of Gas Supply
	Gas (N Ireland) Order 1996	Director-General of Gas Supply for Northern Ireland
Water	Water Industry Act 1991	Director-General of Water Services
Electricity	Electricity Act 1989 Electricity (N Ireland) Order 1992	Director-General of Electricity Supply Director General of Electricity Supply for Northern Ireland
Railways	Railways Act 1993	Rail Regulator
Water merger	Water industry Act 1991	Secretary of State
Airports	Airports Act 1986 Airports (N Ireland) Order 1994	Civil Aviation Authority Civil Aviation Authority

Reproduced from *The role of the MMC,* 3.[23] In the table 'Secretary of State' refers to the Secretary of State for Trade and Industry.

The MMC's reports are presented to Parliament and published as command papers. In recent years it has averaged about 18 reports per annum;

therefore, as may be seen from the 1995 and 1996 total of 1450 acquisitions, cited above, the vast majority of deals go through without MMC intervention. The operations of the MMC are described in two official publications. The manner in which takeovers take place in Britain is unofficially controlled by the City itself. The rules are laid down in the *City code on take-overs and mergers*,[24] issued by the Panel on Take-overs and Mergers, which is located in the Stock Exchange. News, surveys and articles on mergers and buyouts worldwide are provided by the journal *Acquisitions monthly*[25] and *Amdata*, its database equivalent. *FT precedents* offers a similar service. A number of commercial online databases cover merger activity, for example *SDC worldwide mergers and acquisitions*.

References

1   Central Statistical Office, *Standard industrial classification of economic activities 1992*, London, HMSO, 1992.
2   Office for Official Publications of the European Communities, *NACE rev. 1: Statistical classification of economic activities in the European Community*, Luxembourg, Office for Official Publications of the European Communities, 1996.
3   Central Statistical Office, *Indexes to the standard industrial classification of economic activities 1992*, London, HMSO, 1993.
4   Office for National Statistics, *PRODCOM reports*, London, The Stationery Office, quarterly and annual.
5   Office for National Statistics, *Business monitor PA1002: manufacturing summary volume*, London, The Stationery Office, August 1997.
6   Office for National Statistics, *Business monitor PA1003: size analysis of UK business,* London, The Stationery Office, October 1996.
7   *Business point*, British Chamber of Commerce, monthly.
8   Office for National Statistics, *MA23 sector classification for national accounts*, 10th issue, London, The Stationery Office, 1996.
9   Office for National Statistics, *United Kingdom national accounts: the blue book*, London, The Stationery Office, annual.
10 Office for National Statistics, *Sector classification for the national accounts methodological guide*, London, The Stationery Office, 1997.
11 *European system of accounts classification: ESA 1995*, Luxembourg, Eurostat, 1996.
12 Office for National Statistics, *Regional trends: first 30 years*, London, The Stationery Office, 1996, CD-ROM.

13 Office for National Statistics, *Gazetteer for the reorganised statistical regions and local authorities in the United Kingdom*, Newport, ONS, 1997.

14 Office for National Statistics, *Regional trends 32*, London, The Stationery Office, 1997.

15 *The Times 1000 1996*, London, Times Books, 1995.

16 Office for National Statistics, *Monthly digest of statistics*, London, The Stationery Office, monthly. (Electronic version also available as a monthly dataset on disk.)

17 See Reference 5.

18 Office for National Statistics, *Social trends 27*, London, The Stationery Office, 1997. (CD ROM version of the first 25 years of *Social Trends* also available. Subsequent editions published irregularly in electronic formats: ASCII and CD ROM.)

19 Ansoff, H.I., *Corporate strategy*, 2nd rev. edn, London, Penguin, 1988.

20 Hall, H. and Butler, A., 'Mergers and take-overs in the online industry: impacts on information services provision and user satisfaction', *Proceedings of the 19th International Online Meeting*, London, 5–7 December 1995, 267–79.

21 Office for National Statistics, *Acquisitions and margers within the UK*, The Stationery Office, London, quarterly (electronic dataset).

22 Office for National Statistics, *First release: acquisitions and mergers involving UK companies*, London, Office for National Statistics, quarterly.

23 Monopolies and Mergers Commission, *The role of the MMC*, 5th edn, London, The Monopolies and Mergers Commission, 1996.

24 *City code on take-overs and mergers and the rules governing substantial acquisitions of shares*, 5th edn, London, Panel on Take-overs and Mergers, 1996.

25 *Acquisitions monthly*, Tudor House, monthly.

Web site

US Census Bureau   http://www.census.gov/

2 The legal status of businesses

1 Introduction

This chapter discusses types of business, families of firms, company registration and reporting and the use of company and business names. The object of the chapter is to set out the legal basis of business existence, with particular reference to the requirements for the disclosure of information and the role that Companies House plays in the UK as a depository for such information. (Note that in the UK a centralized system for filing accounts operates. In other countries, for example France and Spain, disclosure is made on a regional basis. Disclosure produces leaflets, for example *European corporate filings*, that outline the rules and regulations affecting the disclosure of company information.)

In the UK the Department of Trade and Industry frames British company law and regulates businesses. Reference is made to the relevant Acts of Parliament, the most important of these being the Companies Act, which was implemented in 1985 and amended in 1989. The annual report of the DTI[1] provides information on company law developments and can be used to see proposed changes to the detail of the law described in this chapter.

Note that the role of Companies House as a source of company information is considered with other company information sources in Chapter 8.

2 Types of business

There are three main kinds of business organization: sole traders, partnerships and companies.

2.1 Sole traders

A sole trader is a private person engaged in business. From the point of view of the law, the Inland Revenue, and so on, the sole trader is little different from any other individual. He or she is not required to register the business with anyone, nor to disclose financial details except for tax purposes, including VAT registration if the turnover is above the current VAT threshold. The sole trader's business does not have a legal existence separate from that of the owner. No information is available to the public about a sole trader, other than what he or she chooses to disclose, for example through advertising.

2.2 Partnerships

Solicitors, accountants and similar service professions usually operate as partnerships, which are regulated by the Partnership Act 1890, the Limited Partnership Act 1907, and certain sections of the Companies Act 1985. There two types of partnership – 'general' and 'limited' – and these are distinguished by the different allocations of liability of the partners.

In general partnerships, every partner is personally liable for the assets, liabilities and obligations of the business, just like a sole trader. The business as such has no separate legal existence. A general partnership is an example of an unincorporated association, such as a students' union, sports clubs or youth clubs. The property is jointly owned by the members and liability for contractual obligations falls only on the individual who authorizes the contract, not on the other members, nor on the association itself.

In limited partnerships, certain partners can enjoy limited liability, and the partnership is registered under the Act of 1907. This form is rarely used, as there must be at least one general partner with unlimited liability, and none of the limited partners may take any part in the management of the firm. If *all* partners wish to achieve limited liability, it is necessary to register the business as a limited company under the Companies Act as outlined below.

In general, the law prohibits partnerships of more than 20 persons, the intention being that larger businesses shall be registered limited companies. However, the Companies Act 1985 specifically permits solicitors, accountants and stockbrokers to have more than 20 partners, and the Secretary of State is empowered to make regulations exempting other groups from this rule. Groups exempted include surveyors, estate agents, land agents, estate managers, valuers, auctioneers, actuaries and insurance brokers.

There is special legislation for some unincorporated associations, for example trade unions, which can sue and be sued as separate entities distinct from the members and officers. Another group with special status is building societies, which are governed by the Building Societies, Banking and Financial Services Acts, and regulated by the Building Societies Commission.

2.3 Companies

In order to have any legal duties and rights, an entity must be a legal person. The law recognizes two types, namely 'natural' persons and 'artificial' persons. A natural person has legal rights and duties simply by being in existence, although, of course, they are varied for minors, persons of unsound mind, convicted criminals, and so on. Even the unborn child has certain well-established legal rights. An artificial person on the other hand obviously has no separate physical existence, but has been created by law. The description generally applies to a group of natural persons, in which the group as such has a separate legal personality of its own. These groups are therefore incorporated associations or, more simply, corporations. The concept of the artificial person can be criticized as illogical, but it has proved to be of immense practical value.

There are advantages of operating a business as a company. Firstly, the possession of legal personality means that the corporation can continue to exist, regardless of changes in the individual members. Indeed its 'life' can be terminated only under the law. The company can itself enter into contracts with other legal persons, natural or artificial; has rights and duties under the law; and can sue and be sued in the courts. The legal penalties that can be imposed on it are limited to fines or, in extreme cases, winding-up; imprisonment is not an option.

The second, and perhaps even more important, advantage of incorporation is that of limited liability. This means that the liability of members (shareholders) to meet the debts of the company is limited to the amount they have invested in it in the first place. It is no exaggeration to state that this principle has been a major factor in the development of western capitalism, because it enables limited risk-taking: an investor can decide in advance how much capital to risk, and is not threatened with the loss of other personal wealth if the company goes bankrupt. This, combined with the ability of public companies (these are defined below) to invite investment from the public at large, has meant that business organizations have been able to grow to considerable size, and has encouraged the deployment of large amounts of capital in the development of industry. Thus, although one person may be the only shareholder of a limited company and therefore, in a commonsense view, is indistinguishable from the company, the assets and liabilities of the company are nevertheless quite separate from those of the owner. Hence, the company could be wound up, still owing money to creditors, but the owner-shareholder would not have to meet the outstanding debts from his or her personal assets. Note that, for the protection of the public, in these and other circumstances a director could be disqualified from holding office as a company director for a period of years.

Associations can be incorporated in different ways: by royal charter, by statute, or by registration under the Companies Acts.

Formation of companies by royal charter

Historically, organizations such as the Hudson's Bay Company and the East India Company came into existence by the grant of a royal charter by the Crown. Nowadays, the royal charter is used only for learned societies and the like, and is of no commercial significance.

Formation of companies by statute

A corporation may be brought into existence by a public act of parliament, as was the case of the National Coal Board and British Rail. This method was mostly used to bring about nationalization and, more recently, privatization. In the past, private acts of parliament were also passed in order to create corporations, for example in the 18th century, when statutory companies were instituted in order to facilitate large public works such as canals and docks.

Formation of companies through registration under the Companies Acts

Registration under the Companies Acts is currently the only method of incorporation of any importance.

2.3.1 Defining companies by legal type

Legally, a company may fall into one of four categories: a private company limited by shares; a private company limited by guarantee; a private unlimited company; a public limited company. The main distinctions between these categories relate to liability, how the company may raise money and the number of officers.

Limitation by shares means that the liability of the shareholder is limited to his or her investment represented by the shares bought in the first place, always provided that the shares are fully paid up. If part of the agreed price is still outstanding when the company is wound up, the shareholder would have to pay the balance.

Limitation by guarantee means that a member agrees to pay a fixed sum if the company is wound up. This sum is written into the Memorandum of Association (see 4.2.1) of the company, and any member joining the company is bound by that memorandum. Liability to pay the guaranteed sum lapses one year after the member leaves the company. In practice, companies limited by guarantee are usually non-profit-making bodies such as societies.

An unlimited company resembles a partnership in that all members are individually liable for debts but, unlike a partnership, it has a separate legal personality. Under current law unlimited companies must be private companies, whereas formerly unlimited public companies existed. Unlimited companies are formed to avoid the problems associated with succession following death or bankruptcy in partnerships. An unlimited company does not have to file its accounts with Companies House (see 4.3.2).

A public company is a company limited by shares. (In the past it was possible to have a public company limited by guarantee. From 22 December 1980 no new companies limited by guarantee were permitted to have a share capital. The intention of the law was that public companies would in future be limited by shares only.) A public company's name ends with the words 'public limited company' or the abbreviation 'PLC' (or the Welsh equivalent) and its memorandum states that it is a public company. Public companies may offer shares or debentures for sale to the public at large, whereas private companies can sell shares only by private deals. Another distinction is that a public company must have a minimum issued share capital of £50,000, whereas a private company has no such restriction. A public company must have at least two directors, and a private company at least one. Every company must have a secretary and a sole director may not also act as the secretary. One effect of all this is that both types may have only two directors, of which one is the secretary. How plcs raise capital is discussed in the next chapter.

These and all other regulations governing the formation, management and winding up of companies are set out in the relevant acts, of which the most important is the Companies Act 1985 (amended 1989) which consolidated a variety of previous legislation. For fuller details readers should consult a current textbook related to business law.

2.3.2 Defining companies by size

Private companies are further defined by size. The size category into which a private company falls determines the detail of information to be made public, as will be outlined below. In November 1997 a small company was defined as one which met two of the three criteria since incorporation or, if not within the limits at incorporation, then for the current financial year and the one before:

- Turnover: £2.8 million or less
- Balance sheet total (i.e. total assets): £1.4 million or less
- Employees (average): 50 or fewer

For a medium company the following criteria applied:

- Turnover: £11.2 million or less
- Balance sheet total (i.e. total assets): £5.6 million or less
- Employees (average): 250 or fewer

3 Families of firms

As was pointed out in Chapter 1 there are many mergers and takeovers between companies, and many firms invest in other firms without intending to gain control. Ownership or part ownership of other firms is achieved by buying all or some of the shares of the target company. This process gives rise to families of firms, comprising parents, subsidiaries and associates. The following conventional definitions are often used:

- If firm A owns all the shares of firm B, then B is a wholly owned subsidiary of the parent A.
- If A owns more than 50% of the shares of B, then B is a subsidiary and A has a controlling interest and would be considered the parent.
- If A owns more than 20% but less than 50% of B's shares, the two firms will usually be referred to as associate companies.
- If A owns less than 20%, it will generally be regarded as just another shareholder, albeit a major one.

Holdings above a certain percentage in a public company must be drawn to the attention of the company by the shareholder. Under the Companies Act 1989, holdings of 3% or more must be so notified within two days. Such holdings are reported in the directors' report and accounts of the target company. Under the *City code on take-overs and mergers*,[2] a 30% holding, called the trigger level, obliges the shareholder to launch a full bid for the target company. It should be noted that voting powers at shareholders' meetings are in proportion to shareholdings, so that the owner of more than 50% of a firm's shares can always outvote other shareholders.

Sometimes two or more firms will combine temporarily (though perhaps for a period of years) to form a consortium. This is often done in order to undertake very large projects too big for one firm, such as the European Airbus and large civil engineering projects. A consortium does not involve a formal takeover or merger between firms, rather it is a contract between separate companies, but is usually given a name of its own, so that it looks like a distinct organization.

4 Company registration and reporting

4.1   The role of Companies House

Companies House is an executive agency of the Department of Trade and Industry. Its role is administrative rather than regulatory. It has five main functions:

- to register new companies
- to register documents delivered to it by registered companies under companies, insolvency and related legislation
- to provide company information to the public
- to dissolve and strike companies off the register
- to ensure that companies comply with their obligations in connection with the functions listed above.

The three main offices of Companies House are located in Cardiff, London and Edinburgh. There are satellite offices in Birmingham, Manchester, Leeds and Glasgow. Contact details of each office are given in Table 2.1.

The registration of a new company requires the initial deposit of certain documents with Companies House. Subsequently, existing companies must also make regular returns to Companies House. Companies' disclosure requirements are outlined below.

Table 2.1 *Offices of Companies House*

Office	Address	Telephone
Birmingham	Central Library, Chamberlain Square, Birmingham B3 3HQ	0121 233 9047
Cardiff	Crown Way, Cardiff CF4 3UZ	01222 388588
Edinburgh	37 Castle Terrace, Edinburgh EH1 2EB	0131 535 5800
Glasgow	7 West George Street, Glasgow G2 1BQ	0141 221 5513
Leeds	25 Queen Street, Leeds LS1 2TW	0113 233 8338
London	55–71 City Road, London EC1Y 1BB	0171 253 9393
Manchester	75 Mosley Street, Manchester M2 2HR	0161 236 7500

4.2 Registration documentation

There are several registration documents that a new company must submit to Companies House: the Memorandum of Association; the Articles of Association; Statement of Directors and Registered Office (form 10); Declaration of Compliance (form 12); and, in the case of the public issue of shares, the Prospectus. If everything regarding these documents is in order, a certificate of incorporation is sent within four weeks of receipt. Further details of required registration documentation can be found in the Companies House *Notes for guidance CHN 1*.[3]

4.2.1 Memorandum of Association

The Memorandum of Association represents the external face of the company. For all company types it states: the name of the company (with the addition of 'limited', 'Ltd', 'public limited company', 'PLC' or the Welsh equivalent as appropriate); the country in which the registered office is to be located; and the objects of the company (i.e. the purpose for which it was formed, usually written in as wide a manner as possible). It provides witnessed signatures of its subscribers. Except for private unlimited companies, the limited liability of members is stated. For private companies limited by shares and public limited companies, the share capital registered on incorporation and the number of shares taken up by subscribers are given. The Memorandum of Association for a PLC states that the share capital is the authorized minimum and gives the amount each member will contribute if the company is wound up.

4.2.2 Articles of Association

The Articles of Association represent the internal face of the company. They set forth the rules governing the conduct of meetings, voting procedures, appointment and powers of directors, and other regulations controlling the workings of the company.

4.2.3 Statement of Directors and Registered Office (form 10)

The Statement of Directors and Registered Office gives particulars of the first director(s) and secretary including their names, addresses, dates of birth, nationalities, occupations and details of directorships held in the last five years. Added to this information is the address of the company's registered office to which legal documents should be sent. Often this is not the main trading address of a company. In some cases it will be found that the registered address of a small private company is that of the company's solicitor or accountant.

4.2.4 Declaration of Compliance (form 12)

The Declaration of Compliance is signed by the solicitor engaged in the formation of the company, or by one of the persons named in the articles as a director or company secretary. It is a statutory declaration of compliance with all the legal requirements related to the incorporation of a company.

4.2.5 The Prospectus

Companies going public and existing companies issuing new shares must produce a prospectus, a copy of which must be deposited at Companies House. Designed to enable potential investors to decide whether or not to buy shares, the prospectus contains detail about the firm, such as its history, financial record, products and directors.

4.3 Continuing disclosure requirements

Subsequently, every company must deposit at Companies House an Annual Return and a copy of the company's accounts. Other changes that must be notified include new mortgages, changes of director and increases in the share capital. Companies are also obliged to keep statutory books, normally at the registered office. These contain further information for inspection. (A discussion of accounts in relation to information needs will be found in Chapter 3.) Fuller details of disclosure requirements are given in the Companies House *Notes for guidance CHN 19*.[4]

4.3.1 Annual Return

The Annual Return provides a snapshot of the company at a particular date. It notifies Companies House of the current registered office address, the present issued share capital and the class(es) of shares issued, a list of all shareholders with the amounts of their holdings, and the names and addresses of directors at the end of the accounting period.

4.3.2 Accounts

The accounts include: a profit and loss account (or income and expenditure account if the company is not trading for profit); a balance sheet signed by a director; a directors' report signed by a director or the secretary of the company; notes to the accounts and group accounts (where appropriate). There are reduced reporting requirements for small and medium-sized private companies, and for dormant companies. Unlimited companies do not generally file accounts.

4.3.3 Other disclosure requirements

The indebtedness of a company is a major consideration for investors, shareholders and other interested parties, and mortgages on the company's assets are therefore important items on which information may be sought. All new mortgages must be notified to Companies House, stating the amount, the date and type of mortgage, the assets against which it is charged, and the bank or other institution that has lent the money. Companies House also needs to be informed of appointments and resignations of the company's directors and secretary, changes in their particulars, changes to the registered office address and any changes to the Articles or

Memorandum. If the company goes into liquidation, receivership, administration or voluntary arrangement, Companies House must be told.

4.3.4 Statutory books

Companies are obliged to hold at the registered office (normally) registers of: members; directors and secretaries; interest in shares greater than 3%; directors' interests; debenture holders; and mortgages and charges. Minutes books for members' and directors' meetings should also be available.

4.4 Penalties for late reporting

In the case of public companies there exists, in effect, a bargain between the company and society. The company has the privileges of limited liability and of access to the public market for capital, and in return it should make information available to the public on which it depends. For all notifiable items, the law lays down periods of time within which Companies House must receive information from companies. For example, a public company must deposit a copy of its accounts within seven months of the end of the company's accounting reference period (financial year), a private company within ten months. In recent years Companies House has campaigned strongly to encourage compliance with the registration and filing requirements to be met by companies. In July 1992 late filing penalties were introduced and fines are now levied on those who submit their accounts late. Over 1000 directors are prosecuted personally each year. A compliance rate of under 50% in the early 1980s was increased to around 90% by the late 1990s.

5 Business names and company names

The choice of name for a business is a matter of great importance, since the name should be memorable and distinguish the business from other businesses. Like a trade mark or brand name, the name of a business may come to be associated with its reputation – the 'good name' of the business. For the protection of the public and the business, the use of names is regulated by law.

It is important to distinguish between business names and company names. A business name arises when the owner (person or company) of a business trades under a name which is not the name of the owner. A company name is the *registered* name of a registered company.

As an illustration, suppose the authors of this book were to open a sweet shop. They could put 'Maria Burke and Hazel Hall', 'M.E. Burke and H.J.R. Hall' or even just 'Burke and Hall' over the door and, because they would be trading under their own names, need take no further action. However, if they were to call the business 'Maria and Hazel's Chocolate Box', this would constitute a business name because they would no longer be trading under their 'real' names. Finally, they could register a private company, calling it perhaps 'Burke and Hall Ltd'; this would be the company's registered name. This is summarized in Table 2.2 below.

Table 2.2   *Trading and names*

Proposed shop name	Trading	Action
Maria Burke and Hazel Hall	Using own names	None required
ME Burke and HJR Hall	Using own names	None required
Burke and Hall	Using own names	None required
Maria and Hazel's Chocolate Box	Using a business name	Follow the provisions of the Business Names Act 1985 regarding choice of name and disclosure of information
Burke and Hall Ltd	Using a company name	Follow provisions of the Business Names Act 1985 and Companies Act 1985 (amended 1989) regarding choice of name and disclosure of information

5.1 Business names

Companies very often trade under shortened forms of their names (or own separate businesses with different names) and, as noted above, sole traders may use names that are not their own. This practice is regulated by law. Until 1982, the Registration of Business Names Act 1916 required the registration of such names, and the Register of Business Names, maintained by the DTI, revealed the true owners of these businesses. However, the Register was abolished, amid some controversy, by the 1981 Companies Act. Admittedly, about half of the 2½ million names in the register were said to have ceased trading, or to be inaccurate, but it was potentially a valuable information source. After its abolition, the London Chamber of Commerce tried for a time to operate the register as a private venture, but it was not a success.

The 1981 Act, which was later consolidated as the Business Names Act 1985, however, substituted new requirements which affect all businesses trading under business names as defined. In all such cases, businesses must disclose ownership through quoting the corporate name, name of each partner or individual person's name; and in relation to each person named, an address at which documents can be served. The information must be shown on all business letters, orders, invoices and receipts, and written demands for debts. The information must also be displayed prominently in any premises in which the business is carried on and to which customers or suppliers have access. The guidance notes issued by Companies House[5] state that the information must be 'easily seen' and in large premises businesses are advised that 'they may need to think carefully about the size of the notice and where you display it to make sure that all your customers and suppliers see it'. However, in practice it is often difficult to find such notices in premises where they should appear, and the reader may care to check this personally.

Examples of imaginary cases that would be affected are also given in the *Notes for guidance*.[6] A company called in full ABC Foods (Great Britain) Ltd might trade as ABC Foods, using the convenient short form on its vans, letterheads and so on. Such a company would have to comply with the requirements above. Even the mere omission of the letters PLC would be a case in point. For example, Marks and Spencer PLC uses the form 'Marks & Spencer' on shop signs, stationery and bags. In these instances the company (Marks and Spencer PLC) is using a business name ('Marks & Spencer'). Under the Business Names Act 1985 the correct name and address of the owner must be shown as elsewhere required. This may be verified by inspecting the reverse of any Marks & Spencer till receipt.

Since the Register of Business Names no longer exists, there is no independent way of checking the true owners of a name, and an enquirer would need to inspect the business' premises or its stationery, or consult the business itself; always supposing that the enquirer can in the first place make a guess as to the business or has some clue as to its identity. The law requires that the owner's name and address must be disclosed to anyone, for example a customer or supplier, with whom anything is done or discussed in the course of business, if that person asks for them; but this would not cover an enquiry from a third party, such as a public library. In certain circumstances, what appears to be a business name might in reality be a trade mark. For example, if a sole trader sets up business as a hairdresser and calls his business 'Snippets', it might be a business name, but it might equally be a registered (service) trade mark. In the latter case, ownership of the mark would be more easily established (see Chapter 14 on trademarks and related issues for details).

5.2 Company names

Companies House maintains an index of company names. Limited partnerships must be registered in the index, otherwise they will be treated as general partnerships. Every registered company must have a name, and the choice of name is governed by the Companies Act 1985. A company name will not be registered if (a) it is the same as a name already on the index maintained at Companies House; (b) it contains the words 'limited', or 'unlimited', or 'public limited company', or their abbreviations or Welsh equivalents, *except* at the end of the name; (c) in the opinion of the Secretary of State it is offensive or its use would constitute a criminal offence. In addition, interested parties, for example other companies with similar names, can object to a newly registered name, and the registering company can be directed to change its name within 12 months of registration if the name is too like an existing name. The use of certain classes of words also requires the prior approval of the Secretary of State, as does any name implying a connection with HM government or a local authority. Full details of the regulations, with examples, may be found in the guidance notes[7] issued by Companies House. A company's name must be displayed on the outside of every one of its places of business.

References

1   Department of Trade and Industry, *Companies in 1996–97*, London,

The Stationery Office, 1997.
2   *City code on take-overs and mergers and the rules governing substantial acquisitions of shares*, London, Panel on Take-overs and Mergers, 5th edn, 1996.
3   Companies House, *Notes for guidance 1 – new companies*, Cardiff, Companies House, 1996.
4   Companies House, *Notes for guidance 19 – disclosure requirements*, Cardiff, Companies House, 1997.
5   Companies House, *Notes for guidance 11 – The Business Names Act 1985*, Cardiff, Companies House, 1997.
6   See Reference 5.
7   Companies House, *Notes for guidance 3 – Companies Act 1985 – Sensitive words and expressions*, Cardiff, Companies House, 1996.

Web sites

Companies House	http://www.companies-house.gov.uk
Acts of Parliament	http://www.hmso.gov.uk/acts.htm#acts
Companies Act 1989 (summary)	http://www.hmso.gov.uk/acts/summary/01989040.htm

3 Company finance

1 Introduction

This chapter is concerned with capital structure, company financial accounting and related financial topics. These subjects, especially that of company accounts, are the ones that lay persons often find most difficult to deal with, and generate reactions ranging from boredom, through uncertainty, to near panic. The aim of the chapter is to show that any business information specialist can understand these topics well enough to be able to deal with the relevant information sources; certainly in this field, above all, the sources make no sense without an understanding of the background. The reader may take courage from the fact that neither author of this book is an accountant. The content of this section, therefore, represents the minimum that is considered necessary in order to be able to use information sources effectively. The reader will be able to build on this minimum by wider reading and experience.

There are whole libraries dealing with these areas and the choice of texts is enormous. A general introduction to company finance and non-specialist explanations of company accounts may be found in many texts such as Holmes and Sugden,[1] Oldcorn[2] and Brett.[3] Treatments of business ratios will be found in Holmes and Sugden. A more detailed text for students of accounting is the work by Wood.[4] Further treatment of stocks and shares will be found in Brett and Gough[5] and both of these texts will be found useful in the context of Chapter 4, which discusses investments and the operation of the London Stock Exchange.

2 Capital structure

In order to develop and grow, a business must find capital funds. These funds may be provided by ploughing profits back into the business, but money may also be raised externally by selling shares (subject to the restrictions on private companies noted in Chapter 2 on the legal status of business) and by borrowing. A comprehensive reference work on sources of business finance is the *UK business finance directory*,[6] covering all sectors such as banks, insurance companies, the stock market and venture capital.

The two main kinds of business funds are referred to as share capital and loan capital.

2.1 Share capital

A share represents money invested in a company in return for the hope or expectation of a return. (Note that outside the UK shares are called 'stock'. In the UK 'stock' usually refers to British Government stock or gilts, which are described later in this chapter.) The shareholder is an owner or part-owner of the company. Two kinds of return may be realised: that is, the company may pay a dividend to the shareholder, out of profits, and/or (in the case of public companies) the share may increase in value, and so be sold at a profit. It is equally true that a company does not have to declare a dividend, even if it is in profit and that, in the time-honoured phrase of investment publicity, shares can go down in value as well as up. The workings of the stock market are outlined in Chapter 4 on investments and markets. As was observed in the previous chapter (the legal status of business), a share also represents the extent of liability of the shareholder for the debts of the company. Share capital represents the long-term capital of the company. The various terms used to refer to this capital need explanation.

2.1.1 Authorized capital

Authorized capital is the number, type and nominal value of the shares that a company is empowered by its Memorandum of Association to issue. Thus the authorized capital of a firm might consist of, say, 200,000 ordinary shares of £1 each and 100,000 5% preference shares (see 2.2.2) of £1 each, making a total authorized capital of £300,000. The nominal value of the share is its face value, in this case £1, so that we can also refer to the nominal capital, which is the same as the authorized capital.

2.1.2 Issued capital

A company is not bound to issue, or sell, all its authorized shares. Thus the imaginary company above might decide that it can acquire sufficient resources to start the business with only £150,000 of ordinary share capital. It will therefore have an issued capital of £150,000 and be able to sell a further £50,000-worth of ordinary shares later.

2.1.3 Called-up capital

A firm may sell shares but ask initially only for part-payment. So, 150,000 shares might be offered for sale at par (nominal value). If the company asks initially for a payment of, say, 70p per share, with 30p to be paid later, then the called-up capital will be 70p x 150,000 = £105,000. The remaining £45,000 is the uncalled capital.

2.1.4 Paid-up capital

If all shareholders have paid the amount asked for, the capital is said to be paid-up. This will be the same as the called-up capital, unless some shareholders are in arrears. Suppose, in the case above, that a shareholder still owes £2,000. Then the paid-up capital will be £103,000. If the company has called the full amount of £1 per share and all shareholders have paid, the capital is said to be fully paid up (in this case £150,000).

The market value of a share may be more or less than the nominal value, according to market conditions. New shares may be, and often are, offered for sale at a higher price than the nominal value, or may immediately start trading at a price higher than the asking price. The difference is called a premium. It is, however, illegal to offer shares for sale at a discount to par value.

A company can easily increase its authorized capital according to the regulations set out in its articles. This usually entails a resolution of the shareholders. However, a company may reduce its capital only under strictly controlled conditions, and then only with the permission of the courts. The chief reason for this is that any such reduction would prejudice the interests of the company's creditors, because the capital would be reduced by buying back shares from the shareholders. This would involve a reduction of the assets available to pay debts.

2.2 Types of shares

The two main kinds of shares are ordinary and preference shares.

2.2.1 Ordinary shares

These are sometimes also called equity shares. The ordinary shareholders are the main risk-bearers of a company, because in a bad year they may receive no dividend and the value of their shares may fall. Equally, ordinary shares can increase in value and give high dividends. These shares are the main object of speculation in the stock market.

Because ordinary shareholders take the risks, they are also entitled to a say in the management of the firm (depending on the number of shares held and the status of the shareholder), consequently ordinary shares are the only ones to which voting rights are attached.

2.2.2 Preference shares

Holders of preference shares receive a fixed dividend payment annually (5% in the example above) in preference to ordinary shareholders. Consequently, if a company decides that there is enough money only to pay the preference share dividend, ordinary shareholders will receive nothing. Preference shares are of two kinds; non-cumulative and cumulative. In the former case, if available profits in one year are insufficient to cover the preference dividend, then it cannot be made good in a following year. However, in the case of cumulative preference shares, any deficiency is carried forward (cumulated) and paid later when profits permit.

Preference shareholders bear much less risk than ordinary shareholders, and have no voting rights unless their dividend is in arrears.

2.3 Rights issues

A common way of issuing new shares to raise more capital is by a rights issue, which means that existing shareholders have the right to purchase the new shares before they are made generally available (pre-emptive rights), although they do not have to take up the offer. The offer is in proportion to the shareholder's existing holding and is described as a '1 for X' rights issue. Thus a company with an ordinary share capital of £100 million might make a '1 for 10' rights issue, which means that £10m-worth of new shares would be on offer, raising the capital to £110 million. A shareholder with 5000 shares would be entitled to buy 500 new ones. Rights issues are usually offered at a price lower than the current market price of the share, as an inducement to buy, but after a rights issue the market price adjusts to reflect the fact that the total value of the company is now divided into more shares and therefore each share is worth less. Suppose a firm's shares are currently valued at £2 on the market, and it makes a '3 for 8' rights issue, offering the new shares at £1.75 each. A shareholder taking up the right would have eight existing shares at £2 each (£16) and three new ones at £1.75 each (£5.25), making a total of £21.25 for 11 shares. The value of each share is now therefore £21.25/11 = approximately £1.93, and this is about the price at which the stock market will value the share after the issue.

2.4 Scrip issues

A company will occasionally make a '1 for X' scrip issue, that is it gives shares to shareholders in proportion to their existing holdings. To the uninitiated this looks like something for nothing, and indeed such shares are sometimes referred to as bonus shares, but this is quite misleading. There are two main reasons for making scrip issues:

Division into more manageable units

Sometimes the market price of a share will rise far above its nominal value, especially when a company has had a long period of success. A £1 ordinary share of a company might subsequently be priced at £10. This price might discourage small investors because, for example, only 100 shares can be bought for £1000. The situation could be alleviated by making, say, a '1 for 1' scrip issue, that is for every share currently owned a shareholder receives one new one. However, since there are now twice as many shares as before, the market value will be halved. If there were, say, 5 million £1 shares before the issue, with a market value of £13 each, this would amount to a total of £65 million. After the issue, there will be 10 million shares, each worth £6.50, again making a total of £65 million. In practice, because scrip issues are often made when a company is doing well, the market will usually value the share at slightly above the theoretical new price.

Capitalization of reserves

When a company ploughs profits back into the business, these are shown on the balance sheet as reserves. Such profits may have been used to buy new capital assets such as plant and machinery, but the use of the word 'reserves' makes it seem to the uninitiated that the company is holding on to a lot of cash that could be used, for example, to pay higher dividends. In an extreme imaginary case, suppose a company has £1 million in ordinary share capital, but has been very profitable and has accumulated £9 million of reserves. Of this amount, let us say, £8 million has long since been used to pay for a new factory building and its machinery. These capital assets, of course, belong to the shareholders, just like the £1 million of share capital. To make the situation clear, the company might decide to capitalize the £8 million by issuing new shares in a scrip issue, so that for every one share currently held a shareholder receives eight new ones free of charge. The balance sheet now shows £9 million in ordinary shares and £1 million of reserves. As in the case of a rights issue, the market price will fall to reflect the issue; previously there were 1 million shares worth, say, £13 each, a total market value of £13 millions. There will now be 9 million shares worth £13m/9m = £1.44 each. The shareholder has not gained anything since he/she now owns many more shares but the total value is the same as before. All that has happened is that money has been moved from one heading to another on the balance sheet. Further explanation of reserves will be found later in this chapter.

2.5 Loan capital

As an alternative to issuing shares, companies may borrow money in order to finance growth and development. Loans may be obtained from banks, including merchant banks, and other financial institutions such as factoring companies, credit insurance companies, insurance companies and investment trusts. The company 3i, founded by the Bank of England and the clearing banks, provides finance for small and medium-sized companies. A bank will usually lend money against a specified security, such as land or buildings. In other words a company may mortgage its property rather like a private houseowner. A rarer form of loan stock is where there is no interest, but a promise to pay later a certain capital amount, which is discounted by the implied interest rate when it is taken out.

2.5.1 Debentures

In addition to the above forms of loan, companies are empowered to issue fixed-interest bonds, often called debentures. These might be thought a kind of share, and they may indeed be bought and sold on the stock market; however, a debenture is a loan and the buyer of a debenture is not a shareholder but a creditor. There is usually a fixed rate of interest which must be paid annually, whether a share dividend is declared or not, and the debenture will often be secured against some asset of the company. A debenture may be redeemable, that is repayable, at some specified date; or irredeemable, meaning that it will be repaid only when the company is wound up, or perhaps in the case that the company defaults on the payment of interest.

The security of a loan may be by a fixed charge or a floating charge. A fixed charge is safer for the lender because the loan is secured against a specified asset that does not change, e.g. a building. A floating charge might be on, for example, the trading stock held by the company, but over time this could change with the value of the stock. Often a floating charge will be on all of the assets of the company. If there is a fixed charge, debentures are often referred to as mortgage debenture stock; if a floating charge, debenture stock; if there is no security at all, debentures might be referred to as unsecured loan stock.

If debentures are redeemable, there is usually a range of dates during which repayment will be made. For example, a debenture described as 'XYZ PLC 7% Unsecured Loan Stock 1997/2001' pays 7% (gross) interest per annum, is not secured against any asset, and will be redeemed some time during the period 1997–2001. Debentures typically have very long lives, often 20–25 years, and represent a very long-term investment.

Convertibles are another type of loan. These are debentures or loan stock that can be converted into ordinary shares according to a pre-arranged formula. Until converted a fixed rate of interest is paid; once converted into ordinary shares, the shares are identical to other shares in the issue and earn the same dividend.

2.6 Gearing

It can thus be seen that a company can raise money in two main ways, but the consequences are quite different. In the case of shares, the company is not bound to pay a dividend in any one year if there are no profits (or indeed if there are), but in the case of loans, the interest must be paid even if the company makes a loss. If a company could not meet interest payments and other debts, it could face liquidation. On the other hand, payment of interest on loans can be set against tax as an allowance, whereas dividends cannot.

If carefully applied, loan capital can be applied to expand output and create greater profits, but some over-ambitious companies might borrow too much and run into difficulties. The use of loan capital to increase assets and performance is called gearing ('leverage' in the USA). After the stock market crash in October 1987, it was impossible for a long time to raise money by new share issues, because investors were frightened off, and loan capital became more prominent for a time.

If, say, 90% of a company's capital is borrowed money, it could look very vulnerable in certain circumstances. Because of the relative advantages and disadvantages of share capital and loan capital, investors and company analysts are interested in the relationship between them. This relationship is called the gearing ratio, and a company with a high proportion of loan to share capital is said to be highly geared. Gearing ratios are discussed and defined later in this chapter under the general heading of Financial Indicators.

2.7 Winding up

A company can be wound up (liquidated) either voluntarily (on resolution of the shareholders) or compulsorily (by court order). Voluntary winding up may be because the company is insolvent and has been recognized as such by its management. Alternatively, the company may be solvent but has come to the end of its trading life. Compulsory winding ups are almost exclusively of insolvent companies. In the case of a company being wound up, the law specifies the order of priority for the payment of debts. Omitting some of the detail, this order is:

1   secured creditors with fixed charges (e.g. a bank that lent money against a building as security);
2   the costs of the winding up procedure, including the fee paid to the liquidator;
3   preferential creditors: PAYE and National Insurance contributions to the Inland Revenue for the last six months of trading; VAT to Customs and Excise for the last six months of trading; up to £800 arrears of wages; arrears of holiday pay;
4   creditors with floating charges;
5   unsecured creditors, e.g. other companies that have supplied goods on credit and have not been paid. Their low priority for payment largely explains why companies asked to supply goods on credit to a customer, especially a new one, need to assess the customer's ability to pay (credit-worthiness);
6   the repayment of paid-up capital to shareholders;
7   any surplus to shareholders (preference shareholders first, then ordinary shareholders).

The lowest priority is accorded to the shareholders, which underlines once again, and only too clearly, that they bear the greatest risk.

3 Company accounts

Every company is required by law to keep day-to-day records of receipts and expenditures of money; to maintain a record of the assets and liabilities of the company; and to record stocks of goods and details of sales and of all buyers and sellers of goods (except in the case of retail sales). A company is also bound by law to prepare annual accounts, which must be audited by a qualified auditor. The annual accounts must be deposited at Companies House (and the Stock Exchange if the company is listed), as noted in Chapter 2 on the legal status of businesses, subject to modifications in the cases of small and medium-sized companies.

The annual accounts are therefore a public record and an important source of information for many enquiries. The accounts must comprise a balance sheet and a profit-and-loss account in respect of each financial year (accounting reference period). In addition, companies with a turnover of £2.8m or more, or gross assets of £1.4m or more are expected to conform with *Financial reporting standard 1: cash flow* statements,[7] which requires a cash flow statement. Financial reporting standards are issued by the Accounting Standards Board, which is responsible to the Financial Reporting Council (FRC). Notes to the accounts also form part of a company's accounts. Should a company's accounts not conform to the standards required the courts have the power to order the preparation of revised accounts at the expense of company directors. Earlier standards are known as SSAPs – Statements of Standard Accounting Practice.[8] A number of these, published between 1971 and 1990, remain in force.

The purpose of this section is to show that the basic structure and principles of company accounts are really quite easy to understand, and to indicate their uses for the derivation of information, including the calculation of business ratios.

In Chapter 2 we imagined the authors running a sweet shop under the name 'Maria and Hazel's Chocolate Box', and later registering a company called 'Burke and Hall Ltd'. Suppose that subsequently the company has grown into a chain of shops and that the owners have sold 51% of their shares in Burke and Hall Ltd to a large confectionery manufacturer called Kaye PLC, which uses the Burke and Hall shops as retail outlets for its products (an example of vertical integration). Burke and Hall Ltd is now a subsidiary of Kaye PLC, but M. Burke and H. Hall still personally own a substantial interest. Kaye PLC also has several other subsidiaries, all wholly owned. The accounts of this imaginary company are used to illustrate the explanation that follows. Permitted formats for accounts are laid down in the Companies Act 1985 and the 1989 amendments to it. The ones shown are those in most common use.

3.1 Profit-and-loss account

Figure 3.1 demonstrates how a consolidated profit-and-loss (P-and-L) account for the group, that is for Kaye PLC (the holding company) together with its subsidiaries might be presented. There would probably be no P-and-L account for Kaye PLC on its own, as this exemption is permitted under the Act. Note that all figures are rounded to the nearest thousand, and that the previous year is given for purposes of comparison and because this is a legal requirement. Certain items would be explained in more detail in the notes to the accounts (not shown), which are required by law. A figure in brackets indicates a deduction or a loss and descriptions follow to explain each item in turn.

Consolidated profit-and-loss account, year ended 30 June 1998			
	Notes	1998 £000	1997 £000
Turnover		42,228	31,388
Cost of sales		(33,811)	(25,571)
Gross profit		8,417	5,817
Operating expenses	1	(2,704)	(2,139)
Operating profit		5,713	3,678
Investment income	2	170	173
Interest payable	3	(1,112)	(800)
Profit before taxation	4	4,771	3,051
Taxation	5	(1,670)	(1,127)
Profit after taxation		3,101	1,924
Minority interest		(25)	(73)
Profit for the financial year		3,076	1,851
Dividends	6	(765)	(407)
Retained profit for the year		2,311	1,444
Retained profit brought forward		7,124	5,680
Retained profit carried forward		9,435	7,124
Earnings per ordinary share	7	12.66p	9.48p
The accompanying notes are an integral part of this consolidated profit-and-loss account			

Fig. 3.1   *Profit-and-loss account for Kaye PLC*

(a) *Turnover*

Otherwise known as sales, this is the invoiced value of sales of goods and services, excluding VAT, trade discounts and other items.

(b) *Cost of sales*

This slightly misleading term would include the cost of raw material and labour, production overheads, hire of plant and machinery, and generally any cost directly attributable to the production of goods and/or services.

(c) *Gross profit*

The result of deducting (b) from (a).

(d) *Operating expenses*

This includes other, indirect, costs such as costs of selling and marketing, transport and distribution, research and development, administrative expenses, office services and the like.

(e) *Operating profit*

The result of deducting (d) from (c).

(f) *Investment income*

Could include such things as interest on government bonds, rents from property holdings, and so on.

(g) *Interest payable*

Interest paid on bank overdrafts, debentures and other loans.

(h) *Profit before taxation*

The result of adding (f) to (e) and deducting (g). Profit before tax is a major indicator of company performance.

(i) *Taxation*

Corporation tax is paid on profits after all outgoings, except dividends, have been deducted. In recent years, the rate of corporation tax has been on a sliding scale from 24% to 33%.

(j) *Profit after taxation*

The result of deducting (i) from (h).

(k) *Minority interest*

As was noted above, M Burke and H Hall still personally own a minority share (49%) in Burke and Hall Ltd, which is a subsidiary of Kaye PLC. Profits (or losses) of Burke and Hall Ltd are included in the consolidated statement of the group. If Burke and Hall Ltd were wholly owned, like the other subsidiaries, all final profits could be distributed to the shareholders of Kaye PLC. But, because M. Burke and H. Hall still own a minority interest in the subsidiary, their 49% share (£25,000) of the profits of the subsidiary must first be deducted.

(l) *Profit for the financial year*

The result of deducting (k) from (j).

(m) *Dividends*

Note 6 to the accounts will explain the amount of dividend paid during the year, in the form of so many pence per share. Suppose there are 24,290,000 issued shares, then the dividend per share must be (765,000 x 100)/24,290,000 = 3.15p per share. This could have been paid in two instalments – an interim and a final dividend.

(n) *Retained profit for the year*

Of the total profit of £3,076,000, the directors have distributed £765,000 as dividends and are proposing to retain the rest in the business, perhaps to finance expansion or the purchase of new machinery, or to repay loans.

(o) *Retained profit brought forward*

This is the retained profit brought forward from 1997 (see bottom of 1997 column).

(p) *Retained profit carried forward*

The result of adding (o) to (n). Note that this sum, although retained in the business, belongs to the shareholders, as will be seen later.

(q) *Earnings per ordinary share*

This is the profit earned by each share, and is a useful measure of performance, especially in this case by comparison with the previous year. It is calculated by dividing the profit for the financial year (after tax and minority payments), by the number of shares, i.e. $(3,076,000 \times 100)/24,290,000 = 12.66p$ per share. (This needs to be shown only for listed companies.)

3.2 Balance sheet

Figures 3.2 and 3.3 show the balance sheets of the Kaye PLC group, drawn up in accordance with the two formats specified in the Companies Act 1985 (and the 1989 amendments to the Act). Format 1, used in Figure 3.3, is almost universally used now, but it is helpful to start by studying format 2, which is simpler and illustrates the principles very clearly.

3.2.1 Format 2

Assets and liabilities do not have to be displayed side by side (in the Act, they are shown in one sequence), but are presented here in this way to show clearly how they balance. Note that the Act does not specify which items should balance; the practice described below is almost universal, but deviations will be found occasionally. The following general points should be noted: (a) all figures are rounded to the nearest thousand; (b) there would be numbered notes to the accounts, which are not shown here; (c) the previous year's figures would be given for comparison, but for simplicity's sake are omitted here; (d) unlike the P-and-L account, the balance sheets must be presented separately for both the holding company (Kaye PLC) and the group (the holding company plus its subsidiaries).

ASSETS	Group £000	Company £000	LIABILITIES	Group £000	Company £000
FIXED ASSETS			**CAPITAL AND RESERVES**		
Intangible assets	214	214	Share capital	4,858	4,858
Tangible assets	1,532	1,532	Share premium account	2,356	2,356
Investments	5	345	Revaluation reserve	151	151
			Profit-and-loss account	9,435	9,435
Total	1,751	2,091	Provision for liabilities and charges	103	103
CURRENT ASSETS			CREDITORS: amounts due within one year	17,059	17,112
Stocks	31,665	31,665	CREDITORS: amounts due after more than one year	952	952
Debtors	940	1,194	Minority interest	25	–
Cash	583	17		34,939	34,967
Total	33,188	32,876			
	34,939	34,967			

Group and company balance sheet, year ended 30 June 1998

Fig. 3.2 Balance sheet: format 2

The balance sheet shows the financial state of the company on the last day of its financial year, both as to the value of its assets (although this would not be its market value – see below on historical costs), and the extent of its debts or liabilities. In principle, a company could have a balance sheet for every day of the year, and it is worth pointing out that there are actions a company can take to make its published balance sheet look more favourable.

The left-hand side shows the assets, divided into fixed and current. Fixed assets are mainly tangible ones, such as land, buildings and machinery, which are held over a longer period of time to produce profits in the future. Current assets include actual cash in hand or in the bank, and assets which could fairly easily be converted into cash, such as stocks of raw materials. Current assets can produce profit more immediately. Some explanations are called for as follows:

Intangible assets

This is the value of such assets as patents, registered designs or trade marks, and also goodwill. The latter arises when more is paid for an asset than its tangible value. Thus a shop sold as a going concern may command a higher price than the actual value of the building, fittings and stock, because the shop's existing customers, trade contacts and reputation are also valuable. The excess paid for these intangibles is accounted for as goodwill.

Investments

These are long-term investments, which would include the capital value of shares held in other companies. In the present case, the £345,000 represents, *inter alia*, the investment made by Kaye in its subsidiaries, including the 51% stake in Burke and Hall Ltd.

Stocks

Three classes of stocks are commonly recognized: i.e. raw materials; semi-finished goods (work in progress); finished goods awaiting sale. As noted above, these are in principle convertible into cash at fairly short notice, although obviously semi-finished goods are much less readily encashable than finished ones.

Debtors

Where customers have ordered goods on credit and the goods have been delivered to the customer, who has not yet paid for them, a trade debt arises. Although Kaye PLC has not yet received payment, the money due to it is one of its assets. In the present case the sum of £1,194,000 entered under the company may well include money owed by the subsidiaries for goods delivered to them by the parent.

Everything on the right-hand side of the account is a debt or liability, and the total liabilities must balance the assets, as can be seen from the bottom line. For ease of explanation, we will look at these in reverse order.

Minority interest

£25,000 was paid to M. Burke and H. Hall as the minority shareholders in the subsidiary Burke and Hall Ltd. This is therefore a deduction from the group assets.

Creditors

Long-term creditors (amounts due after more than one year) include holders of debentures, banks which have lent money on longer terms, and so on. The amounts here are those due to be paid back in the long term. Short-term creditors (amounts due within one year) include suppliers who have delivered raw materials, stationery etc., on credit to the company or its subsidiaries, but who have not yet been paid.

Provision for liabilities and charges

This is money set aside for contingencies, where it is expected that a payment will have to be made but the amount or the date when it will be due is uncertain. Items commonly found here are deferred taxation and redemption sums (e.g. money set aside for buying back the company's shares).

Capital and reserves

This group of items gives rise to the greatest misunderstanding and accordingly the explanation has been left to the last. To the uninitiated it would seem that share capital should be an asset, but this is not so. It represents money that would have to be repaid to the shareholders in the event of the company being wound up, and is therefore a liability. Of course the share capital has long since been used to buy buildings, machinery and so on, and these assets would have to be sold (liquidated) in order to pay the shareholders and creditors, should such a winding up occur.

Profit-and-loss account

£9,435,000 was the bottom line on the P-and-L account. It is profit retained in the business. In the future, the directors may use this money to finance new capital assets, but in any case, like the share capital, it belongs to the shareholders and is therefore a liability.

Share premium account

When new shares are sold at a premium the premium itself (the difference between nominal value and selling price) goes into a share premium account. Like the profit-and-loss and the share capital, this money belongs to the shareholders and is a liability.

Reserves

The share premium account, the profit-and-loss balance and the revaluation reserve are all examples of reserves. Reserves arise when a business generates a surplus of assets over liabilities, for example in gaining a debtor or having an asset revalued. In accounts reserves are used as a device which is necessary to demonstrate a balance. The revaluation reserve is a case in point. Companies periodically have their fixed assets such as buildings and land revalued to reflect the higher prices due to inflation, for example. This increases the value of the assets, and there must be a corresponding increase in the liabilities in order to balance the account. Even retained profits may well be eventually converted into additional fixed assets, requiring a similar adjustment to the liabilities.

To make the situation perfectly clear, consider the following very simple example of a balance sheet for a company at the end of year:

Assets	£	Liabilities	£
Fixed assets	15,000	Capital	20,000
Stocks (current assets)	5,000		
Total	20,000		20,000

During the second year the owner, an idle fellow, takes only one action: he sells all the stocks for £6000, yielding a profit of £1000. At the end of year 2, his balance sheet reads as follows:

Assets	£	Liabilities	£
Fixed assets	15,000	Capital	20,000
Cash (current assets)	6,000	P-and-L a/c	1,000
Total	21,000		21,000

Since his assets have increased by £1000, the same sum must be entered under liabilities, in this case as the balance of the profit-and-loss account. During the third year, the owner decides to use the £1000 extra cash to buy a new piece of equipment. At the end of this year, the balance sheet reads:

Assets	£	Liabilities	£
Fixed assets	16,000	Capital	20,000
Cash (current assets)	5,000	Reserves	1,000
Total	21,000		21,000

The fixed assets have increased by the value of the new equipment, and this must be balanced as before, in this case by a capital reserve, which does not exist as cash but is simply there to show that there is a sum of money which belongs to the shareholders, even though it exists only in the form of a piece of equipment. This demonstrates clearly the nature of most reserves.

3.2.2 Format 1

The kind of balance sheet shown in Figure 3.3, which is almost always used, is referred to as the vertical balance sheet, or sometimes the narrative form, because it is designed to tell a better story by revealing more information.

The first difference to note between this and format 2 is that the balance is now between different items, namely net assets and total shareholders' interest. What has happened is that the capital and reserves now stand on

Group and company balance sheet, year ended 30 June 1998

	Group £000	Company £000
FIXED ASSETS		
Intangible assets	214	214
Tangible assets	1,532	1,532
Investments	5	345
Total	1,751	2,001
CURRENT ASSETS		
Stocks	31,665	31,665
Debtors	940	1,194
Cash	583	17
Total	33,188	32,876
CREDITORS: amounts due within 1 year	(17,059)	(17,112)
NET CURRENT ASSETS	16,129	15,764
Total assets less current liabilities	17,880	17,855
CREDITORS: amounts due after more than 1 year	(952)	(952)
Provision for liabilities and charges	(103)	(103)
NET ASSETS	16,800	16,800
CAPITAL AND RESERVES		
Share capital	4,858	4,858
Share premium account	2,356	2,356
Revaluation reserve	151	151
Profit-and-loss account	9,435	9,435
Minority interest	(25)	–
Group shareholders' funds	16,800	16,800

The accompanying notes are an integral part of these balance sheets

Fig. 3.3 *Balance sheet: format 1*

their own and are balanced against the rest. The rest consist of the fixed and current assets as before, from which are deducted both types of creditors, provision for liabilities and charges. Note the use of brackets to signify deductions. This 'side' of the balance sheet is called the net assets – in short it represents total assets minus total liabilities (other than capital and reserves). This layout serves among other things to emphasize the interest of the shareholders, that is all the surplus assets that belong to them when other debts have been paid.

In addition, two subsidiary calculations are made 'on the way' as it were, and incorporated into the account. These are *net current assets* and *total assets less current liabilities*.

Net current assets

This is the difference between current assets and current liabilities (the latter being named on the account 'creditors: amounts due within one year'). In this case, net current assets are £33,188 – 17,059 = 16,129 (000). The net current assets are often taken as an indication of the company's liquidity (ability to pay its debts). Further discussion of this will be found later in this section. The term 'working capital' refers to stocks and debtors less trade creditors. Generally companies aim to keep a low working capital in order to maximize their access to cash.

Total assets less current liabilities

This is more fully expressed as: fixed assets *plus* current assets *less* creditors equals amounts due within one year. In the present case it is given by £1,751 + 33,188 – 17,059 = 17,880 (000). This item is often called capital employed and is used to calculate a measure of company performance, as will be seen later.

3.3 Problems with accounts

With some justification, company accounts are often criticized for being obscure and misleading. It is hoped that this section has cast light on a topic found difficult by the lay person; nevertheless, the reader's attention should be drawn to some key problems.

In the first place, it must be remembered that whereas the profit and loss account can tell a story, the balance sheet represents only a financial snapshot of the company on one day in the year. Certainly, many companies issue interim statements, typically at the six-month interval, but the fact remains that the outsider can know little or nothing of a firm's financial condition during the rest of the year. Moreover firms could, and no doubt do, take steps to present their annual accounts in the best possible light. For example, the distribution of current assets between stocks, debtors and cash could be made to look more favourable by having a sales drive to convert unsold stocks of finished goods into cash, or by putting pressure on debtors to pay outstanding bills.

Accounts are conventionally prepared on the basis of historic costs, that is assets and liabilities, profits and losses, are all stated in terms of the appropriate cost or value of obtaining at the time each item arose. In periods of high inflation, this can lead to severe discrepancies, for example the cost of raw materials purchased at the start of a year, when set against profits made from these materials later in the year, could give a misleading impression of profitability if prices had risen markedly in the meantime. Even at times of low inflation, fixed assets acquired a long time ago would look undervalued unless firms periodically revalued them, as is often the case. Various devices have been tried, or proposed, in order to overcome this problem, for example current cost accounting (CCA). For a few years during the early 1980s the accounting bodies imposed CCA by means of *Statement of standard accounting practice 16*[9] and company reports of that period often contained two versions of the accounts, one drawn up on the basis of historic costs and one in accordance with CCA. *SSAP 16* was suspended in June 1985 after the rate of inflation fell back, but the general problem is not resolved. A full discussion of the issues can be found in a publication of the Accounting Standards Committee.[10]

A further problem arises with off-balance-sheet finance. Company groups have to produce consolidated accounts, that is the financial affairs of a holding company together with its subsidiaries must be fully represented in consolidated or group accounts. Various techniques have been used, however, to ensure that a company does not qualify as a subsidiary under the present definition, even though it may still be effectively controlled by the parent. In such cases, the accounts of the 'subsidiary' are not included in the group accounts, which consequently do not accurately represent the group's financial affairs as a whole. The cynical could be forgiven for assuming that such a deliberate ploy is undertaken for some suspicious reason since, for example, a subsidiary as a liability may not appear in the accounts, although its contribution to profit does. The standard *Financial reporting standard 2: accounting for subsidiary undertakings*[11] issued in 1992 addresses this by stressing the importance of segmental reporting in group financial reporting.

It has often been held that many, if not most, shareholders do not need the full report and accounts that they receive, frequently do not understand them, and may simply discard them unread. They would perhaps be better served by some abbreviated form of annual report. Consequently, a provision was included in the Companies Act 1989, by which all listed PLCs have the option of supplying their shareholders with a summary financial statement. Shareholders may request the full report and accounts if they want them, and companies are still obliged to deposit the full documents at Companies House and to present them at shareholders' meetings.

Company annual reports and accounts have been subjected to other, much more radical, scrutiny. The Institute of Chartered Accountants of Scotland (ICAS)[12] criticized corporate reporting for ignoring the economic reality underlying a company's performance, and for concentrating too much on the legal form and cost of transactions. It recommended that the traditional profit-and-loss statement and balance sheet should be abolished and replaced by a more realistic statement of a company's financial position. The report was partly based on a series of literature surveys[13] commissioned by the ICAS.

Financial reporting standard 3: reporting financial performance,[14] first issued in 1992 and amended in 1993 with provisions for insurance companies, was designed to bring the presentation of the profit-and-loss account closer to the all-inclusive concept of accounting, and thus prevent some earlier forms of creative accounting (and financial scandals such as Polly Peck and Maxwell). Methods of creative accounting had included the possible classification of unusual losses or profits as 'extraordinary', so that reported earnings per share could be enhanced. Under the provisions of *FRS 3* the definition of an extraordinary item was tightened; extraordinary items now have to be calculated into earnings per share and results have to be sub-divided down to operating profit level. In addition, separate disclosure must be made of three items after operating profit and prior to interest: (1) profit or losses on the sale or termination of an operation; (2) costs of a fundamental reorganization or restructuring having a material effect on the nature and focus of the reporting entity's operations; (3) profits or losses on the disposal of fixed assets. When accounts are presented to this standard they give equal prominence to the profit and loss account, the cash flow statement, the statement of total recognized gains and losses and the balance sheet. An example of this is shown in *FRS3*.

Remaining problems with accounting practices in the UK and the steps being taken to resolve them are discussed in the final chapter of Holmes and Sugden.[1]

4 Financial indicators

Many interested parties, including shareholders, customers, suppliers and the company itself, need to be able to assess the performance, efficiency and general financial health of a firm. In particular, it will often be necessary to make such assessments relative to other companies such as competitors. In this context, business ratios are of great importance.

It will be readily understood that comparisons between two or more firms, or between the performance in different years of the same firm, can fairly be made, if at all, only on the basis of ratios. Suppose there are two companies, A and B, both operating in the same kind of business. A might have annual profits of, say, £10 million and B profits of £1 million, but this in no way means that A is ten times as profitable as B. Suppose that A's profits were made on sales of £150 million and B's on sales of £10 million. Then A's profit margin (profit as a percentage of sales) is 6.7%, whereas B's is 10%. B, although much smaller than A in absolute terms, is actually performing better than A on this measure. It is the ratio of profit to sales that cancels out the absolute size difference between the two and enables us to make the comparison.

The profit margin is an example of a business ratio. There are many such ratios which are used by company analysts and others to assess companies' relative performance and financial health. Most of them are based on financial data which can be derived from company accounts. Ratios are expressed either as a percentage or as a decimal fraction, according to convention. It should be noted that the definition of a particular ratio may vary from source to source; therefore, when quoting a ratio, it is important to state how it is defined. The lack of standard definitions makes the collation of data from different sources extremely hazardous.

Business ratios may conveniently be grouped into three main classes: liquidity, performance, and gearing ratios.

4.1 Liquidity ratios

The liquidity of a company is of vital importance to some parties, especially potential suppliers, who will be unwilling to supply goods on credit to a new customer without some indication of the customer's ability to pay.

Such credit-worthiness is partly gauged by liquidity measures, which indicate the amount of cash available to pay debts. In the following paragraphs, the examples are based on the imaginary accounts of the Kaye PLC group shown in Figures 3.2 and 3.3.

Net current assets

This is the difference between current assets and current liabilities, as discussed above, and in this particular case it amounts to £16,129,000, which can be read directly from the balance sheet. Although this sum applies only to the last day of the financial year, it does give some indication of the cash and encashable assets that could be used to pay debts.

Current ratio

This ratio derives from net current assets and is the ratio of current assets to current liabilities. In the example, it is given as: 33,188/17,059 = 1.95.) This ratio shows that at the time the company had sufficient current assets to pay its current debts almost twice over. A current ratio of 2 is generally regarded as satisfactory; anything less than 1 would give cause for concern.

Quick ratio

This is sometimes also called the acid-test or liquidity ratio. Many analysts take the view that stocks such as raw materials and work in progress cannot readily be converted into cash at their true value and should therefore not be taken into account in the assessment of liquidity. The liquid ratio is therefore defined as the ratio of current assets less stocks to current liabilities. In the example this is: (33,188 – 31,665)/17,059 = 0.09. Compared to the current ratio, this reveals a very different and unsatisfactory position.

4.2 Performance ratios

A number of such ratios exist to indicate relative profitability, efficiency, financial return, and the like. Some of the more common ones follow.

Return on capital employed (ROCE)

This is the ratio of profit before tax to capital employed, as a percentage. The former can be read directly from the profit-and-loss account, and the latter from the balance sheet, where capital employed is shown as total assets less current liabilities. In the example the ratio is therefore; (4,771/17,880) x 100 = 26.7%. It is fair to use profit before the deduction of tax for this purpose, since the imposition of tax is made by government and does not depend on any business decision taken by the company; it should not therefore affect our assessment of a company's performance. The definition of capital employed tends to vary and care should be taken when using this ratio.

Operating profit

This is defined as profit before tax as a percentage of sales (turnover). In our example it is: (4,771/42,228) x 100 = 11.3%.

Return on shareholders' funds

Profit after tax as a percentage of shareholders' funds. This is similar to return on capital, but disregards long-term borrowings and similar liabilities, and considers profit only in relation to the shareholders' investment. In the example it is: (4,771/16,800) x 100 = 28.4%.

Sales per employee

The turnover is divided by the number of employees.

Profit per employee

Profit before tax is divided by the number of employees. These last two ratios are useful indicators of the average output per worker. International comparisons between similar firms in different countries can be interesting to observe.

4.3 Gearing ratios

Gearing and loan capital were discussed earlier in this chapter under the heading Capital structure. Various gearing ratios are used to indicate the relationship between loan capital and share capital. The ratios are defined differently according to the views and needs of the definers.

A general gearing ratio

In principle, the company analyst wants to know the relative importance of borrowed money in financing a company. This would be achieved by taking loan capital as a percentage of total capital employed. Loan capital is more precisely defined as long-term loans (creditors: amounts due after more than one year). Capital employed is, as we know already, total assets less current liabilities. In the example, this ratio would be: (952/17,880) x 100 = 5.3%. What counts as loan capital and share capital would vary according to interests. For example, a banker considering the gearing of a client firm might interpret share capital to mean only equity or ordinary shares and be inclined to view preference shares, especially cumulative preference shares, as a form of loan, since they carry a fixed dividend. A bank would also naturally regard bank overdrafts, on which it was charging its client interest, as part of loan capital, whereas a company financial manager might view overdrafts simply as a way of managing cash flow. Very short-term debts, however, such as amounts due to be paid to creditors within one month, would not be taken into account, especially as they would not normally carry any interest charges.

Other ratios will be found in common use. Three in particular are worth specific mention because they are used in *Business ratio reports* published by ICC,[15] an important series which will be considered in Chapter 8 on company information sources. The ratios are:

- borrowing ratio: total debt expressed as a ratio of net worth
- equity gearing: shareholders' funds expressed as a ratio of total liabilities
- income gearing: gross interest paid as a percentage of pre-interest, pre-tax profit.

The reader is invited to study the definition of these ratios in *Business ratio reports*. For a comprehensive treatment of business ratios and their uses, the reader is referred to the standard work by Westwick.[16]

References

1 Holmes, G. and Sugden, A., *Interpreting company reports and accounts*, 6th edn, London, Prentice Hall, 1997.

2 Oldcorn, R., *Company accounts*, 3rd edn, London, Macmillan, 1996.

3 Brett, M., *How to read the financial pages*, 4th edn, London, Century, 1995.

4 Wood, F., *Business accounting*, 7th edn, London, Pitman, 1996.

5 Gough, L., *How the stock market really works*, London, Pitman, 1997.

6 Carr, J. (ed.), *UK business finance directory 1990–*, London, Graham and Trotman, 1990.

7 Accounting Standards Board, *Financial reporting standard 1: cash flow statements*, London, ASB, 1996 rev. edn.

8 Accounting Standards Committee, *Statements of standard accounting practice*, London, Institute of Chartered Accountants, various dates.

9 Accounting Standards Committee, *Statement of standard accounting practice 16: current cost accounting*, London, Institute of Chartered Accountants, 1980.

10 Accounting Standards Committee, *Accounting for the effects of changing prices: a handbook*, London, CCAB, 1986.

11 Accounting Standards Board, *Financial reporting standard 2: accounting for subsidiary undertakings*, London, ASB, 1992.

12 Institute of Chartered Accountants of Scotland, *Making corporate reports valuable*, London, Kogan Page, 1988.

13 Institute of Chartered Accountants of Scotland, *Making corporate reports valuable – the literature surveys*, Edinburgh, The Institute, 1988.

14 Accounting Standards Board, *Financial reporting standard 3: reporting financial performance*, London, ASB 1993 rev. edn.

15 *ICC Business ratio reports*, London, ICC, various dates.

16 Westwick, C.A., *How to use management ratios*, 2nd edn, Aldershot, Gower, 1989.

4 Investments and markets

1 Introduction

Members of the public often invest money without appreciating how the investment is put to use by the organization that takes it. The application of the money belonging to one set of people can create real wealth by allowing others to make and sell products and services. For example, the money that the small investor puts into a bank deposit account will be lent by the bank, perhaps to a local business which will use it to create jobs, produce goods and sell them at a profit. The profits will help to pay the bank the interest on the loan, so that the bank in turn can pay interest to the investor. To the professional economist this analysis would be regarded as simplistic and naïve, but the fact is that the prosperity of an economy depends ultimately on enterprises that create real wealth.

This section reviews briefly the popular ways in which individuals invest their money (as summarized in Table 4.1), examines the workings of the London Stock Exchange, and outlines the main sources of information that are encountered in this field. The reader will discover how the institutions – pension funds, unit and investment trusts, insurance companies, banks and building societies – act as intermediaries with funds that are indirectly owned by ordinary people. An indication of the regulatory framework for the UK financial services industry and proposed changes to legislation is given at the end of the chapter.

2 Investing in bank and building society deposit accounts

Investment in *bank deposit accounts* and *building society shares* of various kinds are too well known to deserve more than a mention. It is, however, worth pointing out that the distinctions between the two types of institution became blurred as a result of legislation in the 1980s, and since then banks have, for example, provided mortgage facilities (a traditional building society function) and building societies have offered cheque accounts to clients. A number of building societies have actually become banks, for

Table 4.1   *Common forms of personal investment*

Approximate level of risk (1=lowest)	Type of investment	How money is invested	Anticipated return
1	National savings accounts	Individual purchases savings certificates and premium bonds or places savings in deposit accounts	Interest on amount deposited
2	Bank/building society accounts	Individual places savings in deposit accounts	Interest on amount deposited
3	Pensions	Individual makes regular payments through employer, bank, building society, life insurance company, unit trust company, investment adviser or Inland Revenue (self employed).	Income in retirement
4=	Endowment policies	Individual pays regular premiums to insurance company	Lump sum on death/maturity of policy
4=	Unit-linked life insurance	Individual buys policy and the insurance company reinvests money in stocks and shares	Lump sum on sale of bonds
6	Guaranteed income bonds	Individual invests lump sum with insurance company	Interest
7	Guaranteed growth bonds	Individual invests lump sum with insurance company	Lump sum at maturity of bond

cont.

Table 4.1 (continued)

8	Annuities	Individual invests lump sum with insurance company	Income
9	British government stocks (also known as gilt-edged securities or gilts)	Individual purchases gilts traded on the Stock Exchange	Interest plus profit on capital growth
10	Personal equity plan (PEP)	Individual buys portfolio of shares through a plan manager: bank, building society or investment adviser	Dividends and profit on capital growth of PEP (plus tax advantages)
11	Unit trusts	Individual buys unit trust comprising a spread of investments from shares and gilts to loans and commodities	Dividends and profit on capital growth of investments
12	Investment trusts	Individual buys shares in investment trust company through stockbroker or agent	Dividend and profit on capital growth of shares
13	Shares in public companies	Individual buys shares through stockbroker or agent	Dividends and profit on capital growth
14	Alternative investments	Individual invests in commodities and objects such as antiques, property or wine	Profit on sale of purchase

example in 1997 both the Halifax and the Alliance & Leicester gave up their mutual status. Interest paid on bank and building society accounts fluctuates with the prevailing rates, which depend on the minimum rate set by the Bank of England. As well as being the most accessible and convenient form of saving, bank and building society deposits are very secure. Unlike the value of shares on the Stock Exchange, the full amount deposited can, within the constraints of the investment account, always be withdrawn. For most deposits, which are backed by the Bank of England's deposit protection scheme, this is so even if the bank concerned gets into financial difficulties. In recent years it has not simply been the security and interest rates that have encouraged investors to keep accounts with the building societies: many have opened accounts primarily in the expectation of the society's conversion to a bank, hoping to cash in on 'free' shares.

3 Investing in government schemes

The British government borrows money from the public through encouraging investment in *British Government stocks* (also known as gilt-edged securities or gilts) and *National Savings*. When investing in gilts the investor lends the government money at a fixed rate of interest for redemption after a certain number of years. Gilts are traded on the London Stock Exchange and their value will rise and fall according to a number of factors including, for example, the levels of government borrowing, inflation and economic activity. If gilts are held to maturity they can be regarded as very secure, although, over a long holding period, inflation can erode the purchasing power of the original amount invested. Gilts can be bought through the National Savings Stock Register, as well as through a broker. The best known form of National Savings is the National Savings Certificate. The first National Savings Certificates were issued in 1916 as War Savings Certificates. By January 1997 there had been 43 issues of certificates. Once the investor buys a certificate it can be kept indefinitely and the interest it gains is added to the value of the certificate until it is cashed in. There are other ways of investing in National Savings such as the National Savings Ordinary and Investment accounts, National Savings Bonds and Premium Bonds.

4 Investing in insurance funds and pension schemes

In addition to taking out ordinary life, fire, property and other similar insurance policies, it is possible to link investment to insurance in various ways. Common forms of investment through insurance include *endowment policies, unit-linked life insurance, guaranteed income and growth bonds* and *annuities*. In a broad sense *pension schemes* may be regarded as a form of insurance and are therefore considered in this section.

An endowment policy, for which a regular monthly or annual premium is paid, provides life insurance cover in case the policyholder dies, or a capital sum with bonuses if (s)he survives. In effect, this is a savings plan with life cover. Unit-linked life insurance often takes the form of a single premium life insurance policy. Investors also have the option of placing their money in a unit linked regular premium plan. The funds are invested by the insurance company in shares, British Government stocks, etc., and the value of the bond rises and falls according to the state of the stock market. A bond is usually held for a longish period, for example ten years. The return could be less than the sum invested in the first place if the bond has been ill-managed. Insurance bonds are a risky investment, like shares, although the risk is spread over a large number of stocks. Guaranteed income and growth bonds allow the investor to invest a lump sum over a fixed period for a fixed rate of return. The income bond provides a regular income from the investment. The growth bond provides its return when the bond reaches the end of its lifetime.

Pension schemes allow workers to make regular savings for retirement. This is achieved through the state scheme of National Insurance contributions, employers' schemes and personal pension plans. As well as providing the security of an income in later years, pension schemes have the added advantage of being very tax efficient. When an investor purchases an annuity a lump sum is exchanged for a stipulated income for life, consisting partly of income on the money paid and partly of return of the capital. Whether this turns out to be a good investment or not depends on how long the investor lives. Often annuities are bought at the point of retirement, when a personal pension plan investment fund is converted into a pension.

5 Investing in stock markets

It has been demonstrated above how a large number of private individuals invest indirectly in *shares* when the money they have deposited with a bank or in an pension scheme is reinvested by fund managers. Investors may also buy shares in individual public companies, through an agent such as a stockbroker, in the hope of enjoying a regular income through the provision of dividends and/or capital appreciation. There are numerous factors which determine the buying and selling prices of shares, ranging from company analyses, through changes in the political environment to the behaviour of those actually buying and selling them. In summer 1997 Newcastle United's share price was adversely affected by injuries to their striker Alan Shearer! How companies raise capital from the issue of shares and put it to use has been described in Chapter 3 on company finance.

Banks, building societies and investment advisers also facilitate private investment in shares through the management of *personal equity plans* (PEPs). A PEP allows the investor to keep a portfolio of investments with a number of tax advantages. Putting money into *investment trusts* is another way of investing in shares. Investment trusts are limited companies floated on the Stock Exchange. One can buy shares in an investment trust, just like shares in any other company. They can be bought and sold at a profit (or loss), and they may provide a dividend. Another means of investing in shares across several companies is to invest in *unit trusts* (also known as 'mutual funds' in the USA). These provide for investment in a large number of companies, perhaps 60 or 70, often with a common theme such as 'small companies' or 'overseas markets'. For the small investor the administration, costs and risks associated with this kind of investment are lower than those when investing in company shares directly.

6 Alternative investments

It is possible to invest in many non-monetary ways, for example by buying art or antiques, jewellery, wine, stamps, forestry, memorabilia, minted gold coins and medallions or other precious metal objects, diamonds, property rents, and so on. Investment can also be made in raw materials, known as commodities and grouped as metals (e.g. copper, lead, zinc, gold), soft commodities (e.g. coffee, nuts, rubber), energy (e.g. crude oil, gas) and grain (e.g. maize, soya beans). These alternative investments are high risk and only for those with specialist knowledge.

7 Markets and the London Stock Exchange

Some aspects of stocks and shares have been considered in Chapter 3 on company finance, since the Stock Exchange is a major source of capital for public companies.

Financial markets are also important in their own right. City institutions provide a large number of jobs, add considerably to the gross national product and generate a substantial proportion of our invisible exports by providing financial services to clients all over the world. This section explains what defines a financial market, examines the London Stock Exchange and considers the way in which securities (i.e. gilts and public company shares) are traded. Much of the information in this section is derived from publicity material issued by the London Stock Exchange, such as the annual *Fact file*,[1] to which the reader is directed for further details. The London Stock Exchange also has a web site (http://www.stockex.co.uk) which describes its services and gives details of publications, many of which can be supplied free of charge.

7.1 Markets and exchanges

The use of the term 'market' here simply refers to a mechanism by which people may trade with one another. Trading might take place at a physical location. Equally buyers and sellers (or their representatives) may be spread geographically and communicate over telephone or computer networks. For each type of investment there is a market: money markets deal in overnight and other short term borrowing; the forex market deals in currencies; futures and options markets deal in derivative contracts (those which 'derive' their value from the prices of other financial instruments such as share prices, index levels or exchange rates); there are markets for commodities such as oil and grain; and stock exchanges are the markets for government bonds and company shares. Over sixty countries have stock exchanges.

7.2 Functions of the London Stock Exchange

Along with the New York and Tokyo stock exchanges the London Stock Exchange, as the UK's main domestic market for dealing in securities, is one of the world's largest. It comprises two functions in one: the *primary* market allows the government and companies to sell new securities to raise cash; the *secondary* market allows traders to buy and sell existing shares.

The London Stock Exchange operates three main markets:

Main Market (Official List)

The Main Market (Official List) permits trading in shares of listed UK and international companies. Joining the main market and conforming to the

Exchange's requirements increases the visibility of a company within the investment community. When applying for a listing on the Exchange companies have to provide a complete picture of their operation: trading history, financial record, management, business prospects, information on the securities to be listed, as well as the terms of any fund raising. The document that includes this information is known as the company's listing particulars. The information contained helps investors make their investment decisions and the company to market its shares. A company hoping to become listed has to be sponsored by a member firm, bank, broker, firm of solicitors or accountants or other financial advisers. At the end of 1996 there were 143 approved sponsors and 2704 companies listed on the main market.

British Government Securities (Gilt-edged) Market

The British Government Securities Market facilitates the buying and selling of gilts.

AIM

The Alternative Investment Market (AIM) was launched in June 1995 as the market for the Exchange's younger and fast-growing companies. The rules for joining are not as strict as those for the Main Market. There were 252 companies on AIM at the end of 1996.

The markets described above are not entirely independent of each other since what happens in one affects the others. This is because investors are always ready to change their investments to maximize the return on their capital.

As well as facilitating companies' raising of capital through the public trading of shares, the London Stock Exchange also provides trading and information services, regulates the listed companies and supervises the member firms that deal on the markets.

At this point it is worth describing the operation of OFEX (http://www.ofex.co.uk). Technically this is not a market, but an off-exchange mechanism whereby shares in unquoted securities can be traded. J.P. Jenkins Ltd is the principal market maker in this unregulated dealing facility which offers little protection to the investor. It is not part of the London Stock Exchange, but important because it is here that the shares of a number of well known companies, such as Glasgow Rangers, are traded.

7.3 Trading on the Main Market of the London Stock Exchange prior to 1986

Until October 1986, the International Stock Exchange in London operated on the basis of face-to-face trading on the floor of the Exchange. An investor wishing to buy or sell shares would engage a stockbroker to act on his or her behalf. The broker would buy from or sell to a stock-jobber, who dealt on the Exchange. The roles of broker and jobber were strictly separate. The jobber bought and sold shares on his own behalf, making his profit in doing so. The broker was not allowed to buy shares on his own behalf and then sell them to the client, but acted as an agent, taking a commission on the sale. This separation of functions was intended to protect the investor from malpractice. A broker would obtain quotes for both buying and selling prices from several jobbers, and then select the best for his client. Rates of commission were fixed. Jobbers were not permitted to deal with investors, but only with brokers.

7.4 Trading on the Main Market of the London Stock Exchange from 1986

7.4.1 Changes brought about by 'Big Bang'

In 1986, the system was deregulated by the government, the change taking place on 27 October 1986, known as 'Big Bang' day. Essentially, the rules were changed as follows:

- The distinction between jobbers and brokers was abolished.
- Stock Exchange member firms (i.e. those permitted to trade shares) could be owned by outside organizations, so that, for example, Barclays Bank bought up a broking firm and a jobbing firm to create a single market maker called Barclays de Zoete Wedd. (In 1997 the company announced plans to sell off some parts of this business.)
- A member firm could be a broker/dealer able to act both as an agency broker in the old way and as a principal (i.e. an intermediary between buyer and seller), buying and selling shares on its own account; or a member firm could become a committed market maker. (Market makers

earn money by taking the difference between buying and selling prices. They lend liquidity to the market since a potential buyer can always buy without having to hunt for a seller, and can therefore easily turn his or her securities into cash.) Market makers were required to make markets at all times in their registered stocks and to adhere to their quoted prices.

- Fixed commissions were abolished and brokers could now quote variable and competitive rates.
- Voting rights at the Exchange were transferred from individual members to member firms.
- Trading ceased to be a face-to-face activity on a single floor in favour of trading by telephone using computerized systems in brokers' offices anywhere in the UK.

The intention behind deregulation was to make the London stock market more competitive, so as to attract international financial business. At the same time the protection for the investor, provided by the old system, disappeared, so that other regulations were created for the purpose.

After Big Bang and a number of successful privatization issues, for example British Telecom and British Airways, there was a huge boom in trading, with many outside firms entering the market and setting up as broker/dealers or market makers. Share prices soared on the London market and for a time fortunes were made, at least on paper. Unfortunately, the expansion was too rapid and a crash came in October 1987, with prices plummeting in London and elsewhere. With hindsight it is now clear that up to this point investors had been taking too optimistic a view of the prospects for the economy, inflation, interest rates and corporate earnings. When the bubble burst, prices fell back sharply into line with more established valuation levels. The sudden fall in prices scared many small investors away from the market and, as the outlook for the economy worsened, a number of Stock Exchange member firms ceased trading.

The 1987 crash highlighted the fundamental tenet of investment: investors can achieve higher than average returns only by bearing higher than average levels of risk. Over the short term prices of shares and gilts can be volatile, but over the longer term the returns are generally higher than those available on safer instruments such as bank deposits. For example, over the 20 years to December 1996, equities yielded an annual real (i.e. above the rate of inflation) return of 12.1% compared to a 6.3% real return on gilts and a 3.7% real return on cash.[2]

7.4.2 Trading in new share issues

When public companies float new shares they usually do so by a public *offer for sale*, as was the case with the large privatization issues, such as British Gas. A prospectus is issued and a copy of it must be deposited at Companies House (see Chapter 2 on the legal status of businesses). The sale is advertised, typically by a full-page advertisement or perhaps even a mini-prospectus, in the *Financial Times*,[3] together with an application form. Members of the public can apply to purchase such shares direct from the company's agent and no commission charge is made in these cases. New shares may be issued by a *placing*, which means that the issuing house or company's broker makes private deals with clients (the big institutions) to take up the shares. If a company has many shareholders it may simply want permission for the shares to be dealt in on the Stock Exchange. An *introduction* is a relatively cheap way of doing this and does not involve raising any new capital.

Going public and issuing new shares are expensive procedures, considering the cost of Stock Exchange fees, administration and publicity. An issuing house, such as a merchant bank (known as an 'investment bank' in the USA), is employed to organize the issue. To ensure success, the issuing house arranges for the issue to be underwritten, that is some financial institutions agree to purchase any shares not taken up by the public. In return, they are paid an underwriting fee. It is essential that all shares be sold, otherwise the Registrar of Companies will not issue a trading certificate.

7.4.3 Trading in established shares using SEAQ, SEATS PLUS and SETS

Contrary to the popular movie image of share trading, UK brokers and dealers nowadays work in front of screens and with telephones, rather than on the floor of an exchange, except for in the futures and options markets. (Some overseas markets still operate by face-to-face dealing, for example Wall Street.) Even the role of the telephone is slowly diminishing, due to the introduction of new, sophisticated computerized systems.

When investors engage brokers to buy or sell established shares on their behalf, the brokers are bound to obtain the best price for their clients. SEAQ, SEATS Plus and SETS are systems that support this through permitting computerized trading.

SEAQ stands for Stock Exchange Automated Quotation System. As a continuously updated database of market maker prices it is used to discover current bid (i.e. buying) and offer (i.e. selling) prices and up to four market makers offering the prices quoted. SEAQ International applies to the international equity market.

SEATS Plus works in a similar way in support of the trading of all AIM companies and those listed UK equities whose turnover is insufficient for the market-making system. (SEATS originally stood for Stock Exchange Automated Trading System. 'Plus' refers to the software upgrade. Now SEATS is treated as a noun, rather than an acronym.)

October 1997 saw the introduction of the Stock Exchange Electronic Trading Service (SETS) for the shares of the UK's 100 largest companies. This is an order matching system in which member firms display their buy and sell orders to the market on an electronic order book. When prices match, orders automatically execute against one another on screen, thus improving speed and efficiency of transactions. Orders remain on the book until execution, or until the order is deleted, or when the specified expiry time has passed. Market makers dealing in shares of the largest 100 companies no longer place buy and sell orders by telephone. It is anticipated that shares in other companies will continue to be traded under the SEAQ structure pending a review of the progress of the order book.

7.5 Indices

Stock market indices designed to indicate industry performance have existed for a number of decades. In 1984, as part of the preparations for Big Bang, a new stock market index was launched to give a real-time indication of the performance of the leading companies in the stock market. Since then a range of real-time indices has grown to meet the requirements of investors and analysts. Together they are known as the FTSE (pronounced footsie) indices and are owned and managed by FTSE International, established by the Stock Exchange and the *Financial Times* in 1996. (The FTSE International web site at (http://www.ftse.com) which provides background information, press releases, access to daily stock databases, closing values and links to all FTSE company web sites.) The organization is advised by index users on issues such as the revision of indices so that they remain relevant and objective, how complex events are likely to affect calculations and how companies should be classified within industry sectors. Calculations are made by FTSE International for two main series of indices – the UK and the European – and the ISE/Nikkei 50, which is an index of leading Japanese shares quoted in London. Table 4.2 summarizes the main indices of the UK series.

Table 4.2 *The main indices of the UK series*

Index	Covers
FTSE 100	100 largest UK companies, calculated each minute
FTSE 250	250 next largest companies after FTSE 100
FTSE 350	Combination of FTSE 100 and FTSE 250
FTSE SmallCap	Approximately 550 smaller companies
FTSE All-share	Composite index covering the three segments (large, medium and small) of the UK series
FTSE Fledgling	Companies too small to be included in FTSE All-share index

It is the FTSE 100 that is updated by the minute and quoted regularly in news broadcasts. It was established in January 1984 at a base of 1000. By August 1997 it had breached the 5000 level. It is a weighted arithmetic index, meaning that a change in price is weighted by the issued share capital of a company. The effect of this is that a change in the share price of a small company has less weight than that of the same percentage in a large one. The other major index is the FTSE All-share, which is based on about 900 shares, giving a broader indication of the market's performance.

8 Sources of information on investments and markets

There are numerous sources that can provide investment and market data, from high-cost, real-time commercial online systems, through freely accessible Internet sites to print publications. Information on individual companies is important to those making investment decisions or analysts checking out markets. Readers are therefore encouraged to consider the content of this part of the book alongside Chapter 8 on company information.

8.1 Secondary sources for identifying online material on investments and markets

For a newcomer to this aspect of business information, there are some secondary sources that are particularly useful in providing an overview of what is available in the dominant electronic format. To identify the commercial online sources of relevance Amor's *Online manual*[4] can be consulted. Using the fifth edition of this work, it can be seen that databases of interest are mounted on commercial systems such as DataStar, Datastream, DIALOG, Dow Jones Interactive Publishing (formerly known as Dow Jones News/Retrieval), Dun and Bradstreet, ESA/IRS, FT Profile, Global Scan, ICC Information Ltd, IFR Securities Data, Infocheck Equifax, Jordans, NEXIS, Questel-Orbit, Reedbase Kompass Online, Reuters Business Information and Waterlow Signature. The subject headings 'company financials', 'economics', 'news and business' and 'securities' can be used in the *Online manual* to identify commercial online databases on markets. The manual also points to sources on pensions, personal finance, financial services and insurance.

For Internet users, Webber provides links to stock market data and personal investment advice web sites at http://www.dis.strath.ac.uk/business. RBA Information Services (http://www.rba.co.uk), also links to several sites of relevance. The 'larger' Internet directories provide routes to sites that are appropriate to the business information professional searching for investment and market data, for example, Yahoo's business and economy section (http://www.yahoo.com). Readers are reminded that web sites often have limited life-spans and change location. The sites identified in this section were accessible in the locations cited in summer 1997: whether they are still there, or are now as useful, can only be discovered by checking online.

8.2 Primary sources on investments and markets

8.2.1 Investments and market information sources offered by commercial online hosts

Of the commercial hosts, one of the most important is Datastream/ICV, which, as well as covering the subject areas of equities, bonds, corporate accounts and indices in real-time, provides historical and forecast data and offers software services. Bloomberg offers similar services. The forecast information is supplied as purchasable extras by third parties such as Hemmington Scott or Edinburgh Financial Publishing. Readers of the *Financial Times* will note that many of the graphs supplied in the newspaper are derived from Datastream. A number of financial information products and services are marketed by the Thomson Financial Services group: *Technical data*, a source of online analysis for traders, sales people, researchers and portfolio managers; *CDA spectrum*, a database of share ownerships; and *IFR securities data*, which provides new issues, mergers and corporate transaction data. The Dialog Corporation's *Profound* service and Reuters Business Information focus much of their work on equities and financial indices. Dow Jones Interactive gives securities and historical information and history on several thousand world-wide share issues.

It is possible to use the data from these services with software that customizes the information. For example, Dow Jones customers can set up a portfolio to track investments and their value, receive up-to-date news on these and analyse the information further with ratios and other market data. Multimedia facilities are demonstrated on services such as Reuters Equity Focus and Bloomberg Financial Markets. These services distribute information services of news, data, and analysis of global financial markets and business, furnishing users with real-time financial information over a network. Users may also subscribe to the multimedia TV desk-top packages sold by these companies.

Stockbroker reports, which offer opinion on the performance and prospects of individual companies, whole industries and the economy are accessible on databases such as *Brokerline* and *ICC stockbroker research reports*. Thomson Financial Services provides stockbroker reports through *Investext* and its off-shoot *First Call*, which brings together market commentary and company specific updates from brokers. Thomson's *Pipeline* indicates citations database to investment research reports. These databases can be searched as dial-up services, or on CD-ROM. The web-based *Profound* service accesses analyst reports from broker houses as well as economic forecast information sources. It is worth noting that some hosts, such as ICC, act as distributors in the area of stockbroker research and do not have proprietary products.

8.2.2 Investments and markets information sources on the Internet

The Internet is used by financial services companies keen to attract investment. A number of sites have been designed to help the independent investor (and generate advertising revenue for the marketing professionals who maintain them). For example, readers may consult Omnium Communication's Financial Services Internet Directory (http://www.find.co.uk), which provides links to a number of financial services companies offering various products and services from mortgages to financial advice. The Electronic Share Information site (http://www.esi.co.uk), aims its services at the independent individual investor. Marketing companies that earn their revenue through publicizing services of other commercial companies offer a greater range of free services. For example, a directory of UK stockbrokers, financial glossary, useful links (including a page of links to stock exchanges), daily market report and 'closing news' aimed at the small investor are given at the MoneyWorld web site: (http://www.money-world.co.uk). An Internet site offering full (free) analysis of UK investment trusts, graphical analysis and details of fund managers resides at http://www.trustnet.co.uk.

Many of the web sites identified by the secondary sources described above provide much information free of charge. For example, at http://www.ft.com the *Financial Times* gives closing prices of 3000 equities on the London market, links to other stock exchange web sites and company information. An important web site that provides an equities directory of share prices of UK listed companies, historical graphs and brief financials is that of Hemmington-Scott: http://www.hemscott.co.uk/hemscott/. However, often what is mounted on these sites for public viewing is just sample material to attract users to the fee-based services. For instance, Primark allows limited access to its Web services, such as Datastream/ICV at http://www.datastream.com, as a taster for potential subscribers. Users need to be aware that when a service welcomes them with IDs and passwords for future use, this does not mean that they are permitted to mine a valuable suite of information sources free of charge. At the discovery on a Web page of the existence of a report likely to meet all current information needs, a user will often find that the service switches from free to fee-based. It is also important to check the time delays associated with any market data presented over the Web. For access to real-time data a subscription to a fee-based service is necessary.

8.2.3 Broadcast investments and markets information sources

One source of market information in the UK that is easily overlooked is that provided on teletext through the BBC's Ceefax and ITV's Oracle. The major latest share prices, indices and news stories can be accessed free of charge from these broadcasts.

8.2.4 Hard copy investments and markets information sources

A number of hard-copy publications are regularly consulted by business information managers in the financial services sector. The *Financial Times* newspaper can be counted amongst these, as can the Risk Measurement Service of the London Business School, which runs a subscription service that supplies information on investment risks. However, the majority of the hard-copy sources relevant to investments and markets are directories, examples of which are given below. The London Stock Exchange's *Daily official list*[5] is used to establish past official share prices for quoted companies. Edinburgh Financial Publishing's monthly serial *TED*[6] (*The estimates directory*), gives data on stockbrokers' buy and sell recommendations and earnings forecasts for quoted companies. This is also available in CD-ROM format. Hemmington-Scott's monthly *Company REFS*,[7] provides data on every UK equity including its five-year history, individual brokers' estimates, graphs and statistical information. It also provides ranking tables, so, for example, it is possible to identify companies by fastest growth rate. The CD-ROM version of the hard copy issues is known as *CD REFS*. To establish share ownership Fulcrum's *Index of nominees and their beneficial owners*[8] can be consulted. This publication makes it possible to trace shareholders who have nominated share accounts with private banks. Types of investment other than shares are also covered by directory publications such as the *FT unit trust year book*,[9] which is a guide to trusts operating in the UK and authorized by the Securities and Investment Board.

For further information on the pros and cons of the various forms of investment described above and details of other means of investing money (for example in derivatives, futures, options etc.) the reader should turn to specialist textbooks such as Gough,[10] Brett[11] and the *Which? way to save and invest*[12] edited by Filmer. Investment magazines such as the weekly *Investors chronicle*[13] and the broadsheet newspapers can be used to aid personal finance decisions. Those making significant investment decisions consult professional financial advisors. Note that this book does not purport to provide information on the basis of which readers should be able to make investment decisions.

9 Regulation of financial services in the UK

Concurrently with the 1986 deregulation of the stock market, the government introduced new controls through the Financial Services Act 1986. In contrast with the very strong, centralized control in the USA represented by the Securities and Exchange Commission, the British government opted for a form of self-regulation by the market, a decision that did not please everyone, and the wisdom of which has been called into question by subsequent cases of insider dealing and other City fraud.

The system is coordinated by the Securities and Investment Board Ltd (SIB), a limited company responsible to parliament. Its function is to approve financial service businesses and to authorize them to operate. The SIB's web site is at http://www.sib.co.uk. It is assisted by a number of self-regulating organizations (SROs), each of which implements rules of behaviour for its own field. The main SROs are: the Personal Investment Authority (PIA), which covers stockbrokers and independent financial advisers (this replaced the Financial, Intermediaries, Managers and Brokers Regulatory Authority and the Life Assurance and Unit Trust Regulatory Organization, commonly known as FIMBRA and LAUTRO); the Investment Managers Regulatory Organization (IMRO), covering managers of pension funds and other investment funds (http://www.imro. co.uk); and the Securities and Futures Authority (SFA), which regulates operators in futures and equities markets. The Recognized Professional Bodies (RPBs), such as the law societies and the institutes of chartered accountants, are also classed as regulatory bodies in so far as their members carry on investment business.

Within a couple of weeks of taking office in 1997 the new Labour government announced that responsibility for banking supervision would transfer from the Bank of England to the Securities and Investment Board. In a second phase of regulatory changes the other SROs would be merged with the SIB to create a single statutory authority with powers over banks, financial services, companies and markets. This announcement prefaced the overhaul of the 1986 Financial Services Act planned for late 1998 at the earliest. The problems of the fragmented and inefficient provision from 1986 onwards will be addressed in the new legislation to improve the protection of the public's investments and maintain confidence in the UK's financial services sector.

References

1   London Stock Exchange, *Fact file*, London, annual.
2   Hughes, M., *Barclays de Zoete Wedd equity-gilt study*, London, BZW, 1997.
3   *Financial Times*, London, Financial Times Information, daily.
4   Amor, L., (ed.), *The online manual*, 5th edn, Oxford, Learned Information, 1996.
5   *Daily official list*, London Stock Exchange.

6 *TED (The Estimates Directory)*, monthly.
7 *Company REFS*, Hemmington-Scott, monthly.
8 Davies, R. (ed.), *The index of nominees and their beneficial owners*, 7th edn, London, Fulcrum Research, 1996.
9 *1997 FT unit trust year book*, London, Pearson Professional, 1997.
10 Gough, L., *How the stock market really works*, London, Pitman, 1997.
11 Brett, M., *How to read the financial pages*, 4th edn, London, Century, 1995.
12 Filmer, E. (ed.), *Which? way to save and invest*, London, Penguin, 1997.
13 *Investors chronicle*, London, Financial Times Information, weekly.

Web sites

Bloomberg	http://www.bloomberg.com
Datastream	http://www.datastream.com
Edinburgh Financial Publishing	http://www.efasia.com
Electronic Shares Information	http://www.esi.co.uk
Financial Times	http://www.ft.com
FTSE International	http://www.ftse.com
Hemmington-Scott	http://www.hemscott.co.uk/hemscott/
Investment Managers Regulatory Organization	http://www.imro.co.uk
London Stock Exchange	http://www.stockex.co.uk
MoneyWorld	http://www.moneyworld.co.uk
Ofex	http://www.ofex.co.uk
Omnium Communications Financial Services Internet Directory	http://www.find.co.uk
RBA Information Services	http://www.rba.co.uk
Securities and Investment Board	http://www.sib.co.uk
Trustnet	http://www.trustnet.co.uk
Webber's business information web site	http://www.dis.strath.ac.uk/business
Yahoo	http://www.yahoo.com

Part 2
Defining information sources

5 Information in business

1 Introduction

Before discussing actual business information sources it is worth consider-ing the characteristics of information in business so that the context of the book might be set. It is not the intention here to provide a treatise on the nature of information: it's a great topic for stretching the intellect, but of little concern to businesses! This section, then, defines information for the purposes of this work, demonstrates how every firm can be regarded as an information system and looks at the differing information needs of busi-nesses.

2 From data to knowledge management
2.1 Data and information

For the purposes of this work the word 'data' is used for raw facts with undefined uses and applications. Information is data that has been processed – for example, by filtering, summarizing or organizing – to make it meaningful in a new way. Taking retail sales as an example, a printout of a till receipt comprises data; a sales report based on the till receipt is information. Information has certain characteristics and values that data do not share, as summarized in Table 5.1.

General textbooks on systems management elaborate on the themes summarized in Table 5.1. For example, Cooke and Slack[1] discuss the char-acteristics and cost of information in the context of decision support, and Martin and Powell[2] cover data and information, desirable characteristics of information, and its value and costs from a systems perspective.

For a broader view of the nature of information readers should turn to the information management press. Meadows[3] and Walker[4] draw together two series of essays. The former considers the information chain and how it contributes to the creation of knowledge; the latter provides a broader view of information management with a focus on social organization and lifestyles. Contributions in the early part of this work discuss information and the nature of information science. McGarry[5] provides a useful introduction to the topic in the first chapter of his book. Readers will discover that the treatment of the topic easily extends beyond the confines of business information management into subject areas such as philosophy, ethics and social policy.

Table 5.1 *Characteristics and value of information*

Information has:	Valuable information:	The value of information is realized through decisions which lead to:
• purpose	• assists the organization in its survival	• reduced costs
• identified user(s)	• increases knowledge	• eliminated losses
• timeliness	• reduces uncertainty	• increased sales
• particular volume and level of detail		• better utilization of resources
• channel of communication	• corrects, updates and adds to existing information	• prevention of fraud
• flow	• confirms that accuracy of existing information	• alternative courses of action
• cost	• increases control	
• value	• aids planning	

2.2 Knowledge and knowledge management

The term 'knowledge management' became a buzzword in the late 1990s and it is worth considering here the relationship between information and knowledge. Knowledge is classed as the understanding that is derived from information. So, to continue with the simple retail sales example given above, the recognition of the product that is providing the shop with the best profit would count as knowledge.

The concept of knowledge management has received much media attention in the popular business magazines and the business and management pages of the quality newspapers, and a number of textbooks on the topic have been published.[6, 7, 8, 9] In this literature businesses are urged to realize the wealth of their intellectual capital through identifying and sharing both explicit and tacit information in open, extended enterprises. It is argued that organizations often do not appreciate what 'they' know, least of all the 'knowledge' built up through the experience and learned behaviour of their staff. To take advantage of the understanding and skills of these people, and transform 'the learnt *know-what* to the experienced *know-how*',[10] organizations need to create a knowledge culture. In such an environment, team working is facilitated through information sharing, and

supported by new technologies that can integrate information provision –
for example intranets (which are discussed further in Chapter 6), video
conferencing and groupware. The company KPMG[11] provides a number of
practical applications of knowledge management activity. A worked example of how it can contribute to the bottom line is given by Bonaventura.[12]

To some commentators knowledge management has the appearance of
an abstract proposition describing just another management fad.
Holtham[13] discusses knowledge management's longevity in his paper 'Will
knowledge management survive until the twenty-first century?'. It might
be argued that it is a simple development of the established processes of
information auditing and strategy (described in the next chapter), with the
bonus of being of interest to decision makers from beyond the information
management community. For a discussion of the role of information specialists with regard to knowledge management readers are referred to the
essay by Klobas.[14]

3 The firm as an information system

It can be argued that a firm is an information system. Whatever it may
produce (or provide as a service), it must generate, process, acquire and use
information. Indeed, if one looks at the complex structure of a large manufacturing company, down through the various levels and functions of management and supervision, it is clear that apart from the pressers of buttons
and the pullers of levers on the shop floor, employees are mainly concerned
with information processing and transmission. The monitoring of performance and breakdown; the creation and communication of instructions,
advice and policies; the exchange of experience and knowledge; the scanning of the business environment; major and minor decisions at all levels
– all consist of or depend on satisfactory information. Table 5.2 shows
where information plays a role in the life-cycle of a product or service.

When looking at the firm as an information system, it is helpful to make
a distinction between internal and external information. Firms generate
and use information about their own internal workings: production and
sales figures; stocks of raw materials, work in progress and finished goods;
financial information such as accounts, profit and loss, and financial performance indicators; labour turnover and absenteeism; research and development reports, etc. Much of this information is quantitative in nature,
especially in the financial area, and this has led to the development of computer systems for handling the data from which it derives. These systems
are commonly referred to as management information systems (MIS) or

decision support systems, and a whole profession and body of study have grown up around them. Managers use these systems in order to study and improve the firm's processes and efficiency, to account to its shareholders for the use of resources and for its performance, and to meet legal requirements under company law and other statutes and regulations.

Table 5.2 *Information in the life-cycle of a product or service*

Product life-cycle activity	Information need/activity
Generation of ideas for products/services	Brainstorming where data from diverse sources is linked, e.g. trade advertisements, announcements, market activity.
Screening product/services ideas	Pitching of ideas against the firm's objectives and targets.
Market analysis of the potential for the product/service	Study of the market place.
Competitor and collaborator analysis	Company information.
Research and development into product/service	Technical, environmental, legal and patent information.
Testing of product/service	Demographic information.
Introduction of product/service	Sales – to verify commercial viability and assess the full market potential.
Production of product/service	Production control (internally generated).
Logistics of product/service handling	Distribution, warehousing, stock control, transport.
Product/service growth	Monitoring of competition and promotion of the product/service.
Throughout the entire process	Management control, education and training.

Every firm exists within a multitude of overlapping and increasingly turbulent environments. In order to survive, let alone flourish, the firm must understand, respond to and even manipulate those environments. A simple model will illustrate the nature of these environments. Figure 5.1

shows the firm within an immediate environment containing the major factors and players with which it must contend, while Figure 5.2 lists some of the aspects that affect the business environment. The firm needs information on these two sets of factors. As Drucker[15] has pointed out: 'A serious cause of business failure is the common assumption that conditions – taxes, social legislation, market preferences, distribution channels, intellectual property rights, and many others – *must* be what we think they are or at least what we think they *should* be.'

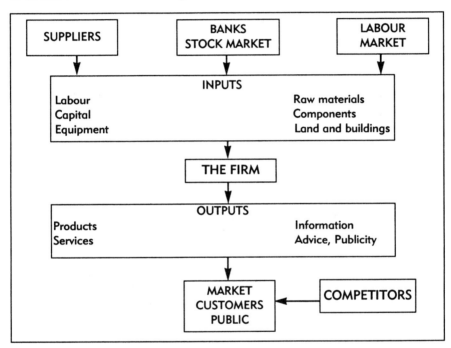

Fig. 5.1   *The firm in its environment*

New science, technology, inventions
Legislation and regulations
Taxation
Economic trends
Social trends
Political trends
Intellectual property
Standards, test methods, codes of practice
Consumer behaviour
World markets

Fig. 5.2   *The wider environment*

Within the immediate environment, the firm is modelled as an input-output system, taking in resources from its environment and converting them to outputs, which are returned to the environment in a process of exchange. Its major inputs of labour, capital, equipment and the like are obtained from the key sources indicated, such as other firms supplying equipment and raw materials; the financial market providing capital, loans and overdrafts; and so on. Major outputs are products and/or services, but it should not be forgotten that firms selling products often also provide technical information and advice on the application of their products; firms also generate other intangible outputs such as public relations and publicity. Outputs are aimed at and taken up by customers in the marketplace and by the public in general. However, unless the firm has a monopoly, it will have competitors who are also engaged in an exchange with a closely similar environment. In terms of business-to-business marketing, it is worth underlining that the firm's immediate environment contains three other highly significant kinds of firm: suppliers, customers and competitors.

The information implications of this scenario are considerable. The firm must study the needs and wants of the market in order to produce and sell the right outputs. It must be aware of new sources of supply, alternative raw materials, cheaper supplies, mergers and takeovers between suppliers, and their implications for its own supplies – in short any change that destabilizes its own supply position. Likewise, the firm must monitor the new products, advertising campaigns, pricing policies, organizational changes and other activities of its competitors, in order not to be left behind in the struggle to maintain or perhaps increase its share of the market.

All this is taking place against a background, in the wider environment shown in Figure 5.2, of new legislation; political, economic and social change; scientific and technical developments; regulatory systems; pressure groups such as the green lobby; constraints imposed by intellectual property rights. Even long-term population trends cannot be ignored in the planning process. For example, the expected increase in the number of older people in Britain and reduction of the teenage population have serious implications for the suppliers of goods and services, to the elderly on the one hand and to the teenage fashion and pop market on the other. Finally, as if this were not enough, every facet of the model can be multiplied many times if the firm has to operate and compete at an international level.

Monitoring and acquiring information on these multifarious aspects of the environment constitute an enormous task, if it is to be done comprehensively. Relating this information to the firm's own information and decision system, so that it can respond effectively to change and maintain its position, is even more difficult.

4 Information needs of businesses

There have been many studies of the need for and use of information by different groups of users – such as managers, scientists and engineers – and in different kinds of organization. The nature and content of information has been examined in various ways. It is not proposed to review these matters in detail here, but we can identify a few key characteristics of the information scene as it appears in the context of the firm and its wider environment. Readers interested in a fuller treatment on how information needs are assessed should refer to the work by Nicholas.[16]

Some industries are more information intensive than others and information needs vary with differing levels of information intensity. For example, large, highly structured firms that are export-orientated and operate technology-driven production processes have high needs for information on markets, competitors and the prevailing economic and political climates. Knowing what drives an industry helps determine the information needs of the companies that operate in it. For example, if competition within the industry is vigorous, a competitor analysis service finds a ready market; if substitute products are a threat a new product current awareness service may be useful. Efforts should be made to focus information provision along the crucial points of a product or service's value chain: for example in pharmaceuticals this is research and development; in fashion it is distribution; and for the manufacture of cosmetics and perfume marketing is important.

Just as information needs vary from industry to industry, attitudes to formalized information services differ according to corporate cultures. A company where decisions have to be made with reference to formally published material such as research publications and market intelligence, or where management decisions are made according to previous practice, would be more receptive to formal information services than one where decisions were made as a result of brainstorming sessions.

With regard to offering business information services, practical experience demonstrates some of the problems in responding to user information needs. Users often find it difficult to articulate their information request. After all, they are often looking for something that they have not encountered before – they may not know, for example, what format it takes, nor its size – so it can be difficult to describe. The need itself might present itself as a demand, a desire, a requirement, or be framed in terms of actual information sources to be used. Business information professionals are used to dealing with the 'wrong' question (along the lines of 'What is the capital of Paris?'), one put too generally (the user makes a vague general request because he or she believes this makes it easier for the information services staff), or put too specifically (when an inappropriate source might be named). If the information requested is not the information needed, then the resulting information presented will not be the information wanted.

For example, a user of a public library business information service based in the Midlands might express a need to see a business directory published for West Lothian. The librarian could go ahead and source the business directory. This is likely to involve contacting the West Lothian Business Centre in Livingston and arranging for the directory to be sent. Alternatively, prior to acting on the request, the librarian might enquire as to the purpose of consulting the directory. If it is simply the case that the telephone number of a company based in West Lothian is sought, then the request for the directory is redundant, since this information is available from the *Yellow Pages* directory, held on the shelves in the reading room of the public library. This demonstrates how an information *demand* (i.e. what the user asks for) needs clarification before being classed as the actual information *need*.

At the other end of the scale are users who are happy that their information needs are being met through readily available sources. They prefer to use informal sources such as other employees and professional colleagues, in-house memoranda and reports, personal files, or simply their own experience and instincts rather than formal documentary sources such as those described in Parts 3 and 4 of this book. They will often go to extraordinary lengths through personal and informal channels to find information that is readily available (and possibly of greater value) in their company library or information centre. Business information professionals need to publicize the services they offer to prevent this wasted effort. This theme is examined more closely in the context of intranet development in Chapter 6.

It is worth considering here attempts to meet business information needs on a national scale in the UK. The development of the Business Link network (Business Shop network in Scotland), announced by the Department of Trade and Industry in 1992, was initiated to respond to problems of business support, including the provision of information. The major local providers of business services – such as training and enterprise councils, chambers of commerce, enterprise agencies and local authorities – were encouraged to set up partnerships to provide business support services ranging from account management to information, advice, counselling and consultancy. The focus was to be on small and medium-sized enterprises, concentrating on those with 10–200 employees. It was felt that a coordinated approach to the provision of business information services would lessen the fragmentation and general confusion over the remit and facilities of the many types of organization that claimed to be information providers. The first Business Links were launched in 1993 in six pilot areas. By November 1996 there were 70 Business Links at 160 sites.

The growth of the network points to its success. However, there have been criticisms of its operation, particularly with regards to the level of training of business information personnel and the involvement of established business information services in public libraries in the scheme. A study of the Business Link initiative published in 1995[17] raised concern over the degree of non-involvement of the public library services. Abell and Smith's review,[18] which appeared a year later, demonstrated that there had been a change and that the majority of Business Links were developing links with libraries. This report discusses the problems associated with public library participation in such schemes, as well as the advantages.

Taking into consideration that there is no national strategy for information in the UK as a whole, let alone for business information (except the business information plan outlined for Scotland in 1993[19]), the Business Link network makes a significant contribution to information service provision. In the best examples it is evident that policy makers have acknowledged the links between information and economic policy, which play an important role both in meeting the information needs of local firms, and encouraging their prosperity.

References

1   Cooke, S. and Slack, N., *Making management decisions*, Englewood Cliffs, Prentice Hall, 1984.
2   Martin, M. and Powell, P., *Information systems: a management perspective*, London, McGraw-Hill, 1992.
3   Meadows, A.J., *Knowledge and communication: essays on the information chain*, London, Library Association, 1991.
4   Walker, G. (ed.), *The information environment: a reader*, New York, G.K. Hall, 1992.
5   McGarry, K., *The changing context of information: an introductory*

analysis, 2nd edn, London, Library Association, 1993.

6 Nonaka, I. and Takeuichi, H., *The knowledge creating company*, New York, Oxford University Press, 1995.

7 Skyrme, D. and Amidon, D.M., *Creating the knowledge-based business*, London, Business Intelligence, 1997.

8 Stewart, T., *Intellectual capital: the new wealth of nations*, New York, Doubleday, 1997.

9 Von Krogh, G. and Roos, J. (eds.), *Managing knowledge: perspectives on co-operation and competition*, London, Sage, 1996.

10 Bonaventura, M., 'The benefits of a knowledge culture', *Aslib proceedings*, 49 (4), 1997, 82–9.

11 *The power of knowledge: a business guide to knowledge management*, London, KPMG, c.1997.

12 See Reference 10.

13 Holtham, C., 'Will business knowledge management survive until the twenty first century?', in Raitt, D., Blake, P. and Jeapes, B. (eds.), *Proceedings of the 21st International Online Meeting, London, 9–11 December 1997*, 79–85.

14 Klobas, J.E., 'Information services for new millennium organizations: librarians and knowledge management', in Raitt, D. (ed.), *Libraries for the new millennium: implications for managers*, London, Library Association, 1997, 39–64.

15 Drucker, P., 'The information executives truly need', *Harvard business review*, January–February 1995, 54–62.

16 Nicholas, D., *Assessing information needs: tools and techniques*, London, Aslib, 1996.

17 Hyde, M., A *review of Business Link information services and their association with public libraries*, BLR&DD report 6178, St Albans, Cimtech–University of Hertfordshire, 1995.

18 Abell, A. and Smith, C., *Public sector involvement with Business Links*, London, TFPL/BLRIC, 1996.

19 Mackay Consultants, *Business information plan for Scotland*, Glasgow, Scottish Library and Information Council, 1993.

6 Information as a resource

1 Introduction

For a long time information managers hankered after recognition of the contribution of efficient information services provision to organizational success. From the mid-1990s media interest in the Internet (both negative and positive), and a number of well-publicized surveys on topics such as information as an asset,[1] information overload[2] and the employment opportunities for knowledge workers[3] generated awareness of information as a resource. The *Financial Times* made it official in March 1997 when Earl stated 'our concept of management is going out of date. Information is the new resource'.[4]

Building on the material presented in Chapter 5, the aims of this chapter are to demonstrate (in broad terms) the value of information to business organizations, to discuss how too much information can be a hindrance in the workplace, to introduce the established concepts of information auditing and strategy, and to outline how business information sources hold the most value when managed by business information staff offering integrated information services. Since much has been published elsewhere on these themes, readers are encouraged to follow up the references provided to further material.

2 The value of information as a resource

There are several ways in which information is regarded as a resource. Information supports businesses in the achievement of their objectives as a tool for corporate decision making, even at the most basic level of facilitating communication across the enterprise. The benefits of the strategic management information resources identified as aiding survival, providing internal trade-off, encouraging competitive advantage, leading to stability and reducing uncertainty are summarized by Davenport and Cronin.[5] Awareness of organizational information resources allows companies to save money and effort by removing the temptation of individual departments to maintain separate information systems. With adequate information on the external environment they can consider their future requirements and build up a degree of protection against change by anticipating it. Innovation is encouraged through investment in information when, for example, one firm's competitors are not investing as much as the other in research and development or market research.

Stonier[6] examined the economic importance of information in the early 1980s, concluding that in a post-industrial society, with a decline in the importance of manufacturing industries and growth of service industries, information can generate wealth. In some instances information *per se* is valuable, for example clients pay veterinary surgeons for advice on how to nurse their pets back to health following illness. In manufacturing industries it is the adding of value to a process – for example in providing technical knowledge for creating goods or options for the logistics of distribution – that is important. For high-value manufactured goods, information regarding the derivation of the product is responsible for competitive advantage: many consumers like to be seen sporting the 'right' brand of clothing or driving a certain make of car. It is interesting to note here that the business information industry, one that generates income for access to sources, has been identified as the second most profitable service industry after water.[7]

A number of studies have been made to assess the value of information as a corporate resource, to which readers are referred for further examples.[8,9] *The value and impact of information*[10] and *The value of information to the intelligent organisation*[11] collect together several essays and case studies by different authors. Other texts, for example that by Kingma,[12] look at the economics of information and issues such as information markets, economic research on information topics, and cost benefit analyses of information goods and services. Snyder and Davenport's *Costing and pricing in the digital age*[13] considers the value of networked information services and includes worked examples of how values can be translated into charges for information services provision.

3 Too much of a good thing: information overload

Where there is a superabundance of information, some of which may be irrelevant or of dubious quality or arrives too quickly, it becomes information overload, which can be damaging to employees and their business. In these cases the value of information is severely diminished. Research conducted in industrialized nations of Europe, the United States and Asia Pacific demonstrated that the problems associated with information overload are tangible: 49% of managers felt that quite often or very frequently they were unable to handle the information they received and two-thirds of them believed that information in their organizations was under-utilized. Some managers were even 'reluctant to admit personally such sufferance for fear of being seen to fail in their job responsibilities'.14

The cause of information overload can be attributed to a number of factors. The focus on information as a resource and the replacement of management hierarchies with matrix, or flat, management structures have altered communication processes within organizations. In the past individuals had a fixed place in the chain of command and were locked into certain relationships that brought with them a formal set of information filters. A diminution in the power of perceived status evident from the organizational chart invites more people to access one another more frequently. This freedom to approach individuals is facilitated by the widespread adoption and use of new technologies, some of which were previously accessible only to the privileged few. There are so many different channels of communication open to those who want to contact others, all advertised on organizational literature, including individuals' business cards.

Poor information management techniques (of often well-meaning colleagues) contribute to the impact of information overload. The ready availability of software and other equipment for the creation and duplication of documents enables a single employee to adopt the role of author, publisher and distribution agent: it does not take much effort to relay information with an undisciplined enthusiasm, regardless of information content or quality, or whether it matches the information needs of the recipients. In an electronic environment the sender takes advantage of the strengths of computers for communication purposes: speed (the message/document will reach the recipients quickly) and storage (the recipient will have plenty of space to store this message/document). The 'overloader' is not discriminating enough in what is sent to whom, and works in tandem with computer distribution systems that are incapable of making improvements to the quantity or quality of information conveyed.

Those who receive unsolicited information by these methods can tolerate a certain degree of overload. Uncertainty about future developments encourages the maintenance of individual storage systems for 'just-in-case' information that, although irrelevant at the time of receipt, might be important in the future. However, for many the rate at which both solicited and unsolicited information reaches them exceeds their information processing capacity as human beings. This is pertinent if they carry out very complex tasks with important consequences, under great pressure to frequent deadlines, in a highly charged environment.[15] This also applies to those who support others working in such an environment.

Problems associated with information overload may be emotional, social or political. The time spent handling the incoming flood of documents and messages, and then trying to locate the high-value information content in material received, has been identified as a major difficulty. When too much time is spent on information activities, other tasks are neglected: 47% of the managers interviewed for the Reuters survey[16] said that the collection of information for decision making distracted them from their main job responsibilities, and many believed that the cost of collecting information exceeded its value to business.

An attempt to gather all relevant information pertinent to any decision can delay work and actions, especially when the information finally gathered is diverse. Waiting for all available information leads to procrastination that may become open-ended. More information offers more choices, increasing the complexity of decision making, yet in theory decisions should be made faster because the organization has invested in new technologies and information services to make the processes easier.

Irrational behaviour may manifest itself in bizarre decision making because the overloaded individual is overwhelmed by the amount of information to hand. Conversely, certain workers may no longer be able to recognize important information and are in fact *under*whelmed. Aligned with this is frustration and stress 'caused by not knowing whether the crucial information exists or if it exists, of not being sure where and how to locate it . . . caused when we know where some essential information is located but we are not sure how to access it' and the claim that 'the worldwide burden of keeping up with the information explosion has led to soaring executive stress, loss of job satisfaction and physical ill-health'.[17]

Various strategies can be employed to cope with information overload. Some employees find it easier to ignore certain information sources and work without them. Others rely on the delegation of information-handling activity. Improved information literacy through training helps individuals to learn effective means of searching for information, particularly with reference to the ratio between recall (i.e. the amount of material uncovered) and precision (i.e. the relevance of what is found). To avoid paralysis, where decisions are delayed in anticipation of the arrival of further information, employees should learn to be 'maximizers' rather than 'satisficers',[18] Whereas maximizers aim to uncover every detail prior to action, satisficers use just enough information to make a decision. Business information services staff can play an active role in minimizing organizational information overload.

4 Maximizing information value through information audit and strategy

Some organizations have created information strategies to ensure that information resources are put to best use and to lessen the problems described above. Information strategies derive from an initial consideration of existing information resources, the use of information within the organization, human and technical resources dedicated to using information and the costs and values involved in corporate information flows. This process, for which there are various approaches,[19] is known as information auditing. Information activities are matched with the objectives of the organization as a whole. Where there are gaps or shortcomings – for example the company may have stated plans to enlarge its market share for a product or service, but has no access to specialist market research information sources – strategies for overcoming them are documented, and then implemented. A information strategy document also discusses how the strategy will be monitored and updated, and the responsibilities of the staff involved in maintaining it.

With an information strategy it is argued that problems associated with poor information handling in organizations (such as the collection of information that is not required; the storage of information long after it is needed; inaccessibility of information to those who want to use it; information overload; inefficiencies in methods used to collect, analyse and retrieve information and the duplication of information related work activities) can be reduced. An information strategy can ensure continuity in planning for information use.

The design of an information strategy and its implementation also serves as a good public relations exercise for information professionals. It admits the crucial importance of information to an organization's success and of those responsible for its provision and management. Control of information-related activity is put into the hands of information management staff, who are seen to be instrumental in identifying the information needs of the organization; stimulating and initiating cooperation across departments; analysing and meeting the need for personnel development with reference to information resources; developing information resources; participating in the planning of information systems and exploiting information technology. It is argued that an organization with an information strategy is less likely to make cuts in information services provision in times of financial crisis.

For further information on information auditing and strategy formulation, including case study examples, readers are referred to Orna's *Practical information policies*.[20]

5 The value that business information specialists add to intranets

The concepts of information auditing and information strategy formulation were originally developed when the most regularly used information sources were hard copy. Now, in the most advanced organizations, employees expect the primary format for the storage and retrieval of information to be digital, and to be provided at the desktop with a free range of web-based tools that allows transparent access to a selection of integrated information sources across the enterprise. Since mid-1995 the term 'intranet' has been adopted for such a system.

It is widely claimed that an intranet is relatively simple to build technologically, is easy to use once implemented and can bring benefits in terms of organizational communication and knowledge sharing, as well as financial savings. For example the automation of transactional information processes shortens turnaround time and reduces printing and document publishing costs. The return on investment can be as high as 1500%.[21] In 1996, for example, the computer manufacturer Sun Microsystems estimated that $25 million per annum was saved in staff time through the use of its intranet.[22]

Much of the information activity over an intranet is transactional. For example, day-to-day messaging that previously used paper-based systems – form filling, memos and the like – for purposes such as the claiming and payment of expenses, migrates easily to a set of intranet exchanges. The first actual information *sources* to be mounted on an organization-wide intranet server are often internally produced files holding relatively static in-house information, for example electronic telephone directories and staff manuals. Internal web pages on the intranet can be used as launch pads to external sources, such as freely accessible Internet web sites. Latterly, externally produced sources offered by the commercial business information providers have been brought to the desktop using the organizational intranet as its vehicle for delivery. This is discussed in the next chapter.

Business information services staff can make a contribution to the development of corporate intranets with the objective of ensuring that the organization derives the maximum value from networked information services. Sometimes business information specialists are engaged from the outset, working with systems teams as intranet architects. At others they are brought in at a later stage to bring a sense of order to a burgeoning succession of difficult-to-navigate web pages that have grown up organically over the lifetime of the intranet. Information services staff provide an interface to the sources available, for example in the creation of subject gateways to both internal and external web sites of interest, so that users know that the information is derived from a reliable source. These roles draw on the business information specialists' training in the discriminatory techniques of the selection, acquisition, abstracting, cataloguing, classification, indexing and packaging of information. Additional skills in negotiation, a knowledge of law relating to intellectual property and the training of end-users come into play as commercial sources (previously accessible only to expert intermediaries) are rolled out to the desktop. The established basic principles of information services provision – that is (a) offering expertise in the content and selection of the best available sources and (b) demonstrating commitment to putting knowledge to work, linking information users to the right resources at the right time – help organizations realize the value from networked information.

White[23] provides a fuller treatment on business information and intranets in a report that covers Internet and intranet technology, the business impact of intranets, intranet and the business information and industry, intranet implementation and profiles of companies offering intranet services. For a discussion of the involvement of information services staff in the collection development of web resources see Hall and Russell.[24]

6 The value of information services

This book is concerned primarily with business information sources and discusses print and electronic material that can be used in the support of business functions. For example, using the text it is possible to identify the major sources on the advertising and distribution of products and services (Chapter 12), or patents (Chapter 13). It is not the purpose of this book to discuss the technical or administrative duties related to the maintenance of the sources that it describes (for example, how to set up a CD-ROM juke box, how to relegate stock, etc.), nor the general management functions that allow business information managers to meet user information needs (for example, how to recruit and train information services staff, how to manage budgets). However, in the context of a discussion of the value of information as a resource, it is worth pointing out that an agile, integrated information service built around business processes offers greater value to an organization than the individual sources that comprise such a service. As more information sources are distributed from the 'centre' there is the danger that end-users of business information may perceive the 'visible' *sources* accessible from the desktop as representing the entire information *service*. As a consequence, they will undervalue the information service, at the extreme believing that a completely DIY approach to information handling will satisfy all information needs. Business information practitioners know that this leads to a variety of problems, many of which have been described above: information overload, duplication of effort in maintaining information systems, etc. At worst, the organization may decide to do away with a dedicated information service and its staff. As well as promoting information as a valuable organizational resource then, business information managers have to promote their services, making explicit how the sources in regular use are supported by a specialist team, which adds value to information services provision across the entire enterprise. After all, a resource can only be such when managed properly by professionals with appropriate training.

References

1 Reuters Business Information, *Information as an asset: the invisible goldmine,* London, Reuters, 1995.
2 Reuters Business Information, *Dying for information?*, London, Reuters, 1996.
3 Create, *Tomorrow's people*, Tunbridge Wells, Create, 1997.
4 Earl, M., *Financial Times*, 19th March 1997.
5 Davenport, L. and Cronin, B., 'Strategic information management – forging the value chain', *International journal of information management*, **1**, 1988, 25–34.
6 Stonier, T., *The wealth of information*, London, Methuen, 1983.
7 Business information industry, *What's new in business information*, 1997, 8, 64.
8 Burk, C.F. and Horton, F.W., *Infomap: a complete guide to discovering corporate information resources*, 2nd edn, Englewood Cliffs, Prentice Hall, 1988.
9 Best, D. (ed.), *The fourth resource: information and its management*, Aldershot, Gower, 1996.
10 Feeney, M. and Grieves, M. (eds.) *The value and impact of information*,

East Grinstead, Bowker Saur, 1994.

11 HERTIS Information and Research and TFPL, *The value of informa-tion to the intelligent organisation*, Hatfield, University of Hertfordshire Press, 1994.

12 Kingma, B.R., *The economics of information*, Englewood, Libraries Unlimited, 1996.

13 Snyder, H. and Davenport, E., *Costing and pricing in the digital age*, London, Library Association Publishing, 1997.

14 See Reference 2.

15 See Reference 2.

16 See Reference 2.

17 See Reference 2.

18 Driver, M.J. et al., *The dynamic decision maker*, San Francisco, Jossey-Bass, 1993.

19 Ellis, D. et al., 'Information audits, communication audits and infor-mation mapping: a review and summary', *International journal of information management*, **13**, 1993 134–51.

20 Orna, E., *Practical information policies*, Aldershot, Gower, 1990.

21 Bannister, N., 'Now, get to grips with your baby net', *Guardian*, 26 April 1997, 41.

22 Gilhooly, C., *Blazing a trail in intranet usage*, http://www.techweb.com/.

23 White, M., *Business information in the intranet age*, London, TFPL, 1997.

24 Hall, H. and Russell, A., 'Resource management in an electronic envi-ronment: company library web pages and collection development prin-ciples', *Proceedings of the 20th International Online Meeting*, London, December 3–5 1996, 471–5.

7 Information formats

1 Introduction

Since it is an information need, rather than an information format, that drives an information user to seek a particular information source, the approach throughout this book is to examine information sources by their function. For example, there is a section on sources that provide information on companies and another on sources that help identify trade marks and their ownership. Where appropriate, there is comment on the formats in which the information sources appear. However, the priority is that the information need is met. Whether this is achieved by consulting a book or a web page is immaterial, provided that the source is fit for the purpose at an acceptable cost.

The aims of this chapter on information formats are:

- to point to the wide variety of formal and informal sources
- to demonstrate that for locating primary information, secondary and tertiary sources can be used
- to highlight that people and organizations can be used as business information sources
- to show how business information professionals keep up to date with business information sources
- to make some general comments on the growth of business information online.

At the end of the section some criteria for the evaluation of information sources, regardless of format (print, online or grapevine), are given. Relevant web sites are listed at the end of the chapter.

2 Formal and informal information sources

For the purposes of this book, a formal information source is one that is published in the public domain. It may appear in print, as an online database, as a web page on the Internet, or as a contribution to a discussion in a news group. Clearly there are levels of formality within these categories: a complaint about the service of a business information supplier broadcast to the UK Online User Group e-mail discussion list would be regarded as less formal than an article on the same subject published in a refereed journal.

Formal information sources may be for quick reference – for example dictionaries, encyclopaedias, directories, yearbooks, databooks, manuals or alert services. This category of information source also includes straightforward monographs and serials, as well as technical publications such as patents and standards. Despite the spectacular growth in electronic media in the late 20th century, print sources are alive, well and staunchly defended (see, for example, Crawford and Gorman[1] and Stoll.[2] However, it is important to note that electronic media are dominant in many aspects of business information provision, notably on investments and markets, as outlined in Chapter 4, and, in some instances, the only available source on a particular subject may be electronic.

The category of informal sources covers word-of-mouth alerts, rumour and speculation that cannot be substantiated by any 'published' format. Many companies, failing to exploit the formal sources relevant to their business activity, rely heavily on informal sources. For example, an examination of the Scottish high-performance textile industry demonstrated worrying reliance on informal sources.[3]

3 Tertiary and secondary information sources

Given the plethora of information sources, business information managers need to be able to identify quickly the best one(s) to consult for the work to be completed. Familiarity with the sources at their immediate disposal makes this possible in the longer term, but a new user of business information sources relies on the use of tertiary and secondary sources in order to find the primary source where the actual information sought resides. For those unfamiliar with the use of the terms 'tertiary' and 'secondary' in this context, an example can illustrate their meaning. The principle is to remember that tertiary sources of information direct users to secondary sources of information, and secondary sources point to primary sources of information.

For example, a request for journal articles on research into a particular chemical process is made to the information manager of a special library of an engineering company. The information manager is not used to receiving such requests so consults the database catalogue of the online hosts to which the company has access. The information manager identifies relevant bibliographic databases for the purposes of the search. The information search is completed and the information manager has ten citations to relevant journal articles. The journal articles may be found within the stock of the special library or requested through interlibrary loan mechanisms.

In this example the primary information is in the journal articles, the secondary sources used to identify them were the bibliographic databases on the hosts, and the database catalogues served as tertiary sources in identifying which bibliographic databases the information manager needed to consult. Had the information manager found full text articles online, the database catalogue would have served as the secondary source pointing to primary sources in electronic format.

Students will see that a bibliography presented at the end of an essay can be used a secondary source should the person reading the work want to follow up the references given. To a degree this textbook serves as a tertiary or secondary source, since in many of the sections it refers readers to primary business information sources, where answers to specific reference enquiries may be sought. The Internet search engines and directory services serve as secondary sources, as they direct users to specific Internet resources such as web pages.

A few general tertiary and secondary sources are mentioned here due to their importance as keys to the literature in many subject areas. It is also worth pointing out that business information enquiries do not necessarily demand the use of specialist business information sources, and therefore the business information manager needs to be aware of these general sources. For example, as well as aiding enthusiasts to link up others who share their passion for skateboarding, computer games or Christian fellowship, the *Directory of British associations*[4] can identify contacts for further information for the serious business information enquirer by pointing to organizations such as trade associations.

The major British, multipurpose subject directory is *Walford's guide to reference material*, which is produced in three volumes.[5, 6, 7] Volume two covers business. *The reference sources handbook*,[8] comprises chapters by different experts commenting on, and listing, sources by format. The *Aslib directory of information sources in the United Kingdom*[9] provides references to organizations, publications and collections with contact details.

More specialized secondary and tertiary sources are published to cover particular formats of information. These include: *Current British directories*[10] and Dawson's *Top 4000 directories and annuals*,[11] which describe directory publications; *Benns media*[12] and *Willings press guide*,[13] which concentrate on serial and media sources; and the Clover publications – *Newspaper index*[14] and *Information index*[15] – which route the user to news stories in the press. To identify online sources the most comprehensive sources are the *Gale directory of databases*[16] and the two volume *Multimedia and CD ROM directory.*[17]

3.1 Tertiary and secondary business information sources

This book is a discursive text, as opposed to a directory, and therefore provides examples of sources rather than exhaustive lists. This section outlines some of the major general tertiary and secondary sources in the business information field. Tertiary and secondary sources of particular relevance to other material discussed in the book can be found in the appropriate sections.

3.1.1 Identifying business information sources in all formats

Business information basics[18] from Headland Business Information is a survey of business information resources giving examples of key UK, European, US and international print and electronic publications, as well as organizations, with evaluative comment. Croner's *A–Z of business information sources*[19] comprises an alphabetical list of subjects showing the relevant sources, and lists directories, periodicals, statistics, market reports and institutional sources such as trade associations. Its loose-leaf format is updated quarterly. With specific reference to Britain, The *Macmillan directory of UK business information sources*[20] identifies sources by industry according to NACE Rev 1 Standard Industrial Classification codes.

There are numerous secondary and tertiary sources dedicated to specific types of business information source. For example, *Business information from government*[21] allows users to identify business information sources held by government departments and official bodies; Euromonitor's *World directory of trade and business journals*,[22] available in hard copy and on CD-ROM, limits reference to serial publications. Newspaper and journal articles can be accessed through print or online abstracting and indexing services. To locate public access collections of business information sources the *World directory of business information libraries*[23] can be consulted.

3.1.2 Identifying electronic business information sources

Learned Information publishes a number of tertiary sources of use to the online community working with business information. The *Online manual*[24] provides, in directory format, coverage of the main online hosts servicing business information needs, with listings of databases and their characteristics. *Online company information*[25] is an extension of the Company Information chapter of the *Online manual*, giving detailed analysis of the financial and reference content of 150 of the main company information databases. Headland Business Information's *Online/CD ROM business sourcebook*[26] evaluates significant business databases, with an emphasis on UK and European services. As well as comment on the online hosts, the Internet, filtered services and CD-ROM databases are also discussed.

The lack of formal editorial control on the Internet poses problems for the business information manager. There are two main options, should the location of the primary information source be unknown.

The first is to check sites that have built up collections of business links such as that maintained by Sheila Webber at Strathclyde University and Karen Blakeman of RBA Information Services. From here users can follow the links. The library web pages of the major UK universities offering strong business programmes, such as the London Business School, can be used in this way. Through the British Electronic Libraries Programme (eLib), a one-stop information gateway for the business studies and economics community in higher education has been developed. With the support of the Association of Business Schools, Biz/ed collects, assesses and describes quality educational resources of use to its target audience. Whilst many of the links from the site are provided for the interest of teaching staff and students, a number of them are worthwhile as launching sites. For example, there are links to the web sites of the UK business schools and their libraries. Croner publishes a regular directory of web addresses as *Business information bulletin: A–Z of useful Internet sites*. This comes as part of the subscription to the *A–Z of business information sources* mentioned above.[27]

The second option in tracking down sources on the Internet is to use an Internet search engine or directory service such as AltaVista or Yahoo. Winship and McNab's *Student's guide to the Internet*[28] provides tips for searching for subject specific information on the Internet. While this is primarily a guide for students, much of the material can be useful outside academia, and since it is specific to the UK it is a more valuable introductory textbook on searching the Internet than the majority of expensive US-based publications.

A third, and somewhat haphazard, means of tracing information over the Internet is to guess at the name of sites that might be useful. This is easier for some types of information than others. For example, most UK company site URLs start with the company name and end with .co.uk.

4 Using organizations as business information sources

Business information managers need to use other people and organizations as information sources from time to time when, for example: they do not have access to the resources required from their own workplace; their workload is such that sub-contracting a project, or part of it, to an information consultant is necessary to meet deadlines or maintain confidentiality; specialist skills and knowledge not available within the organization are sought. A business information manager may simply conduct the work at the institution which holds the stock to be accessed, for example many Scottish users rely on the large collection on annual reports held by the Scottish Business Information Service at the National Library of Scotland. Fee-based information services such as those operated by universities (for example the Manchester Business School), independent information brokers (for example Karen Blakeman of RBA Information Services) or larger consultancy firms (for example the Financial Times Business Research Centre) will undertake work on behalf of clients. Trade associations, the editors of trade journals and company librarians have access to unique information in specific industries and may be approached when published sources cannot help with meeting information needs.

5 Keeping up-to-date with business information

Business information managers maintain their own professional awareness through reading, memberships of professional groups, and attending seminars, training courses and conferences.

To keep up-to-date with business issues in general, business information managers follow the stories in the mainstream media. Radio and television news reports and documentaries set the context of business developments in the UK. Further detailed comment is provided in the press, such as the daily *Financial Times*.[29]

Headland Business Information, an imprint of Bowker-Saur, produces the major titles for business information current awareness: *Business information review*30 (quarterly) carries feature articles, reviews and the annual survey of business information; *European business intelligence briefing*31 (monthly) evaluates information sources on European companies, markets and products; *Online/CD ROM business information*32 (monthly), provides news and reviews of electronic business information sources, and *What's new in business information*33 (20 issues per annum), is devoted to new developments in business information sources.

Other more general information management publications cover business information sources as part of their remit. For example, the main trade journal for online information in the UK, *Information world review*34 (monthly), provides news and reviews of business information sources alongside material on sources in areas such as the arts and humanities.

Active involvement in professional gatherings serves as a means of keeping up to date with business information sources, and developing a deeper appreciation of aspects of business information work not covered by journal articles and textbooks such as this. Those involved in business information work hold memberships with organizations such as: The Library Association (and its sub-group, the Industrial and Commercial Libraries Group, known as ICLG); the Institute of Information Scientists; the City Information Group; the UK Online User Group and the European chapter of the Special Libraries Association. The ICLG produces a list of special interest groups with contact names. These groups are listed in Figure 7.1 opposite. Many run e-mail discussion lists, which facilitate remote debate of current issues. They also offer opportunities for professionals to meet at organized events.

A number of commercial firms promote activities in which business information managers participate. TFPL, an independent information services company with offices in London and New York, runs regular training programmes, and organizes a series of business information conferences on the UK, New York and Europe, known respectively as UKBIC, NYBIC and EBIC. Other organizations well known for their training programmes include the London Business School, and Informed Business, an independent information services company. The annual Online conference and exhibition hosted by Learned Information in December brings an international audience to London, where new products and services are demonstrated alongside an academic conference on online information services provision.

Accountancy Library and Information Group
Aerospace and Defence Librarians Group
Aslib
Association of Information Officers in the Pharmaceutical Industry
Association of Law Librarians in Central England
Banking Information Group
Bristol Law Librarians
British and Irish Association of Law Librarians
Business Information Network
City Law Librarians Group
Construction Industry Information Group
Information for Energy Group
Insurance Librarians and Information Officers Group
Marine Librarians Association
Property Information Group
Scottish Law Librarians Group
SINTO: the Sheffield Information Organization
Special Libraries Committee (The Library Association)
Welsh Law Librarians Group

Fig. 7.1 *Special interest groups identified by ICLG*

6 Online information

6.1 The term 'online'

In the context of information management, the term 'online' refers to the interrogation of computer systems to answer requests for information. Until the advent of databases on CD-ROM in the late 1980s, anyone talking of performing an online search meant accessing commercial databases on remote host systems, such as DIALOG or DataStar, using a complex command language and paying for the services on the basis of a calculation that took into account the amount of time spent connected to the system and the information retrieved. Systems such as these are now considered as traditional commercial search services. From the mid-1990s, when the term 'Internet' entered the vocabulary of common usage and interest in networked services grew, the term 'online' was adopted for services *in addition to* the traditional ones mentioned above, from companies' attempts at marketing products and services from their own web pages to packaged services, such as America Online (AOL), aimed at the home market. Videotext and broadcast teletext may also be classed as online information services.

6.2 The growth of the traditional online industry

The traditional online industry came about because of the convergence of data processing, new techniques in information science, growth in public data networks and the computerization of print publications. Its antecedents lie in the manual abstracting and indexing work of the late 19th century. Indeed, some titles available then in print format live on in online manifestations. For example 1884's *Engineering index* is the Victorian ancestor of *Ei Compendex*. Automation of the labour-intensive and time-consuming work involved in manual abstracting and indexing resulted in the construction of databases that could be searched in batch mode from the late 1960s. These were offered as live commercial services from 1972 onwards, the initial files being bibliographic in content, giving references to primary material in response to requests made in host-specific command languages.

6.3 Business information online

The growth in business information online took off in the 1980s, when online information companies sought commercial opportunity through promoting full-text, menu-driven systems, such as Reuters' *Textline*. It was anticipated that the hosts would deal directly with subject specialists who would carry out their own searches, bypassing the corporate library. In all but a few cases – for example among those who were willing to pay large amounts of money for information required urgently from a limited number of specialist databases that demanded a high level technical knowledge of the subject – responsibility for online searching remained with trained intermediaries. Further design developments brought proprietary Windows interfaces to the market in the mid-1990s, hotly pursued by web interfaces for users familiar with web browsers such as Netscape. These included *DataStar Web*, ICC's *Plum* and MAID's *Profound*. As is the case with mainstream computer products, the new interface releases met with mixed reaction: searchers used to the functionality of command-language searching levelled criticism at poor access to web pages that overused slow-loading graphics. The idea of connect charges became an issue since web access does not depend on a continuous connection to the source. It would appear that the hosts underestimated the difficulties in designing complex graphical systems, and in persuading existing customers to use them.

Since the mid-1990s there has been the option of hunting for material from publicly available Internet web sites at no charge, other than the regular fee paid to Internet service providers. However, business information professionals have been wary of the Internet as an information source, broadly owing to access problems and a lack of faith in the information mounted. In the main, its use is regarded as complementary to the more formal sources offered by print publishers or the commercial online hosts. It is interesting to note, however, that the complaints of slow, unreliable connections to web sites echo comments on the difficulties faced by users of the commercial business online systems in the early 1980s, and it is predicted that as these problems are resolved, consulting a web page in response to a reference enquiry will become more routine. As is seen throughout this book, high-quality web pages can be valuable to the business information manager, and as businesses adopt web technologies for more of their own work (from simply offering a web presence, through providing additional communication links with customers and using the Web as a strategic marketing tool, ultimately to selling products and services online) the number of useful sites will grow. Company web sites have already established themselves as a first port of call in response to trade literature enquiries, as demonstrated by the National Museums of Scotland: 'Curators were recently looking at the history of medicine and the properties Coca Cola was supposed to have when it was introduced – Coca Cola's web page had the history we needed, where we would otherwise have had to have consulted a series of sources to find this information'.[35]

The Internet is also increasingly used as the primary communication forum for information professionals through activity such as one-to-one e-mail and discussion list debate, and more recent initiatives contribute to its potential as a business information current awareness service. For example *Free pint* was set up in November 1997 by the information consultancy Willco as a free bi-monthly e-mail newsletter (complete with ISSN) for people in any business or organization who use the Internet to find information to help with their work. The editor hoped to encourage business information professionals to share their experiences of finding reliable, good-quality information on the Internet through the provision of feature articles and lists of tips and tricks.

6.4 The market for online business information

The market for online business information in Europe was valued in 1996 at between £450 million and £500 million, with revenue growth averaging between 10% and 15% in the years 1994–6. The UK is the largest European market, accounting for 50% of all European users and 60% of revenues. France and Germany are significant, and together France, Germany and the UK represent 75% of the market share.[36] The largest market in Europe for online services is the financial community with its demands for real-time information. The next biggest is the market for historic information and is aimed at information professionals, for example at those who search for patents in the pharmaceutical industry or use general sources such as news databases.

In the late 1990s the focus of market opportunity fell on new user groups. The hosts and database producers failed to attract a significant end-user following in the 1980s owing, in the main, to technical limitations of the products and for other reasons such as the lack of widespread computing facilities at the desktop. From the end of the 1990s the online companies sought to attract the new market through promoting web interfaces to a community now adept at using personal computers for general purposes. It is interesting to note the opinion offered by librarians and information officers questioned on growth of the end-user market in 1996, and contrast it with that of the end-users themselves. Those used to playing the role of intermediary in supplying business information to colleagues saw a likely increase of 6% per annum in end-user participation; end-users predicted 28% growth in spending over the same period of time (Learned Information, 1997).[37] In the past, when the hosts and database producers were unsuccessful in tapping into the end-user market, business information specialists acted as information gatekeepers. As systems become more user-friendly and the issues relating to costs and charging mechanisms are addressed, the role of the information specialist with regard to online information provision will be that of facilitator: choosing resources for the company; making them available; and teaching users the value of information and how to assess information sources. The 1997 European Business Information Conference took partnerships between the online companies and in-house business information specialists as one of its main themes, recognizing that whatever the uptake of end-user online work, its management should be coordinated from the corporate information centre, where are placed staff who can negotiate the best deals, be it loading files on to the company intranet or promoting particular products for certain user groups.

When Learned Information carried out the industry report on the online business information market in Europe in 1996 it was reported that the most important business information hosts were Knight Ridder (with the services of DataStar and DIALOG), FT Profile and Reuters. Together they accounted for 45% of the total market measured by both users and revenue. MAID and Lexis-Nexis were building their market share, but were some way behind the three market leaders.[38] The purchase of Knight Ridder by MAID in November 1997 changed the balance of Learned Information's findings, with the creation of the new company, the Dialog Corporation. (For comment on the impact of acquisitions and merger activity in the online industry on information services provision see Hall and Butler.[39])

7 The evaluation of information sources

Taking into consideration the investment (in terms of both time and money) committed to building an adequate collection to meet the business information needs of any organization, skills in the evaluation of information sources are important. There are several criteria by which business information managers evaluate information sources. These are related to the content, means of access, presentation and data provenance of the information sources under consideration, as summarized in Table 7.1. These criteria are common to all sources, regardless of their format. Once it has been established that a purchase is to be made, the decision process may continue, where arguments for and against a print, online or CD subscription have to be determined if the source is available in more than one format. Online information sources often offer more features than their print equivalents. Therefore, when business information managers are faced with a subscription decision, or have to determine which of the hosts at their immediate disposal to consult on a particular occasion, a number of other criteria come into play. For example, the facility of searching across several databases at once using one host is more efficient than logging into several databases on another host to achieve the same end; the options for downloading and manipulating the information retrieved need to be assessed; and the quality of customer support can be an important issue. Building virtual collections through the provision of web pages linked to remote Internet web sites brings its own problems, where the ease of adding to stock without financial or physical limitations can tempt the zealous to create elaborate interfaces to material that may only rarely be of any real value. The ultimate check when evaluating any information source is to judge its success in meeting user information needs.

Table 7.1 *Criteria for the evaluation of information sources*

Criteria	Check
Content	Coverage is comprehensive enough
	Coverage does not duplicate existing resources
	Level
	Accuracy
	Currency
	Frequency of updating
Access	Quality of indexing
	Ease of access
	Speed of information retrieval
	Cost and cost effectiveness
Presentation	Consistency
	Attractiveness
	Errors
Provenance of data	Reliability of data sources
	Legitimacy of data sources
	Reputation of supplier

References

1 Crawford, W. and Gorman, M., *Future libraries: dreams, madness and reality*, Chicago, ALA, 1995.
2 Stoll, C., *Silicon snake oil: second thoughts on the information highway*, London, Macmillan, 1995.
3 Hall, H., 'Information strategy and manufacturing industry – case studies in the Scottish textile industry', *International journal of information management*, **14** (4), August 1994, 281-94.
4 *Directory of British associations and associations in Ireland*, CBD Research, 13th edn, 1996.
5 *Walford's guide to reference material: volume 1 Science and technology*, 7th edn, London, Library Association Publishing, 1996.
6 *Walford's guide to reference material: volume 2 Social and historical sciences, philosophy and religion*, 7th edn, London, Library Association

Publishing, 1997.

7 *Walford's guide to reference material: volume 3 Generalia, language and literature, the arts*, 6th edn, London, Library Association Publishing, 1995.

8 Lea, P.W. and Day, A. (eds.), *The reference sources handbook*, 4th edn, London, Library Association Publishing, 1996.

9 Reynard, K.W. and Reynard, J.M.E. (eds.), *Aslib directory of information sources in the United Kingdom*, 9th edn, London, Aslib, 1996.

10 *Current British directories*, 13th edn, Kent, CBD Research, 1996.

11 *Top 4000 directories and annuals*, Wellingborough, Dawson, annual.

12 *Benns media*, Tonbridge, Miller Freeman, annual.

13 *Willings press guide*, Teddington, Hollis, annual.

14 *Clover newspaper index*, Biggleswade, Clover, weekly (print) with quarterly or monthly cumulations (CD-ROM).

15 *Clover information index*, Biggleswade, Clover, quarterly (print and CD-ROM).

16 *Gale directory of databases*, New York, Gale, annual.

17 *The multimedia and CD ROM directory (volume 1: marketplace; volume 2: titles)*, 17th edn, London, TFPL, 1997.

18 Foster, P. (ed.), *Business information basics*, East Grinstead, Headland Business Information, biennial.

19 *A–Z of business information sources*, Kingston-upon-Thames, Croner, updated quarterly; *Business information bulletin: A–Z of useful Internet sites*, Kingston-upon-Thames, Croner, quarterly.

20 Tudor, J. (ed.), *Macmillan directory of UK business information sources*, 3rd edn, Basingstoke, Macmillan, 1992.

21 Lampard, L. (ed.), *Business information from government*, East Grinstead, Headland Business Information, annual.

22 *World directory of trade and business journals*, London, Euromonitor, 1995.

23 *World directory of business information libraries,* London, Euromonitor, 1996.

24 Amor, L. (ed.), *The online manual*, Oxford, Learned Information, annual.

25 *Online company information: the directory of financial and corporate databases worldwide*, Oxford, Learned Information, annual.

26 Foster, P. (ed.), *Online / CD-ROM business sourcebook*, East Grinstead, Headland Business Information, annual.

27 See Reference 19.

28 Winship, I. and McNab, A., *The student's guide to the Internet*, London,

Library Association, 1996.

29 *Financial Times*, daily.

30 *Business information review*, Headland Business Information, quarterly.

31 *European business intelligence briefing*, Headland Business Information, monthly.

32 *Online/CD-ROM business information*, Headland Business Information, monthly.

33 *What's new in business information*, Headland Business Information, 20 per annum.

34 *Information world review*, Learned Information, monthly.

35 Sylge, C., 'Managing information at National Museums of Scotland', *Managing information*, **3** (6), June 1996, 17–18.

36 Learned Information, *Online business information market in Europe*, Oxford, Learned Information, 1997.

37 See Reference 36.

38 See Reference 36.

39 Hall, H. and Butler, A., 'Mergers and take-overs in the online industry: impacts on information services provision and user satisfaction', *Proceedings of the 19th International Online Meeting*, London, 5–7 December 1995, 267–79.

Web sites

AltaVista	http://altavista.digital.com
America Online	http://www.aol.com
Biz/ed	http://www.bized.ac.uk
Bowker-Saur	http://www.bowker-saur.co.uk/service
Dialog Corporation	http://www.dialog.com
Euromonitor	http://www.euromonitor.com
Financial Times Information	http://www.info.ft.com/
FT Profile	http://www.ft.com
ICC	http://icc.co.uk
Informed Business	http://www.informed-ibs.com
Institute of Information Scientists	http://iis.org.uk
Learned Information	http://www.learned.co.uk
Lexis-Nexis	http://lexis-nexis.com
The Library Association	http://www.la-hq.org.uk
London Business School	http://www.lbs.lon.ac.uk

Manchester Business School	http://www.mbs.ac.uk
RBA Information Services	http://www.rba.co.uk
Reuters	http://www.reuters.com
Special Libraries Association	http://www.sla.org
TFPL	http://www.tfpl.com
UK Online User Group	http://www.ukolug.demon.co.uk
Webber	http://www.dis.strath.ac.uk/business/
Willco	http://www.willco.demon.co.uk
Yahoo	http://www.yahoo.com

Part 3

Identifying business information sources

8 Company information sources

1 Introduction

This chapter reviews the information sources that are of use for enquiries regarding individual business enterprises. The word 'company' is used here in its broadest sense (and not in the legal sense as outlined in Chapter 2 on the legal status of businesses). Since there exist several useful secondary sources that cover company information sources (see Chapter 7 on information formats) this chapter does not aim to provide an exhaustive review. Rather, it highlights some of the more significant and unique sources in the context of typical company information needs. Note that the category of company information includes financials, such as share prices, and these sources have been covered in Chapter 4 on investments and markets, to which the reader is referred.

Readers will discover that it is far easier to track down information on certain types of business organization, most notably PLCs, than others such as sole traders and partnerships. This is due in the main to the information disclosure requirements described in Chapter 2. Of even the registered companies, around 44% are classed as 'small' or 'medium' and therefore are not subject to full disclosure requirements so information about them is not as comprehensive as for the larger firms.[1]

2 The importance of company information: users and uses

Company information is by far the largest part of total business information activity, representing, for example, about half of all enquiries received in business libraries. Requests for information in this field can vary widely, from a few basic details about a firm to a full-scale company profile, from the correct name of a director to its complete annual report and accounts. In order to envisage the different types of information need, it is helpful to consider the different types of enquirers and their motives.

Other companies

Companies need information on other companies for a variety of reasons. For example, a supplier asked to sell goods on credit to a new customer will need to know something about the customer's reputation and ability to pay. Equally, a customer seeking sources of supply wants to know if a potential supplier can deliver the right goods to specification and on time, whether it perhaps operates a quality control system in accordance with the British Standard, and what its reputation is among other customers. Competitors in the same business need to monitor each other's activities, new products, associations with other companies, advertising and publicity, and so on. Yet another kind of enquirer is the company looking for targets for takeover or merger. It needs to examine the suitability of a target company, in terms of undervalued or under-used assets, a depressed share price, or perhaps the complementary strengths it could bring to the acquiring company.

Investors

Investors and their advisers look closely at firms, especially with regard to their financial performance. A potential investor is interested in a company's dividend record, its share-price movements, its prospects for growth, or the likelihood of its being taken over. Others with special interests in this field include stockbrokers, market-makers, fund managers and financial advisers.

Market researchers

Market researchers, studying the market for consumer or industrial products and services, are especially interested in a company's brands, new product developments, price structures, production or sales figures, and share of the market.

Employees

Employees and their trade unions need information to help them make appropriate claims for better pay and conditions. They are therefore interested in a company's profits and the pay and conditions of its employees, and their negotiations will be assisted by a knowledge of comparative conditions in other firms, both at home and abroad.

Job seekers

Job applicants have a natural interest in the companies to which they are applying, if only because it is advantageous to be able to display knowledge at an interview.

Pressure groups

Lobbyists and pressure groups, such as the environmental groups, have a legitimate interest in the behaviour and policies of companies with regard to such issues as equal opportunities and the pollution of the environment.

This brief review by no means exhausts the list of possible enquirers and their motives, but it is broadly representative of the market for company information. It must not be assumed, of course, that the information sought can always be found: this is far from being the case. At the same time, it is sometimes surprising how much can be assembled by the systematic use of a wide variety of sources and by careful collation of the results. Nor should the seeker think only in terms of documentary sources. As will be seen, there are other ways of finding out and they are often more productive than the sources more obvious to the information professional.

3 Identifying company information sources

The general secondary business information sources outlined in Chapter 7 on information formats point to company information sources as part of their remit. For example, Headland Press (the business information imprint of Bowker-Saur) publishes the biennial *Business information basics*,[2] which includes in its coverage listings of company directories, company financial data, ranking data sources and company director guides. A number of secondary publications dedicated primarily to company information sources also exist. *European companies: guide to sources of information*[3] lists sources of information on business enterprises in Europe. The two main guides for commercial online sources are

Learned Information's *Online company information*[4] and *World databases in company information*.[5] What was said regarding Internet sites in Chapter 7 applies equally to searching for company information. Webber's business information site provides links to company sites and trade directories; Yahoo is also a useful tool for this purpose.

It is worth noting here that online and print versions of the same source do not necessarily contain identical information. This is especially true of newspapers on the Internet, where it is quite obvious that content is selective. Even with the more formal online media (CD-ROM and commercial databases) there are significant differences between the electronic and the hard-copy versions. For example, because of copyright restrictions, CD-ROM versions of newspapers may be limited to providing only the articles from the original paper that were written by its staff writers. In this case the content of the electronic version is smaller than that of the print original. The reverse applies in other cases. Kompass UK as file 591 on DIALOG, for example, incorporates information from a number of print directories including *Kompass UK*,[6] *Kelly's directories*[7] and the *Directory of directors*.[8] Business information managers need to be aware of these format differences when attempting to complete a comprehensive search for company information.

It will be seen that there are various options facing the business information professional when it comes to researching companies. Decisions on strategy are taken with relation to the timescale and budget available.

4 Sourcing information from the company itself

It must not be forgotten that a lot of useful information emanates from the firm itself. The following are some of the main avenues worth exploring in this context.

Annual reports

As was noted in Chapter 2 on the legal status of businesses, companies have a statutory duty to deposit reports, accounts and other documents at Companies House and to make them available in various ways. Annual reports are particularly important because they often contain useful information that a company chooses to reveal, in addition to that which it must disclose by law. Of course, thousands of reports drawn up by small firms consist of little more than a few pages of typescript containing the bare minimum of information, but those issued by the larger companies are conceived of as prestige public relations documents, which aim to project a particular image of the firm to the public at large. Consequently they may be attractively produced, informative and widely available. In addition to the statutory directors' report and accounts, other useful material often found includes the chairman's statement (which might contain interesting comments on the trade or latest news of the company); a breakdown of sales by types of product or by regions or countries; descriptions of new products; advances in research and development; and so on. Much information of this kind can often be found nowhere else but in the annual report.

Many larger libraries maintain files of annual reports, sometimes basing the selection on some ranking directory such as *The Times 1000*[9] (described in Chapter 1 on the structure and growth of business). Such files have their problems of course; the documents are free, but the files are time-consuming to maintain, especially if firms cannot be relied on to supply recent reports regularly, which entails a lot of checking and chasing up. For this reason subscriptions to online services offering access to annual reports are useful. Increasingly companies are now making annual reports accessible from their web pages.

Press releases

The larger companies issue many statements for publication in the media, for example during a takeover battle, in conjunction with a new share issue, when there are changes to the board of directors, or on the announcement of interim results. Frequently the annual general meeting is an occasion for announcements or comments by the chairman in his or her statement introducing the annual report. Such press releases may contain unique information, but are fugitive documents. They can be picked up if they are reported in the media. To access them the news sources should be used. These are described below.

Trade literature and catalogues

Huge quantities of trade literature appear annually, ranging from one-page leaflets to thick catalogues. Trade literature can add substantially to the total picture of a company. In addition to details of the company's products or services, it may well reveal other useful data, such as prices, research and development in progress, location of production units, laboratories or sales offices, names of sales staff, and so on. Like annual reports, trade literature is usually free and readily available to the enquirer. Increasingly trade literature and catalogues can be found on company web pages (see below).

House journals

Two kinds of company house journals are commonly encountered: the staff magazine with news of social events, staff retirements and the like; and technical journals with articles on company products, research and development, or product applications. These publications can be used to add further details to a company profile, with clues about company staff policies, profit-sharing schemes, staff consultation procedures, as well as technical developments and product news.

Advertisements

One kind of advertisement, appearing for example in trade journals, gives information about the company's products or services, and this may be especially important if it reveals a new line of development. In addition, job advertisements can sometimes be revealing, indicating the establishment of a new department or facility, or expansion in a particular part of the firm.

Patents

Firms engaging in a lot of research and development will probably protect their inventions by patenting them. A patent search under the company's name may well reveal details of specifications that indicate the lines of research being undertaken. A full treatment of patents will be found in Chapter 13.

Periodical articles and conference proceedings

Company employees, such as research workers, may present conference papers, or publish articles in scientific or technical journals reporting on their work, and the authorship will usually reveal their company affiliation. In many cases, of course, such publication will take place only after the company has applied for patent protection for any inventive aspect of the work. In any case, such papers and articles may give a valuable insight into a company's technical developments. Articles might be observed by regular monitoring of likely journals, or retrieved from databases where affiliations, or perhaps brand names, can be used as search terms.

Web sites

A web presence is now important to many companies. Details provided may be as minimal as company contact details. Since the mid-1990s, some high-tech companies, such as Sun Microsystems, have offered much more sophisticated services over the Web, such as allowing prospective customers to download software from their web sites. As the possibilities for Internet commerce widen, more and more companies will be using their web site as a shop window for their customers, thus improving information access to the business information professional.

As may easily be imagined, the accessibility of some of the above sources tends to vary according to the status of the enquirer. Those working in information units in businesses, whose brief includes the regular monitoring of his or her employer's competitors and other companies, will scan a variety of media for news, advertisements and announcements, and may well pick up in this way items that would be difficult to find by retrospective search.

5 Sourcing company information from organizations

Two company information agencies are worth describing separately due to their importance in the field of company information. These are Companies House and FT Extel. Information brokers also have a particular role to play in matching users' company information needs, as do other company contacts. These are all described below.

5.1 Companies House

The broad functions of Companies House have been described in Chapter 2. Here Companies House is considered for its role of providing company information to the public as of right, as set out in the Companies Act 1985 (amended 1989). This act also requires the Registrar of Companies to use the *London gazette*[10] (or *Edinburgh gazette*[11]) to publish certain matters relating to the receipt or issue of documents at Companies House. Hence the *Gazettes* contain notifications of incorporations of companies, winding-up orders and changes of registered offices.

Companies House holds historical data from as far back as 1844. Over a million British companies (using the legal definition of 'company') are registered with Companies House. In addition, information on Northern Irish companies is available from any of the Companies House offices, and there is also some limited information available on other categories of business enterprise such as industrial and provident companies, limited partnerships, companies registered outside Great Britain with established business locations in Great Britain, Scottish assurance companies and certain unregistered companies.

Individuals may access the information held by Companies House by personal visit to the search rooms, by post, by fax and by courier. The charges for these and other search services (such as the Premium search service that can respond to requests in 20 minutes and archive searches for companies dissolved over 20 years ago), are given on the Companies House web site (http://www.companies-house.gov.uk/).

At the search rooms the in-house database allows users to discover a company's registered number, type and date of incorporation; a list of all documents filed in the previous five years; details of serving directors and secretaries, and those who have recently resigned and a list of disqualified directors. The actual company records are available on a series of three microfiches: the A fiche contains annual returns and accounts; the M fiche gives details of charges and mortgages; the G fiche contains all other documents of the company and includes the incorporation and capital documents. From 1999 microfiche will no longer be the primary format of information held at Companies House, as the organization moves to electronic recording and dissemination of its records under a project known as Strategy 2000.

Three subscription services are offered by Companies House. *Companies House monitor* delivers documents relevant to companies that a customer needs to track. *Companies House direct* is a live online service that allows users to search for information on accounts, mortgages, dissolutions and directors, as well as general company details. *The CD ROM directory*, issued monthly, provides access to details of approximately 1.3 million current and recently dissolved companies.

An initiative for Companies House in the late 1990s was to join forces with its equivalent agencies in Europe to contribute to the establishment of the European Business Register (EBR), which allows users to create company profiles from networked resources.

It can be seen that the files at Companies House are a fundamental original source. Many of the commercially produced sources, both print and online, depend on these to build their own services. It is therefore worth noting that if a company is in default or late in delivery of documents, then the Companies House files are out of date, and also therefore the published services dependent on those files.

The reason why some business information professionals prefer to use other agencies to access information originally derived from Companies House files is that the commercial services add value to the basic information that has been supplied in response to a legal requirement. Information prepared by the commercial services is processed further; for example it may include ready-calculated figures such as the return on capital employed, or provide data from a number of years for key account items. This saves the business information manager the trouble of doing this extra work.

5.2 FT Extel

The *FT Extel*[12] service is a part of Financial Times Information. *FT Extel* provides information on around 10,000 companies (UK-quoted and major unquoted and large international) in the main formats of print, online and CD-ROM. The print version provides company information on a series of cards. An annual card is produced for each company, based on its annual report and accounts. This gives background directory-type information with financial data. Regular cumulative news cards update the service with major financial news and corporate events. The hosts DIALOG Corporation (with services DIALOG and DataStar), FT Profile, and Nexis provide online access to Extel, as either one or two databases. For example, on the DIALOG service the equivalent files are *Extel international financial cards* and *Extel international news cards*; on DataStar the two series of cards are merged as one database, *Extel international cards*.

5.3 Information brokers

In Chapter 7 the main functions of the major information services companies and information brokerages were identified as executing work on behalf of clients unable to do so themselves due to time constraints, skills deficiencies or a need for confidentiality. Some of these information brokering companies maintain large company information collections, which include annual reports, interim statements, circulars and prospectuses and offer services in quick repackaging of company information for their fee-paying clients. For example, Disclosure First Contact undertakes work ranging from providing responses to quick reference requests to preparing detailed research reports; the Extel Information Centre provides a research service and can supply annual reports and other documents from the in-house library of 15,000 international files.

5.4 Other company contacts

5.4.1 Banks

One naturally expects bankers to be secretive about clients' accounts, and this is indeed generally the case. However, a bank will express a guarded opinion, in certain circumstances, about a company whose account it handles, when approached by credit agencies (see below). In some cases a bank client negotiating a deal with another company may cite the bank as a referee, and in such cases the bank will respond, but information revealed in this way is of course available only to the company that requested the reference. In criminal cases a bank may be compelled by law to disclose information, but access to such information is naturally restricted to those legally entitled to it.

5.4.2 Stockbrokers

Stockbrokers and other financial advisers collect information and offer opinions about companies whose shares an investor may be thinking of buying. Brokers offer advice and supply information to their clients both in individual cases and in the form of regular bulletins or report series. Further information on stockbroker reports can be found in Chapter 4 on investments and markets.

5.4.3 Chambers of commerce and trade

Business people are often members of the local chamber, which can be a source of informal gossip and news about other companies and trade developments generally.

5.4.4 Trade contacts

Companies have many contacts with each other, as suppliers, customers or competitors, and a lot of news and information is therefore gathered by sales representatives, purchasing officers and the like. The written reports and memoranda of representatives are valuable sources of information that have not always been as fully exploited in-house as they could. This is beginning to change as companies recognize the importance of internally generated information as part of their knowledge management strategy, and share information more freely over corporate intranets. With trade contacts there are, of course, limits to the transfer of information because a lot of trading depends on trust and the assumption of confidentiality. Suppose firm A is buying a piece of equipment from firm B. In so doing, A may need to reveal to B all kinds of information about its processes and its production plans, and it naturally wants to be confident that this information will not be passed by B to another of its customers. In some large conglomerate companies, this may even mean that parts of the same firm have secrets from each other. Business people often meet their contacts at trade fairs and these score highly as sources of information in surveys. Trade fair catalogues serve as useful, up-to-date niche directories and many can be accessible on the Internet as well as at the venues of trade fairs.

5.4.5 Industrial espionage

By its very nature, little is known about industrial espionage, but it seems certain that a great deal of such activity goes on, some of it using very sophisticated equipment. Some strategies are quite simple, for example companies can obtain information from competitors by posing as potential customers. In other circumstances it is a chance incident that leads to information being passed from one competitor to another, perhaps when a faxed message is sent to the wrong number, or a conversation is overhead on a train. Another obvious hazard faced by companies is that of the key employee who leaves, taking with him or her a lot of knowledge, trade secrets and expertise. Industrial espionage is an ethical nightmare and it is unlikely that the business information professional will go through life without encountering it in some form.

6 Published company information sources
6.1 Directory information

Since directories represent the dominant media for company information provision *Current British directories*[13] is a useful tool in identifying which of the 4000-plus in existence is the most appropriate for any given company information enquiry. Directories are published by a variety of organizations – broadstream publishers, trade associations, professional bodies and local authorities. Some are sector-specific, others relate to a particular geography. They may be accessible in print format or online. Of the database producers/hosts Dun and Bradstreet and ICC offer the greatest coverage, with over a million and 3 million companies respectively covered on their primary services, *Dun and Bradstreet* and *ICC British company intelligence*.[14]

Print directories are usually revised annually, which means that they are out-of-date almost as soon as they appear, and remain so for a long time. Nevertheless they are often adequate for a quick rundown on any company they list. Some issue supplements between the annual volumes, in an effort to be more up to date, or operate telephone hotlines for subscribers who need to check current accuracy of details. A useful starting point for telephone directories on the Web is http://www.contractjobs.com/tel.

6.1.1 General directories

The humble *Phone book*,[15] the *Yellow pages*[16] and *Thomson local*[17] should not be overlooked for checking addresses, and occasionally a brief note of a company's business. The UK is covered in more than 100 regional telephone books. The separately published index should be used to locate any given place. Advertisements in the *Yellow pages* and *Thomson local* often supply more information, such as a firm's brands and agencies. British Telecom offers subscriptions to online and CD-ROM versions of its directories. There are also Internet telephone directories: *UK freepages, UK electronic yellow pages, Thomson directories*.

It is also worth remembering that, with a little imagination, publications that are not nominally company information directories can be used to answer company information enquiries. For example, imagine an enquiry that requires the identification of the popular drugs in the product range of a particular company. If access to specialist directories and online sources is not possible, the popular home reference book *Medicines: the comprehensive guide*[18] can be consulted since entries for drugs include the manufacturer names.

6.1.2 General company information directories

For ease of reference, the descriptions of the major company directories are given here in alphabetical order. The publishers' web sites are given at the end of the section.

Britain's Top Privately Owned Companies [19]

This directory by Jordans lists, in five volumes, privately owned companies. The first four volumes list the companies by sales turnover. Volume 5 orders them by net tangible assets.

The Company Guide [20]

Hemmington-Scott's quarterly *Company guide* provides tabulated facts and figures on quoted companies. This includes information on activities, addresses, personnel, professional advisers and other main company contacts, as well as announcement dates.

Financial Surveys [21]

ICC's *Financial survey* series provides, in hard copy or on disk, details on trading companies with a turnover or asset value of over £25,000 (public and private) in particular industry sectors. For each company three years' key financial data, such as turnover and pretax profits, are tabulated, and other basic information such as names of directors and the nature of business is given. *Financial surveys* are available in hard copy or on disk.

Kelly's Business Directory [22]

This long-established general trade directory, first published in 1877, provides only minimal information about companies, i.e. address, telephone number and perhaps a phrase indicating the nature of the business, but it is a useful checklist on the existence of over 100,000 companies. The print version of the directory has four sections: the first section comprises product literature advertisements which can be used to send away for brochures; the second lists products and services; the remaining two sections list companies alphabetically, first according to products and services categories, then in a straightforward listing. The

CD-ROM version is known as *Kelly's CD book*. The directory forms part of the online version of *Kompass*, which is accessible via DIALOG and Reedbase Kompass Online.

Key British Enterprises 23

This well-established directory covers the top 50,000 public and private companies, in six volumes. Volumes 1–3 provide an alphabetical list of firms. Volume 4 provides cross references to companies by company name, city, county and line of business. Brand names, export markets and directors' names can be established by the use of volume 5. The top 5000 firms are ranked by sales and employees within geographical and sector groupings in Volume 6. There are two versions of *Key British enterprises* on CD-ROM. One is the exact equivalent of the hard copy, the other, *Key British enterprises PLUS* widens the coverage with details of over 200,000 businesses. On DataStar the online version is called *Key British enterprises financial performance*. The coverage of the database is the 50,000 companies of the print directory with additional financial data.

Kompass UK 24

Over 900,000 companies are covered in the entire series of Kompass, published by Reed Information Services. The five-volume *Kompass UK* provides corporate profiles of 46,000 companies in 41,000 product and service classifications: company information, products and services, financial data, parents and subsidiaries and industrial trade names. Online access to *Kompass UK* is through DIALOG and Reedbase Kompass Online. The CD-ROM version, *Kompass CD Plus*, can be bought in separate volumes (reflecting the volume coverage of the print publication) or as a complete set.

Macmillan's Unquoted Companies 25

Macmillan's unquoted companies provides three-year financial profiles of Britain's top 20,000 unquoted companies in two volumes by turnover threshold. In 1997 volume 1 covered companies with a turnover of above £18 million and volume 2 covered those with a turnover of below £18 million. The directory is compiled by ICC Business Publications.

Macmillan Stock Exchange Yearbook [26]

For companies listed on the London and Dublin Stock Exchanges, The *Macmillan Stock Exchange yearbook* provides a financial profile and five-year financial summary, contact details, director names, parent-subsidiary relationships, merger and takeover details and description of company activities. Detail is given of the companies that have delisted since the previous edition of the yearbook, and companies in administration, liquidation and receivership are also included. The yearbook is compiled by the Economics Department at the University of Exeter. The *Macmillan Stock Exchange yearbook on CD ROM* incorporates *Who's who in the City*.

Price Waterhouse Corporate Register [27]

The *Price Waterhouse corporate register* provides information on fully listed AIM companies, giving details of companies, their directors, officers and professional advisers.

The Times 1000 for Company Rankings [28]

Based on data from FT Extel, *The Times 1000* uses capital employed (i.e. shareholders' funds plus long-term debt, plus inter-group payables, plus deferred liabilities, minus technical reserves) as its main measure of size. This criteria is used as the basis for the listings of company information.

6.1.3 Specialist trade directories

For some trades an alternative approach to company information is offered by directories in special fields. For example, the long-established *Rylands directory*,[29] gives company data and details of products, services, brand and trade names in engineering. This type of directory is helpful for finding out more about companies too small to appear in the major general directories. The basic details often include capital and names of directors. This type of directory is accessible through the directory listing publications mentioned above, or might be discovered through approaching trade or professional organizations.

6.1.4 Directories of company affiliations and company relationships

Enquiries about parents, subsidiaries and associates often present problems. Many of the general sources mentioned above, such as the *Stock Exchange official yearbook*,[30] list the main subsidiaries of the parent companies described, but they are no help in understanding this relationship in reverse. For this purpose Dun and Bradstreet's *Who owns whom*[31] should be consulted. It is published in hard copy annually with quarterly updates and is also available both on CD-ROM and mounted on DataStar. There are six regional volumes of the hard copy and CD-ROM versions. Volumes 3 and 4 cover the UK and Ireland. There is an index to all the companies featured in the publication, showing the chains of relationship. The online version is updated the most frequently (monthly), but care needs to be taken when using such a source given the speed of business events. For this reason news sources should be used to supplement information discovered through *Who owns whom*.

Crawford's directory of city connections[32] lists the stockbroker, financial adviser, auditor and solicitor for quoted and unquoted companies. Addresses, contact details and clients are also given for stockbrokers, advisers, auditors, solicitors, PR consultants, pension fund consultants and actuaries.

6.1.5 Directories of personnel

Directory of Directors [33]

The long-established *Directory of directors* lists the directors of over 14,000 companies. There are two volumes: volume 1 gives details of directors, showing company, post held, etc.; volume 2 is organized by company name, showing directors, addresses, type of business and financial data.

Who's who in the City [34]

Who's who in the City is a compilation of biographies, providing information on over 16,000 individuals, ranging from their current position and directorships, to their hobbies and date of birth. There are company and sector indexes to complement the arrangement by individual. The *Macmillan Stock Exchange yearbook on CD-ROM* incorporates *Who's who in the City*.

6.2 News and comment on companies

News information is important for commentary on company activities. Sources of stories range from the daily newspapers and serial journal literature, for example the *Financial times*,[35] *Investors chronicle*[36] and *Financial weekly*,[37] to commercial online databases such as *FT profile* and *Reuters business briefing*. News information can be important as actual 'news', i.e. as a story breaks, or to provide a historic perspective of an event in context. Comment on news events, made at some distance from the event, can also be important to business. For listings of, and comments on, the major Internet news sites see Blakeman.[38]

6.2.1 News sources for company information

Breaking stories first reach the public domain through the broadcast media, and for this reason business information managers follow the 'serious' news and documentary programmes such as those broadcast by BBC television (for example, 'The money programme') and Radio 4 (for example, the business news reports on the 'Today' programme). Teletext pages are also useful for checking headlines and developments with reference to companies, as are the headline services on the major Internet directory and search engine sites.

Print is still an important medium for disseminating news stories. Daily newspapers provide announcements sooner than the information will reach the directory publications outlined above. For example, the *Financial times* is a vital source for news of new directorships, meetings, dividend payments, takeovers, etc. In many information units scanning the press and providing a cuttings service to the organization is an important daily task. Another means of accessing the pertinent press stories is for the organization to subscribe to a press cuttings agency service, where bulletins are compiled for clients early in the morning and then delivered to customers in time for their arrival at work. The press cuttings agency may be instructed to cover company information on competitors, or to track news stories that mention the client organization.

FT McCarthy[39] comprises a number of services in print on card, on microfiche, on CD-ROM and online. News articles from about 80 business publications are selected and indexed according to company name, industry, country and type of news. Subscribers can access a portion of the service if interested in cards or microfiche, for example the UK quoted company service, which covers all London and Irish stock exchange companies, or the industry service, which provides coverage of more than 60 industry sectors and includes statistics and comment. The online and CD-ROM versions encompass the entire range of services.

The provision of news information to the executive desktop is seen by the commercial online information providers as an obvious market for intranet products. Desktop data's *NewsEDGE* is an example of such a product. It is a real-time news alerting service with feeds from information provided by more than 650 news and information sources, such as Reuters.

6.2.2 Accessing news reports through indexes and online services

While some individual newspapers have indexes (for example, *The Times* and the *Financial times*), advances in technology have diminished their prominence for researching news stories. It is far easier to search across the content of an entire title on CD-ROM, or several titles online, than check through several print indexes. Clover's *Company data supplement*,[40] available in print or CD-ROM, acts as an index to company news stories across several titles. The *Research index*,[41] published every two weeks, indexes business material from 70 newspapers, trade journals and magazines. Some of the newspaper sites on the Internet provide archive files, for example the *Financial times* keeps stories online for 30 days, but for a thorough search the major commercial services should be consulted. Of the online services *FT Profile* and *Reuters business briefing* are the major sources for news information. The British Library publishes *News information: online, CD-ROM and Internet resources*[42] in its Key Resource series. This serves as a tertiary source for the identification of news information sources and includes details on publishers and information vendors.

6.2.3 Comparative company comment

It is often useful to look at an industry sector or geography to assess and compare company performance. ICC publishes *Business ratio plus*,[43] which is a series of 165 reports on specific industry sectors, each focusing on the performance of between 50 and 150 leading companies of the sector. Competitor firms can be compared across performance league tables, industry averages and commentary. The sectors covered are: advertising, PR and marketing; business service and finance; construction; electrical and electronics; engineering; films, music and photography; food and drink; furniture, fittings and interior design; leisure and travel; medical and chemical; metals; paper, printing and publishing; retail and consumer services; textiles, footwear and clothing; transport and the motor trade. The reports are available in print or on CD-ROM, where it is known as *ROM: BUS*. Other ICC publications that deal in comparative data include *Regional reports*,[44] which provides company information by region, and *UK industrial performance average*,[45] which looks at UK industry sectors as a whole. Dun and Bradstreet publishes *Key business ratios*,[46] which can be used to discover how well a company is performing compared to the industrial average.

6.3 Financials

See Chapter 4 on investments and markets for details of the main sources of information related to company financials.

6.4 Credit information

The credit-worthiness of potential customers is a matter of some importance to suppliers. Ways of assessing liquidity were outlined in Chapter 3. A number of commercial credit reference agencies specialize in the provision of status reports which sometimes give opinions about a business's credit-worthiness and reliability. Of these Dun and Bradstreet, Experian (formerly CCN), Infocheck Equifax and Jordans are among the best known. The information processed by credit-rating agencies is based on the records at Companies House and research performed by the agency itself, for example through conducting interviews with key personnel, or asking companies to complete questionnaires that assess the speed at which customers pay bills. There are some difficulties with reliance on credit-ratings databases: some recommended credit limits for the same company have been found to differ greatly from database to database. A report on 'The money programme' broadcast on BBC2 on 19 October 1997 revealed how mistakes taken in good faith from a credit-ratings agency can be detrimental to business.

References

1   Murphy, C. and McLaughlin, J., 'Discover: financial information', *Managing information*, supplement, March 1997.

2 Foster, P. (ed.), *Business information basics*, East Grinstead, Headland Business Information, biennial.

3 *European companies: guide to sources of information*, 4th edn, Beckenham, CBD Research, 1992.

4 *Online company information: the directory of financial and corporate databases worldwide*, Oxford, Learned Information, 1997.

5 Armstrong, C.J. and Fenton, R.R. (eds.), *World databases in company information*, East Grinstead, Bowker-Saur, 1996.

6 *Kompass UK*, East Grinstead, Reed, annual.

7 *Kelly's business directory*, East Grinstead, Kelly's Directories, annual.

8 *Directory of directors*, East Grinstead, Reed, annual.

9 *The Times 1000 1996*, London, Times Books, 1995.

10 *London gazette*, London, The Stationery Office, four issues per week.

11 *Edinburgh gazette*, Edinburgh, Stationery Office, two issues per week.

12 *FT Extel*, London, Financial Times Information.

13 *Current British directories*, 13th edn, Kent, CBD Research, 1996.

14 Available in Amor, L. (ed.), *The online manual*, 5th edn, Oxford, Learned Information, 1996.

15 *Phone book*, London, British Telecommunications, annual.

16 *Yellow pages*, London, British Telecommunications, annual.

17 *Thomson local*, Farnborough, Thomson Directories, annual.

18 Morton, I. and Hall, J.M., *Medicines: the comprehensive guide*, 4th edn, London, Bloomsbury, 1997.

19 *Britain's top privately owned companies*, Bristol, Jordans, annual.

20 *The company guide*, London, Hemmington-Scott, quarterly.

21 *Financial surveys*, London, ICC, annual.

22 See Reference 7.

23 *Key British enterprises*, High Wycombe, Dun and Bradstreet, annual.

24 See Reference 6.

25 *Macmillan's unquoted companies*, London, Macmillan, annual.

26 *Macmillan Stock Exchange yearbook*, London, Macmillan, annual in print, quarterly on CD-ROM.

27 *Price Waterhouse corporate register*, London, Hemmington-Scott, quarterly.

28 See Reference 9.

29 *Rylands directory*, London, Thomas Telford Information, 1992.

30 See Reference 26.

31 *Who owns whom?*, High Wycombe, Dun and Bradstreet, annual with quarterly updates.

32 *Crawford's directory of city connections*, Tonbridge, Miller Freeman, annual.

33 See Reference 8.
34 *Who's who in the City*, London, Macmillan, annual.
35 *Financial Times*, London, Financial Times Information, daily.
36 *Investors chronicle*, London, Financial Times Information, weekly.
37 *Financial weekly*, London, Financial Weekly, weekly.
38 Blakeman, K., *Business information on the Internet*, 2nd edn, Caversham, RBA Information Services, 1997.
39 *FT McCarthy*, London, Financial Times Information.
40 *Company data supplement*, Biggleswade, Clover, weekly (monthly on CD-ROM).
41 *Research index*, Broadmayne, Business Surveys, fortnightly.
42 *News information: online, CD-ROM and Internet resources*, London, British Library, 1997.
43 *Business ratio plus*, London, ICC. (Individual reports on hard copy; *ROM: BUS* provides the reports collectively in CD-ROM format, updated quarterly.)
44 *Regional reports*, London, ICC.
45 *UK industrrial performance averages*, London, ICC.
46 *Key business ratios*, High Wycombe, Dun and Bradstreet.

Web sites

Bowker-Saur	http://www.bowker-saur.co.uk
Companies House	http://www.companies-house.gov.uk/
Desktop data	http://www.desktopdata.com
DIALOG Corporation	http://www.dialog.com
Disclosure First Contact	http://www.disclosure.com
Dun and Bradstreet	http://dbisna.com
European Business Register	http://www.ebr.org/
Financial Times	http://www.ft.com
FT Information	http://www.info.ft.com/
Hemmington-Scott	http://www.hemscott.co.uk/hemscott/
ICC	http://icc.co.uk
Infocheck equifax	http://www.infocheck.co.uk
Jordans	http://www.jordans.co.uk
Kellys	http://kellys.reedinfo.co.uk
Learned Information	http://www.learned.co.uk
Lexis-Nexis	http://lexis-nexis.com
Macmillan	http://www.macmillan-reference.co.uk
Miller Freeman	http://www.mfplc.com
Reed Information	http://www.reedinfo.co.uk

Research Index	http://www.researchindex.co.uk
Reuters	http://www.reuters.com
Sun Microsystems	http://www.sun.com
Telephone directories on the web	http://www.contractjobs.com/tel/
Thomas Telford Information	http://www.t-telford.co.uk
Thomson directories	http://www.inbusiness.co.uk/
UK electronic yellow pages	http://www.eyp.co.uk/
UK freepages	http://www.freepages.co.uk/
Webber's company web site directory listing	http://www.dis.strath.ac.uk/business/directoriesUK.html
Webber's electronic trade directory listing	http://www.dis.strath.ac.uk/business/trade.html
Yahoo company web sites	http://www.yahoo.com/Business_and_Economy/Companies/

9 Marketing information sources

1 Introduction

Marketing is a massive subject area and as such its coverage in this book has been split between two chapters. This chapter will outline the general nature of markets and the marketing process, and will consider some key sources of information relevant to marketing. Chapter 12 will look in some detail at the advertising and promotional aspects of marketing.

This chapter is organized under a series of sub-headings which include definitions of markets; discussions of the factors affecting markets; market research including the key companies which produce market reports; a brief discussion regarding access to market information and the different format; and finally the identification of a few bibliographies of market reports and related web sites.

According to the Chartered Institute of Marketing, marketing is 'the management process which identifies, anticipates and supplies customer requirements efficiently and profitably'. Although at first sight this definition appears to confine the term to the activities of a marketing department, it actually implies something much wider. The management process indeed refers to the internal organization of marketing, but other elements implicitly present include market research (identifying and anticipating); correct design and delivery of product or service (customer requirements); and satisfactory pricing policy (profitability). The modern view of marketing, indeed, is that it is not just a separate function of a specific department of the firm; rather, a marketing stance should be taken by all departments and employees of the company, if the business is to prosper.

A classic analysis of marketing breaks it down into four main elements: product, price, place and promotion (the four Ps, or marketing mix). Successful marketing means not only that these four elements must be correctly positioned individually, but also that they should be consistent with each other to produce a synergistic effect. Thus, a product that is correctly designed for the chosen type of customer must be priced accordingly, appropriately distributed at the right places, and suitably advertised and promoted. However one looks at it, correct marketing must be the top-rank objective of any business, and all other activities contribute to this aim. In this sense, marketing is the concept that unifies all activities of the firm.

A detailed discussion of the marketing process and the marketing mix is inappropriate for this book. The interested reader will easily discover a vast literature on the subject. Two books in particular can be recommended. The first by Kotler[1] is very comprehensive and covers all aspects of marketing from analysis, through planning and implementation and finally looks at how to control the marketing process. This book is updated every few years and at the time of writing was in its ninth international edition. The second book which can be recommended is that by Dibb[2] – here the author gives a more general overview of marketing ideas and concepts and also includes sections on marketing analysis.

2 Definitions of markets

In its narrowest sense, a market is simply the types and number of customers for a given product or service. However, in a wider view, a market may be considered to be the entire exchange system of producers, wholesalers, retailers and customers dealing in the product or service. Markets can be classified in different ways, as follows.

2.1 Consumer and industrial markets

It is sometimes helpful to distinguish between consumer markets and industrial (or business-to-business) markets. In the case of mass-produced branded consumer goods, for example, the manufacturer has thousands of unknown buyers who purchase the product through retail outlets; in the case of industrial equipment and supplies, there may be only a handful of firms who buy the product and they are well known to the manufacturer, who may cultivate their business carefully on an individual basis. The terms on which goods and services are sold to other businesses are quite different from those applying to consumer markets, and industrial marketing and market research are indeed a separate branch of the marketing profession.

2.2 Goods and services

An obvious distinction is between goods and services and, within goods, between consumables and durables. One can also, of course, have combinations of classifications, hence we can talk about consumer durables, for example. It is also worth pointing out that markets may not be mutually exclusive, thus many businesses buy food, drinks and other consumable items commonly retailed in the consumer market. Another concept commonly encountered is that of fast-moving consumer goods, sometimes abbreviated to FMCG, meaning foods, drinks, chocolate countlines, household cleaning materials and a host of similar items which turn over very quickly. One of the reasons for introducing these terms is that sources of information are often structured in corresponding ways. Thus, some market reports or compilations of statistics may concentrate on, or be confined to, some particular class of goods or services, and it may help to bear this in mind, especially when evaluating new sources. It is worth mentioning at this point that there is much more published data on consumer markets than on industrial ones.

2.3 Geography

A further analysis of markets can be made on a geographical basis, an obvious distinction being between home and export markets. A moment's thought is sufficient to realize the host of additional problems presented by export – as opposed to home – markets, foreign languages, overseas standards and regulations, transport and distribution problems, representation abroad, different patterns of market behaviour, and so on. Another geographical analysis of markets might distinguish between local markets (e.g. the market for fresh fruit, or haircuts); regional markets (such as the hire of farm machinery in the south-east); national markets (e.g. for women's magazines); and international markets (e.g. oil).

2.4 Buyers and sellers

Finally, markets can be classified by the number of buyers and sellers. In a competitive market, there are plenty of buyers and sellers, so that, for example, no one seller can impose prices on the buyers. In a completely monopolistic market, a single seller could dictate terms and prices to the buyers. For this reason, in modern economies monopolies are usually outlawed, apart from some state monopolies. An oligopoly means that a small handful of sellers dominate a market, and may act to maintain their position, without of course breaking the law. Petrol is a case in point, with the large suppliers like Shell and Esso tending to charge the same price, so as to avoid rocking the boat. Finally, an uncommon situation is represented by the little-used term monopsony, which means that there is only one buyer in a market, who could therefore unduly influence prices and terms of trade.

3 Factors affecting markets

The behaviour and structure of markets are influenced by a complex network of factors, some of them represented by the above considerations of geography and the number of buyers and sellers. Other important factors include the following.

3.1 Transport facilities and costs

Good or bad transport facilities, whether by road, rail, air or sea, are powerful determinants, and poor facilities may prevent a market from existing at all. The markets for perishable foods have been greatly extended in recent times by a fast motorway network and the existence of refrigerated container vehicles.

3.2 Trade tariffs

Governments impose tariffs (import duties), quota restrictions on quantities permitted to be imported, or even outright bans on certain goods. Tariff barriers between members of the European Union have long since disappeared, but the UK imposes import duties on many products imported from countries outside the Union. Rates of import duty into the UK, and information on quotas, customs procedures, import and export prohibitions, anti-dumping measures, etc, may be found in the *Integrated tariff of the United Kingdom*,[3] but for the most up-to-date information on tariffs and quotas both at home and abroad reference should be made to the tariff section of the British Overseas Trade Board.

3.3 Consumer groups and the 'green' movement

Manufacturers and retailers are increasingly being affected by the environmental and consumer lobbies. Many organizations are now having to pay some attention to environmental issues and this has manifested itself in various ways such as less packaging on goods, full information regarding the ingredients of labelled products and the availability of recycling depots at larger superstores.

3.4 Controls on advertising

Certain markets, such as the tobacco and cigarette market, are not free to promote their goods as they wish, and the controls exerted on advertising, both statutory and voluntary, have an effect on consumer behaviour.

3.5 The nature of the consumer

The level of demand for consumer goods is influenced by a variety of factors such as the amount of personal disposable income available for the purchase of optional items. Individual tastes in goods vary, and may be affected by a number of psychological and other variables that are difficult to study and to take account of in marketing. Tastes can, of course, be influenced by group behaviour, as in the case of clothes fashions; and manufacturers can themselves create fashions or tastes in some sectors by clever promotion.

3.6 Prices

Price influences choice in complex ways. Thus, for example, people may buy more fresh strawberries when the price falls than when they first appear on the market at a very high price. But, however low the price may fall, customers will not necessarily go on buying more; they may become surfeited with strawberries, or some other attraction arises, so that the marginal utility of an extra strawberry is seen to be too low. Prices also relate to substitute and complementary goods. In the UK recent cases of BSE-infected meat products have affected the pricing structure of meat products considerably. Buyers have a tendency to switch to other types of foods. In the case of, say, two complementary goods, the supply, demand and prices of both are interconnected. Thus, a rise in the price of petrol may tend to reduce the demand, not only for petrol but also for cars, in the sense that perhaps some customers reduce their motoring costs by buying a second-hand car instead of a new one.

3.7 General social and economic factors

Social and economic factors include changes in the size and composition of the population, such as the current trend in the UK towards fewer teenagers and more elderly people, which will have some effect on the markets for products and services aimed at these groups. Similarly, uneven distribution of income and wealth in society will have an effect on markets. Thus, the lower level of unemployment and greater wealth of the South East of England relative to the rest of the UK means that consumer markets in the South East are likely to be much more attractive to some manufacturers than elsewhere.

3.8 Factors affecting supply

Factors affecting supply include such things as the prices and supply of raw materials, the cost of labour, energy and other operating costs, the efficiency or otherwise of the technology in use, and so on. Also important to consider are the political issues of the moment (which may affect a particular industry) and such things as the economic stability – or instability – of the supplier's country.

4 Market research

Clearly, the factors outlined above have implications for the supply of information. Some of this will come from a company's own in-house files, such as analyses of sales of the firm's products, to indicate likely trends or regional variations. Much information about the market generally, social and economic trends, the fortunes of competitive brands and products, relevant legislation and regulations, and so on, will be available from published sources. Finally, in the absence of required data, a firm may itself set out to research buying behaviour and other aspects of its markets.

Whether research focuses on the marketing of a specific product or on understanding and monitoring a market generally, all types of information from many different sources are likely to be required. From the point of view of the market researcher, the necessary information can be primary data acquired either by fieldwork, for example by interviewing actual or potential customers, or by desk research, which implies the use of in-house data and published or other secondary sources.

4.1 Market research methods
4.1.1 Fieldwork

Companies may operate their own market research departments and/or commission market research agencies to undertake work for them. Methods employed include the following:

Surveys of consumers by interview or questionnaire

These may be done by selecting respondents in the street, or in stores, or on the doorstep, often by reputable market and survey research companies such as the British Market Research Bureau, Marplan Research International, or the Harris Research Centre. This kind of research is open to abuse by unscrupulous salespersons pretending to conduct surveys, but in reality attempting to sell something. Reputable firms may be expected to belong to the Association of Market Survey Organizations, which operates a code of practice; and individual researchers should be members of the Market Research Society and carry an interviewer membership card. The Market Research Society and the Industrial Marketing Research Association also have a joint code of conduct. This kind of survey involves the use of correct sampling and inferential statistical methods, if the conclusions are to be valid.

Market testing

A new product is sometimes test marketed in different areas, perhaps using different packs, prices and promotional methods. Consumers can then be asked for their opinions on the product.

In-store audits

Specialist firms such as Nielsen Marketing Research can be employed by manufacturers of branded consumer goods to monitor the turnover of their brands and those of their competitors in selected retail outlets. Such audits may include not merely statistics of sales but also the effect on the brand of shelf location, and observations of consumer behaviour.

4.1.2 Desk research

As noted above, desk research may draw on both in-house company information and on external published or semi-published materials. The latter is a major concern and the remainder of this chapter reviews the main types of sources that will be encountered, together with examples. What follows is only an outline guide, and further information should be sought from specialist guides such as Key Notes' latest edition of *The guide*,[4] a considerable compilation covering key information sources including a useful section on pan European sources as well as chapters covering individual countries in some detail. The reader may also find it useful to consult the relevant chapter of *Business information basics*.[5]

What may be considered market information will vary considerably, depending on one's needs. The market researcher and the marketer could require information on almost any aspect of business covered by this book, for example standards and regulations, legislation, even patent or design rights. However, for our purposes marketing information sources are considered to be those that primarily provide data, statistics and reports relevant to the nature, composition and behaviour of customers in the market place. Included in this definition are, firstly, market surveys and reports specially aimed at the marketer. Official and unofficial statistical publications that may be used for marketing purposes are covered in Chapter 11.

5 Market surveys and reports

This section reviews the major types and series of published reports and their bibliographical control, and discusses the problems of access to this kind of literature. There are many commercial and some governmental organizations that produce market surveys. They may appear as one-off monographs or in series or periodical form; and they range from the cheap and cheerful to the very expensive. Broadly speaking, those reports that are basically the result of desk research tend to be relatively cheap. These may offer some estimates of their own or report what they describe as 'trade estimates', but by and large they are secondary reports based on published data such as official statistics, which are readily available elsewhere. Of course, the information is structured and packaged, with informed comment, and therefore has added value. Reports of this kind may cost about £400. At the other end of the scale, it is possible to pay thousands of pounds for a report based on a specially conducted survey, using highly skilled staff and proper sampling and statistical methods. Such a report may well use secondary data, but the primary investigation makes it very costly. Needless to say, reports in this class are seldom found in public-sector libraries.

There are several mainstream producers of market information reports. The company Frost and Sullivan is a long-standing specialist market information organization which produces comprehensive ranges of industry and consumer market research reports that contain in-depth analysis and forecasts of market trends. MAID (Market Analysis and Information Database), founded in 1985, set out to establish a specialised online database of market research reports in response to the needs of the advertising and marketing industries. Since then both the company and its product portfolio have grown and the provision of market information formerly offered under the names MAID and Profound is supplied in a number of delivery formats, including the Internet. MAID as a product name is no longer used, but the Profound service continues, offered by the DIALOG Corporation.

ICC produce *ICC key notes*[6] and *ICC Business ratio reports*,[7] both of which contain detailed market information on a range of consumer and industrial markets. Datamonitor products include market reports and forecasts on UK consumer markets.

Predicast produces a range of databases: Predicast Promt: Market and Technology, including Predicast Aerospace/Defence Markets and Technology; Predicast Marketing and Advertising which covers the promotional side of marketing; and Predicast forecasts, which provides a comprehensive range of published forecasts.

5.1 Reports

Individual reports are published by a variety of organizations, such as Euromonitor and the Economist Intelligence Unit. Euromonitor is one of the most prolific publishers in the field. A glance at their catalogue[8] reveals some 200 titles covering a wide variety of topics such as the motor industry, catering, travel, food and drink, personal care products, household cleaners and finance. Other sources include:

Top Markets [9]

Published by MAPS, this publication presents full marketing information on a range of topics such as market size and segmentation. Includes 5–10-year forecasts.

Headland Business Information Reports [10]

These reports are clear and comprehensive and consist of three series: the local authority leisure market; the drinks market; and the tourism market.

Market Direction Reports [11]

This is Euromonitor's online version and is a database of over 400 updated market reports. The annual reports cover a variety of market sectors from cars to tobacco. Each of the reports contains detailed information covering aspects such as market overview and size, sources of supply, brands and manufacturing, retail distribution and future outlook. They cover the UK, USA, France, Italy, Germany, Spain and Japan.

BIS Strategic Decisions[12]

This company provides information on the electronic industry and produces a variety of reports on related areas.

5.2 Periodicals

There are several reasonably priced periodicals which are within the budgets of many libraries. They include:

Retail Business[13]

Formerly an Economist Intelligence Unit publication, this is now produced by Corporate Intelligence on Retailing. It comprises *Market surveys* (monthly), with surveys of four consumer goods markets. Included with each edition is also either a *Product sector review*, which gives reviews of broad consumer product groups, a *Technology review*, which assesses key developments in the application of new technology in retailing, or an *Economic review*, which gives detailed consumer spending forecasts and prospects for the UK economy.

Marketing in Europe[14]

This publication, also formerly produced by the Economist Intelligence Unit and now published by Corporate Intelligence and Retailing. It is a monthly periodical carrying special reports on individual products in specific countries, e.g. the soft drinks market in Italy. The publication also contains detailed sector reviews and market surveys.

Mintel International[15]

Mintel publishes four relevant periodicals: *Market intelligence*, monthly, offering short reports on the major fast moving consumer-goods markets, six reports per issue, the whole revised over a two-year cycle; *Retail intel-*

ligence, six times a year, four reports per issue; *Leisure intelligence*, quarterly, six studies per issue; *Personal finance intelligence*, quarterly.

Market Research Great Britain [16]

This is produced monthly by Euromonitor. Each issue contains seven reports on individual products or services.

Market Research Europe [17]

Market Research Europe is a monthly Euromonitor publication with six reports per month covering market sectors in one country or across Europe, and reports on consumer spending and trends in retailing.

Other Euromonitor journals are *Retail monitor international* [18] and the relatively new *Market research international*. [19]

5.3 Series

Some monograph reports appear in series, and cover a regular range of topics, revised and reissued at intervals. The main ones are:

Key Note Reports [20]

The series offers reports on about 200 markets, many of which are updated on an annual basis. The reports are mainly on consumer goods and services, with a few on industrial markets. They are useful in covering a number of service sectors such as credit cards, employment agencies, estate agents and retail banking. More recently, Key Note began a new series called *Market reviews*, which deal with broader areas than the standard *Key Note* reports. Other new series are *Euroviews* and *European overviews*. Key Note reports are also available online in full text on DataStar.

5.4 Market databases and other sources

Other sources include the many databases that are now available such as *MarketLine*. [21] *MarketLine* is advertised as 'the complete market research library in a single product'. Available online or on CD-ROM (*MarketLine OnDisc*) the database provides primary research on over 4000 market segments. *MarketLine* covers markets in the UK, France, Germany, Italy, Spain, USA and Japan. The database provides detailed market sector information and regional analysis as well as many other features. Other companies also provide their information on CD-ROM such as *Key notes on CD ROM, Mintel on CD ROM* and *MAPS Intelligence on CD ROM.*

The Internet is a prime source when starting to research markets. The site produced by Webber of the University of Strathclyde's Department of Information Science is an excellent place to start. The Internet address for this site is given at the end of the chapter. In addition there are two more interesting Euromonitor publications which give information not readily available in other places:

Strategic Management Overviews 22

These reports claim to analyse and compare the markets in the UK, USA, France, Germany, and Italy. These reports contain key trends and developments, major market comparison, market performance and company profiles.

Strategy 2000 Reports 23

These reports deal with the strategic marketing analysis and provide a worldwide overview. This is an irregular publication.

There are various series of reports that are not primarily produced as market reports, but which can be useful background when researching a market. In this context, reports issued by firms of stockbrokers can be invaluable.

6 Access to market reports

As mentioned above, most market research companies now have their data available in a variety of electronic formats, including online, CD-ROM and increasingly accessible through the World Wide Web. Availability of these reports in hard copy can sometimes be more difficult to locate. The cheaper ones may be found in the larger public business libraries, the libraries of the Manchester and London Business Schools, and some university collections. Many of the reports including *Key notes*, ICC *Business ratio* reports, ICC *Financial surveys* and *Euromonitor* reports are available at the Business Information Service of the British Library SRIS, but are for reference only.

7 Bibliography of market reports

Apart from the general guides mentioned above, there are several important bibliographies of individual reports.

Marketsearch [24]

This is an annual bibliography, formerly called the *International directory of published market research*. It lists about 20,000 separately published reports worldwide on both industrial and consumer goods and services.

Marketing Surveys Index [25]

This is a loose-leaf guide to separately published reports, with monthly updates cumulating into an annual volume. It is in three parts: the report directory (alphabetical subject index); report details (annotated listing in accession number order); and publisher details. A glance at this last section will give a good indication of the range and types of organizations in this field.

Reports Index [26]

Issued every two months, this is a subject guide to separately published reports.

Statistics and Market Research Bulletin [27]

This is a monthly subject index to about 50 periodicals taken by Birmingham Public Library's Business Information Department. It is extremely useful as being practically the only index to periodical articles in this field, such as those in *Mintel* or *Retail business*.

Market statistics are also a vital tool for market research and this area is covered in a later chapter.

8 Conclusion

This chapter, then, has served to introduce the user to the nature of markets and marketing in the late 20th century. The whole area of marketing is one that is never static. This chapter has aimed to give the user an overview of market research, outlined the main market surveys and reports that are available and identified a selection of key journals and other relevant sources. Marketing is really about decision making and this closing quotation serves to highlight the importance of information in the marketing industry: 'Timely information improves decision-making. To be effective, the marketer needs to gather enough information to understand past events, to identify what is occurring now, and to predict what might occur in the future. Good marketing information is an extremely valuable management tool because it reduces uncertainty about the risks associated with decision making.'[28]

References

1 Kotler, P., *Marketing management: analysis planning implementation and control*, 9th int. edn, New Jersey, Prentice-Hall, 1997.

2 Dibb, S., *Marketing concepts and strategies*, 3rd rev. edn, London, Houghton-Mifflin, 1997.

3 HM Customs and Excise, *Integrated tariff of the United Kingdom*, 3 vols, London, The Stationery Office, annual.

4 *The guide*, Hampton, Key Notes, 1997.

5 *Business information basics*, Headland, Headland Business Information, 1997.

6 ICC *Key notes*, London, ICC.

7 ICC *Business ratios*, London, ICC.

8 *Euromonitor index: complete publication catalogue 1997*, London, Euromonitor, 1997.

9 *Top markets*, London, MAPS, 1995.

10 *Headland business information reports*, Headland, Headland Business Information, 1997.

11 *1997 market direction reports*, London, Euromonitor, 1996.

12 *BIS strategic decisions*, Luton, BIS.

13 *Retail business*, London, Corporate Intelligence and Retailing Unit, monthly.

14 *Marketing in Europe*, London, Corporate Intelligence and Retailing Unit, monthly.

15 *Mintel (Market intelligence)*, London, Mintel International Group, various.

16 *Market research Great Britain*, London, Euromonitor, monthly.

17 *Market research Europe*, London, Euromonitor, monthly.

18 *Retail monitor international*, London, Euromonitor, monthly.

19 *Market research international*, London, Euromonitor, monthly.

20 *Key Note* reports, Hampton, Key Note Publications, irregular.
21 *MarketLine*, London, MarketLine.
22 *Strategic management overviews*, London, Euromonitor, irregular.
23 *Strategy 2000 reports*, London Euromonitor, irregular.
24 *Marketsearch*, London, Arlington Management Publications, annual.
25 *Marketing surveys index*, Mitcham, Marketing Strategies for Industry (UK) Ltd, in association with the Institute of Marketing, loose-leaf.
26 *Reports index*, Dorking, Business Surveys Ltd, bi-monthly.
27 *Statistics and market research bulletin*, Birmingham, Birmingham Public Libraries, monthly.
28 Zigmund, W. and Amoco M. D., *Marketing*, 4th edn, New Jersey, Prentice-Hall, 1993.

Web sites

DIALOG Corporation   http://www.dialog.com
Euromonitor   http://www.euromonitor.com
Frost & Sullivan   http://www.frost.com
Key Note   http://www.keynote.co.uk
Mintel International   http://www.mintel.co.uk
Webber's marketing page   http://www.dis.strath.ac.uk/
                          business/market.html

10 International trade information sources

1 Introduction

International trade is vital to the UK. This chapter outlines the main issues involved and indicates some key sources of information and guidance. Note that international trade statistics, which are a key source of information in this area, are dealt with separately in Chapter 11, Statistical Information Sources. Trade between Britain and the rest of the world is freer now than it has ever been. This, in part, has been due to major changes that have taken place since the early 1980s. These include the success of the European Union in removing trade barriers; the collapse of the Soviet bloc; the rise of multinational companies; and the developments in communications and technology. Each of these changes and the implications for international trade are discussed below.

1.1 The European Union

The European Union (EU) was established over a number of years, beginning in 1951 with the Treaty of Paris which set up the European Coal and Steel Community. A few years later, in 1957, the Treaties of Rome were signed, which established both the European Economic Community and the European Atomic Energy Community. In 1985 the Single European Act was passed and in 1992 the Treaty on European Union was finally signed and created the European Union as we know it today. The Amsterdam Treaty will complete the Treaty of Rome and is due to be signed in October 1999. By 1998 there were 15 member countries of the EU: Austria, Belgium, Denmark, Finland, France, Germany, Greece, Ireland, Italy, Luxembourg, Netherlands, Portugal, Spain, Sweden and the UK.

The main institutions of the EU are the Council of Ministers (also known as the Council of the European Union), the European Parliament, the European Commission and the European Courts of Justice. Detailed discussion of these institutions are beyond the scope of this book. These and other bodies are fully documented in the publication *The institutions of the European Union*[1] and a variety of other EU publications available from European Documentation Centres and most public libraries.

The EU has affected international trade in that the creation of the Union has expanded the market for goods, made trading easier by removal of trade barriers and the ongoing streamlining of business regulations and control. In addition, the possibility of a mandatory Single European Currency as well as many other EU issues are all presently a matter for further debate.

1.2 The collapse of the Soviet bloc

The Cold War ended in 1989 with the collapse of the communist bloc and the significant 'removal' of the Berlin Wall. Many countries within Central and Eastern Europe have undergone great political and economic changes in the move from a state-controlled economy to a form of westernised market economy.

All of these changes have affected international trade in that they have considerably expanded the market for a range of goods and therefore the market for export. This in turn, has led to the setting up of many new small and medium-sized businesses all of which require information. There is also a need for information about changes and trends in areas such as sociology, technology, economics and environmental and political issues – to name but a few. In addition, the need for accurate market information has led to the rise in the number of publications that cover Central and Eastern Europe.

1.3 The developments in communications and information technology (IT)

In the latter years of the 20th century the world witnessed astounding changes in the ways in which people communicate with each other. Examples of these changes include communication by fax (facsimile machine), by e-mail (electronic mail), the ongoing development and use of the Internet to locate and display information, and many others. All these developments in IT have meant that communication is not only fast but it is also efficient and relatively cheap. This has resulted in the development of the world into a kind of 'global village' in that, as communication and IT have developed, the world has literally become a global market place. This, of course, is not to say that trade has not always been on a global scale, but simply that the speed and ease of communications has made finding information, and therefore trading opportunities, much easier and more convenient for many businesses. For further information on this subject the book *Digital business*[2] is a useful starting point and includes discussion on both the pros and cons of the digital era.

1.4 The growth of multinational companies

Developments in communication and information technology and the improvements in the transport structure have combined to encourage the growth of multinational companies. These companies have grown at a phenomenal rate and there is a view that the rise of giant multinationals is one of the factors leading us towards a complete 'globalization' of the economy, which would, in turn, affect international trade on a vast scale. Due to the importance of this issue a research centre on the Study of Globalization and Regionalization has been set up at the University of Warwick. For further discussion of this very interesting topic the book by Lodge[3] is recommended.

2 GATT and the World Trade Organisation

In addition to the removal of the tariff barriers in the European Union other trade restrictions have also been gradually removed world-wide through the efforts of the General Agreement on Tariffs and Trade (GATT), now replaced by the World Trade Organisation (WTO). In order to understand the context in which these institutions work it is necessary to look briefly at the history of these bodies.

GATT was established in 1947. About 90 countries were members or worked to its guidelines, which covered about 80% of world trade. Its main aims were to reduce tariffs and other barriers to trade and to reach other agreements to standardize policies and procedures. GATT went through a number of 'rounds' of negotiations, such as the Kennedy round of 1964–7. Up to and including this round, GATT was mainly concerned with tariff reduction, but after the Tokyo round addressed many other problems, such as subsidies, government procurement, technical barriers to trade, and the needs of developing countries.

The World Trade Organisation was set up in January 1995 to replace GATT following the successful conclusion of the Uruguay round in 1993. The Uruguay round was of particular significance in that it was established to update and extend the rules governing international trade. WTO covers the previous activities of GATT and aims to supervise and liberalize international trade and supervise the settlements of commercial conflicts.

Despite the progress towards freer trade, there are still many restrictions, notably on exports of military equipment and other 'sensitive' products. There are also of course severe problems of drug smuggling and other illegal trade, including counterfeiting. For further information the article in *Overseas trade*[4] summarizes the situation in the late 1990s.

3 Exporting procedures

Exporting procedures are complex. Problems include the choice of methods of selling (e.g. through agents, export houses, or direct); complex paperwork to meet customs and other requirements; and transport and finance. A list of just some of the documentation required would include sales contracts; commercial invoices; certificates of origin; export cargo shipping instructions; single administrative certificates and bills of lading. At the time of writing work was being undertaken by the Simpler Trade Procedures Boards (SITPRO) to simplify the documentation. Specialist firms, such as export houses and forwarding agents, exist to help exporters. Getting paid can be risky, and special insurance may be needed. In this context, the services of the Export Credits Guarantee Department (ECGD) are available from the Department of Trade and Industry. ECGD insures the British exporter against default by the overseas customer. Short term cover is provided by a commercial firm – NCM Credit Insurance. Current guidance on export credit and finance generally can be found in the journal *International trade finance*.[5]

A useful introductory guide to the problems of exporting and sources of government assistance is *Exporting: a guide to export services*,[6] issued by the DTI. One of the key commercial sources of information for exporters is *Croner's reference book for exporting*[7] which contains current information on export control and a useful glossary of terms. There are also many general books on exporting and the Institute of Export in London can be contacted for a current mailing list. One that can be recommended is *The exporters checklist*[8] which covers all aspects such as payment; insurance; transport and documentation. There are many periodicals devoted to exporting and to individual export markets. An example of a general one is the monthly *Export times*.[9]

4 Sources of assistance and advice

Advice and assistance are provided by various bodies in the UK. The British Government provides considerable help and guidance to exporters. The Department of Trade and Industry (DTI) and the Foreign Commonwealth Office (FCO) together provide a range of services to UK exporters. These are provided under the umbrella of the Overseas Trade Services (OTS) which is in turn part of the British Overseas Trade Board (BOTB). The aim of OTS is 'to help UK firms take full advantage of overseas business . . . by providing support, information, advice and assistance opportunities throughout the exporting process'.[10] This aim is achieved by the provision of a network of contacts throughout the world. The network includes:

* The 'country helpdesks' based in London at the DTI
* Commercial departments at Foreign and Commonwealth Office diplomatic posts overseas
* The Business Links in England, Scottish Trade International and the Scottish Business Shop network for Scotland, the Welsh Overseas Trade Services for Wales and the Industrial Development Board for Northern Ireland.

The Business Links employ Export Development Counsellors who make up part of the International Trade Team. To supplement this service the Business Link Information Centres can also provide information on various aspects of exporting.

Details of all these contacts, including full addresses and telephone numbers, are listed at the back of the DTI booklet *Exporting: a guide to export services*.[11]

A list of DTI export publications, with prices, will be found in the DTI *Export publications catalogue*.[12] News of DTI/FCO export activities and general articles on exporting will be found in the DTI's monthly journal *Overseas trade*.[13] The DTI controls export licensing and other regulations through the Export Control Enquiry Unit in London. This unit provides information to exporters of any imminent changes in regulation that would affect trade. Notices of this kind are also published every Thursday in the daily *Lloyd's list international*,[14] under the heading 'DTI Tradefax'.

Other organizations that can help with exporting advice include chambers of commerce, which are partners in Business Links, local export clubs and trade associations. There are approximately 75 export clubs in the UK and these are made up of groups of business people involved with export who meet from time to time to exchange news and ideas.

The DTI also runs the Language in Export Advisory Scheme, designed to assist small firms with translating and interpreting. As mentioned earlier, the Institute of Export is another useful organization in the field and, in conjunction with a firm called Sources of Supply (UK) Ltd, operates a register of export specialists. This is discussed in more detail in the following section.

5 Export opportunities

Intending exporters must research overseas markets and find specific opportunities to sell their goods. A number of systems exist to help with this.

5.1 Export intelligence

Export intelligence is a computerized information service available via subscription from a company called PreLink Ltd. The subscriber's 'profile', indicating the product and market interests, is matched daily against information received from abroad, and the subscriber is notified by post, fax, telex or electronic mail. Information comes from UK diplomatic posts overseas, the European Union (calls for tender from public bodies in the EU), and other bodies such as the World Bank. The service provides a screen-based one-stop shop for export information, including sales leads for government business in the USA and the EU and other business opportunities in China, Russia and world-wide. Further information can be accessed from the Internet address given at the end of the chapter. Alternatively PreLink can be contacted directly by e-mail on 00074.3703@compuserve.com.

5.2 Registers

There are three major web sites that provide information and registers of exporters that are accessible through the Internet. They are:

http://www.tradeuk.com

This is the official DTI web site and is run in association with SOS (UK) Ltd Information Services. The site provides a means for all UK concerns to register their interest and it is intended that TradeUK will become one of the first 'virtual business parks'. There are two levels of entry. The first is free (for basic information to be posted on the register), while the second gives a comprehensive and detailed overview of the company. To appear at the second level a fee is payable.

http://www.export.co.uk

This is the official Institute of Export web site and is also run in association with SOS (UK) Information Service Ltd. The site operates a register of export specialists as well as general information available from the Institute. Again there are two levels of entry to the register – one for basic information and the other for a detailed overview of the company.

http://www.britishexports.com

This site is run by Reed Information Services which is a business partner with the DTI's Information Society Initiative. The site was originally launched in 1996 and has since developed a number of links including the British Exports Interactive (BEI) database. This is an electronic marketplace for products and services exported from Britain and the database is of particular significance in that it is translated from English into French, German, Spanish and Italian.

5.3 Business in Europe

This is run by the DTI and aims to help British companies compete in the EU. It provides current information and advice and as such is useful as a 'first' point of contact.

5.4 Tenders electronic daily (TED)

In the EU, tenders for public-supply contracts above a certain value must be published in the *Official journal of the European communities*.[15] Calls for tender from Japan, the European Free Trade Area and other countries associated with the EU are included. The file of information is added daily to a computerized database known as Tenders Electronic Daily (TED), can be accessed via the web and online through various hosts, including FT Profile and Echo, and via various commercial hosts such as UK Context Ltd which acts as the official UK gateway for TED. The Stationery Office (formerly HMSO) also produces a diskette version of TED and a CD-ROM version is available from Eurobases. There is also now a system known as TED Alert whereby a profile is created of a company's interests and TED is then searched by the agency to check on relevant tenders. This system is available through European Information Centres which are discussed in more detail later.

5.5 BC-NET (Business Co-operation Network)

BC-NET is a system designed to help smaller businesses find export opportunities and overseas business partners. BC-NET is accessed through the major chambers of commerce. Entries for businesses throughout the EU are made on a computer in Brussels, which matches likely pairs. This service is very useful as it is adjusted to the requirements of every company that wishes to take advantage of the many opportunities for business within the EU.

5.6 Business Co-operation Centres

This system is designed to allow companies to advertise their requests in the EU using the local chamber of commerce and European Information Centres as the contact. Opportunities remain viable for six months but can then be renewed for a further six months.

6 Export markets

Sources of information and publications on individual overseas markets are legion. Some of the key ones are listed below.

6.1 Overseas Trade Services

The Overseas Trade Services provide excellent information services including:

The Export Market Information Centre (EMIC)

This is a major collection of overseas directories and statistics and the site can also be visited through the Internet or contacted by e-mail at emic@xpd3.dti.gov.uk. EMIC will also carry out research, for a fee, through the Export Market Research Information Service. (The service is run by the Institute of Export and Business and Trade Statistics Ltd.)

Market Menus

This system outlines the services and literature available for each of the top 80 UK export markets. Information is also available on the Internet at the address given at the end of this chapter. Market menus plus additional information concerning case studies and economic information are also available on CD-ROM.

Market Campaigns

Sometimes referred to in the press as 'trade missions', these are usually aimed at specific markets and aim to publicize particular overseas markets. Details are usually advertised in the journal *Overseas trade*.[16]

Global Information on Science and Technology (GIST)

Until summer 1997 this was known as the Overseas Technical Information Service (OTS). GIST aims to circulate information on scientific and technological developments in other countries. The service provides a newsletter called *GIST news* (previously *OTIS news*), which includes abstracts, features and news. There is online access to the GIST database which is run by Pera Business Connection.

The Market Information Enquiry Service (MIES)

MIES, which is run by the DTI, will supply information about a market and will arrange for an initial free meeting with the exporter.

6.2 Technical Help for Exporters (THE)

Technical Help for Exporters (THE) is based in London and is a branch of the British Standards Institution (BSI). THE will assist with information on any legislation or general regulations regarding specific overseas countries and regions.

6.3 The British Library

The British Library Business Information Service in London provides detailed market information in particular areas.

6.4 European Documentation Centres (EDC) and European Information Centres (EIC)

Both these centres will provide detailed market information. To understand the difference between the two centres it is necessary to provide a little background information.

European Documentation Centres are collections of the published documentation of the EU, established to encourage the academic study of Europe. The EDC project is administered by the Directorate General for Information of the European Commission. There are more than 40 EDCs in the UK, mostly in university libraries which grant access to the public. The documents are supplied by the EC free of charge. The natural first port of call for anyone seeking relevant documents is the *EC Official journal of the European Communities*[17] together with other relevant documentation which can be found in the EDC.

The European Information Centres are another initiative of the European Commission. Unlike the EDCs they are not intended as academic support systems, but are designed to help small and medium-sized businesses with practical advice and information.

6.5 Commercial sources

A wide-ranging review of EU industry – the *Panorama of EU industry*[18] covers over 200 sectors of manufacturing and service industries and is published annually by the EU publications office. Other examples would include publications such as the Economist Intelligence Unit's very comprehensive *Country reports*. Euromonitor publish information about specific regions which are listed in the catalogue, *Euromonitor index*.[19]

A readily accessible source of information on overseas markets is the *Financial times*,[20] which publishes occasional surveys on individual countries. The journal *European business intelligence briefing*[21] provides a valuable service that includes general surveys and a country update each month including updates on Eastern Europe.

Two recent comprehensive directories of sources are *the Directory of networks and other European sources*[22] published by the Commission and the comprehensive *European Union information: a directory of sources.*[23]

7 Central and Eastern Europe

There is an increasing number of companies wishing to export to the 'new' markets which form Central and Eastern Europe. The first point of contact for this kind of information would normally be the East European Trade Council (EETC) which is located in London and houses a very extensive East European business information collection. EETC was set up in 1967 to help assist and promote business in Central and south-east Europe and the former Soviet Union. EETC also produces the *East European bulletin*[24] which aims to 'promote business within the countries of Central and Eastern Europe, Central Asia and Transcaucasia'. The Central European Research and Development Unit (CERDU) at Glasgow University is another useful source of Central and East European information. The information service housed within the Unit provides current information (for a fee) on most aspects of export and related business matters.

Two of the key directories in this area are Headland Press's *East European business information*[25] and the London Business School's *Central and Eastern European business information sources.*[26] Both these publications list information on a range of Eastern European services and products. London Business School also runs the Commonwealth of Independent States: Middle Europe (CISME) Centre, which specializes in Central and Eastern European Information.

The East European Risk Service is run by the Economist Intelligence Unit and provides valuable information on the state of a country's economy to potential exporters. There are also some interesting web sites one of which is listed at the end of this chapter. Finally, there are articles on this subject in the professional library and information press such as the one by Shelley in *Business information review.*[27]

8 Asia-Pacific

Until the Hong Kong stock market crash in late 1997 the area known as Asia-Pacific was undergoing a period of market development – giving rise to general comments in the media such as 'the rise of the Asia Pacific nations'. The nations to which this sort of reference was made included Japan, North and South Korea, Indonesia, the Philippines, Singapore,

Brunei, Burma, Malaysia, Thailand, Cambodia, Laos, Vietnam, China, Mongolia, Hong Kong, and Taiwan

The reasons for the increase in interest and trade in these countries during the 1990s were twofold. First, as mentioned earlier, this group included some of the world's fastest-growing economies – and some of the most well-populated ones. Second, as in Europe, trade barriers are gradually being removed. For example, in 1995 Thailand, Indonesia and the Philippines launched unilateral programmes to cut tariffs.

However, since October 1997, press reports now tend to refer to the 'Asian Meltdown' and even suggest the possibility of a full-scale global recession. These claims are evidenced by the well-publicized collapse of three previously strong Japanese financial institutions – Sanyo Securities, Hokkaido Takushoku Bank and Yamaichi Securities.

Another term – Asean – refers specifically to the seven nations of southeast Asia – Indonesia, Malaysia, the Philippines, Singapore, Thailand, Vietnam and Brunei. These countries are working collaboratively towards a 'free trade area' which, it is hoped, could be in force as early as 2003. It will be interesting to see if events in 1997 affect this drive towards further free trade. Further details on this turbulent and rapidly changing subject can be found in the *Financial Times*[28] which runs regular surveys on Asian financial markets.

Each of the countries within the Asia-Pacific region has its own Department of Trade and Industry Country Helpdesk which would normally be a first point of contact for information. Some of the key sources in this area include the relevant Kompass directories and publications by Euromonitor and other major business information publishing companies. For example, Dun and Bradstreet publish the *Duns Asia/Pacific key British enterprises*,[29] while another key source of information in this subject area is the *Asia-Pacific handbook*.[30] Other useful sources include publications of the Economist Intelligence Unit such as *China's leading industrial companies: the top 50*.[31]

Periodicals that cover Asia-Pacific include *Asia, Inc.*[32] which is also available online, by subscription, through the *Asia, Inc.* web site. Other relevant periodicals include the American periodical *East Asian: executive reports*[33] which gives legal and economic information aimed at professionals such as attorneys and accountants. For something of a more academic nature, the *Asia-Pacific business review*,[34] acts as a forum for discussion of all economic and market issues relating to the relevant countries.

Other journals deal specifically with particular countries in this region. Two of particular note are the weekly *Beijing review*[35] and the monthly

China – Britain trade review: the journal of China – Britain trade group.[36] As one is published in China and the other in the UK it is interesting to compare the two for differing perceptions of similar situations, particularly in the period just before and just after the return of Hong Kong to the Chinese.

9 North America

There is a variety of trade information sources available for the USA. Relevant and well known US directories such as the *Thomas register*[37] contain information on over 150,000 US companies. Increasingly there is more and more useful information available via the web as the US Government and most US companies have quite comprehensive web pages. One of the major sources of information is a web site known as Stat USA (previously called National Trade Data Bank). Webbers' description neatly sums up the aim of the site as being to 'provide a huge amount of economic, business and social data on the USA and overseas information of areas to US exporters . . .'. Other useful web sites include Fedworld which gives access to US government sources and publications. Finally there are various newspapers and journals which provide invaluable current information such as the *Wall Street journal,*[38] *Forbes USA*[39] and *The business journal.*[40]

10 Conclusion

Export is a complicated area that changes as new markets emerge and old markets subside. The recent major and historical changes which were discussed at the beginning of this chapter have provided many new priorities for UK export and the Government and the DTI has not been slow to realize this. Because of this realization there is a very strong framework in the UK which includes many initiatives and schemes such as the Languages in Export Advisory Scheme. Elsewhere there has been a steady increase in trade; the reduction of barriers to trade really has made an impact in the size and diversity of markets available for export. A variety of frameworks and schemes have been set up to give assistance to those who wish to export goods in order to improve both the economy of individual countries and to have some impact on the economy of the world in general.

References

1   European Commission, *The institutions of the European Union,*

Luxembourg, Office for Official Publications of the European Union, 1995.

2 Hammond, R., *Digital business*, London, Coronet, 1997.

3 Lodge, G. C., *Managing globalisation in the age of interdependence*, San Diego, Pfeiffer & Company, 1995.

4 Knight, P., 'Keep business flowing', *Overseas trade*, February 1997, 22.

5 *International trade finance*, London, FT Finance, twice monthly.

6 *Exporting: a guide to export services*, London, Department of Trade and Industry, 1997.

7 *Croner's reference book for exporters*, Surrey, Croner Publications Ltd, looseleaf.

8 Twells, H., *The exporters checklist*, London, Institute of Export, 1997.

9 *Export times*, London, Nexus Media Ltd, monthly.

10 *Exporting: a guide to export services*, London, Department of Trade and Industry, 1997.

11 See Reference 6.

12 *Export publications catalogue*, London, Department of Trade and Industry, 1997.

13 *Overseas trade*, London, Brass Tacks Publishing on behalf of OTB, monthly.

14 *Lloyd's list international*, Colchester, Lloyd's of London Press Ltd, daily.

15 *Official journal of the European Communities*, Luxembourg, Office for Official Publications of the European Union, monthly.

16 See Reference 13.

17 See Reference 15.

18 *Panorama of EU industry 1997*, Luxembourg, Office for Official Publications of the European Union, 1997.

19 *Euromonitor index*, London, Euromonitor Publications, 1997.

20 *Financial Times*, London, Financial Times Information, daily.

21 *European business intelligence briefing*, St. Anne's, Headland Business Information, monthly.

22 *Directory of networks and other European information sources*, Luxembourg, Office for Official Publications of the European Union, 1996.

23 *European Union information: a directory of UK sources*, London, NCC, 1996.

24 *East European bulletin*, London, EECT, six per year.

25 *East European business information*, St. Anne's, Headland Business Information, 1996.

26 *Central and Eastern European business information sources*, London, London Business School, 1997.

27 Shelley, W., 'Business information from Central and Eastern Europe: the CIS', *Business information review*, 245–9.

28 See Reference 20.

29 *Duns Asia/Pacific key British enterprises 1996/7*, Melbourne, Dun and Bradstreet Information Services, 1996.

30 *Asia-Pacific handbook*, London, Extel (part of FT Information Ltd), 1997.

31 *China's leading industrial companies: the top 50*, Hong Kong, Economist Intelligence Unit, 1997.

32 *Asia, Inc*, Asia, Inc Ltd, Hong Kong (People's Republic of China), monthly.

33 *East Asian: executive reports*, Washington, International Executive Reports Ltd, monthly.

34 *Asia-Pacific business review*, London, Frank Cass & Co. Ltd, quarterly.

35 *Beijing review*, People's Republic of China, Beijing, weekly.

36 *China–Britain review: the journal of China–Beijing Trade Group*, London, China–Britain Trade Group, monthly.

37 *Thomas register of American manufacturers*, New York, Thomas Publishing Company, annual.

38 *Wall Street journal*, New York, Dow Jones & Company, daily.

39 *Forbes USA*, New York, Forbes Inc., bi-weekly.

40 *The business journal*, Texas, American City Business Journals, weekly.

Web sites

Department of Trade and Industry	http://www.dti.gov.uk
Overseas Trade Service	http://www.dti.gov.uk/ots
Export Market Information Centre/	http://www.dti.gov.uk/ots/emic
Prelink	http://www.prelink.co.uk
Russia and East European	http://www.pitt.edu/~cjp/
Studies	rees.html
Scottish Business Shop Network	http://business.dis.strath.ac. uk/advice/scotland.html
Central European Research &	http://business.dis.strath.ac.
Development Unit (CERDU)	uk/advice/europe.html
Office for National Statistics	http://www.emap.co.uk/ons/
Stat USA	http://www.stat. usa.gov
FedWorld	http://www.fedworld.gov
Thomas Register	http://www.thomasregister.com
ONS	http://www.emap.co.uk/ons/

11 Statistical information sources

1 Introduction

Compilations of statistics, both official and unofficial, are vital to the success of any business. Statistics are not confined to specific business data such as import or sales figures; demographic data from the census and social data relating to health and education may also often cast light on the potential market for a product or service. This is a very large topic and this chapter can do no more than outline the main features. Governments across the world produce vast quantities of data and together with privately published compilations, and this represents an enormous body of information which can be used for many different purposes. The UK government's own free pamphlet *Government statistics: a brief guide to sources*[1] is as good a guide as any to the uses of statistics in business. It identifies uses in marketing; contracting (e.g. using price indexes to determine cost escalation clauses); accounts (for example the use of price indexes in current-cost accounting); the buying of raw materials and supplies (use of producer-price indexes); management efficiency; finance and investment; and social change.

This chapter is organized into four main sections, starting with a full explanation of the changes in the Government Statistical Office and the way in which official British statistics are now organized. This is followed by sections on unofficial statistics and international trade statistics, and the chapter closes with a discussion on some of the problems that can sometimes arise when dealing with statistics.

2 Official British statistics

The British Government collects and publishes large quantities of data, but it should be understood that this operation is largely for the benefit of the Government itself, to help with planning and guiding the economy. This has inevitably led to discussion in some quarters about the way in which statistics are presented (for a discussion of this point of view see the article by Hibbert).[2] Much of the data collected by the Government is published; if the information happens to be useful to outsiders, including businesses, all well and good, but that is a secondary consideration from the Government's point of view. This has always been the case, although it is certainly even more so since the recent reorganization.

In line with its general policy of reducing the burden of reporting and form-filling placed on businesses and, with the stated intention of improving the quality of government statistics, the system has undergone the following changes in the last few years:

Pre 1989

Prior to July 1989, the Central Statistical Office (CSO), while itself publishing a number of major series such as the *Annual abstract*, had the role of coordinating the activities of the various agencies, such as the Business Statistics Office (BSO) of the DTI, and the Department of Employment's statistical division. Collectively, the various departmental divisions of statistics, the Office of Population Censuses and Surveys (OPCS) and other agencies, together with the CSO, constituted the Government Statistical Service.

1989–1996

On 31 July 1989 the enlarged CSO became a separate department responsible to the Chancellor of the Exchequer, and assumed responsibility for the BSO and all statistical series of the DTI, including *Overseas trade statistics* and the *Retail prices index*, formerly the responsibility of the Department of Employment. (The full story up to this point can be read in articles in *British business*.)[3, 4, 5, 6]

Post April 1996

The most significant recent change, however, was in April 1996 when the new Office for National Statistics (ONS) was created by the merger of the CSO and the OPCS. One of the main objectives of the ONS is to 'establish and maintain a central database of key economic and social statistics drawn from the wide range of Government Statistical Service and produced to common classification, definitions and standards'.[7]

The ONS is responding to the ever changing environment by following an internal change management programme called ONS 2000 which aims to maintain a distinct culture and a reputation for excellence within the Service. Developments in government statistical policy and services can be followed in *Statistical news*[8] on the very comprehensive ONS web site.

The range of publications of the Government Statistical Service is very wide. The pamphlet *Government statistics*,[9] mentioned above, indicates the range of publications available, but the serious user of government data should start with the *Guide to official statistics*[10] (also available on CD-ROM). This compilation gives detailed annotations on all government statistical publications and is essential for establishing the precise subject coverage of particular ones, how data are compiled and edited, changes in scope and so on. In addition to government series, the guide also refers to some major non-governmental publications.

It should be noted that many government statistics are repeated in different sources at different times. Thus, key economic statistics such as the *Retail prices index*[11] are given in press releases and are therefore immediately announced in the media.

It is not possible to list here all the publications that could be useful to business but many a business information manager's top 20 would include the *Annual abstract of statistics* (annual summary tables, often with ten years' data, and a useful starting point for many purposes); the *Monthly digest of statistics*,[12] *Overseas trade statistics*[13] and the *Business monitors*[14] generally; the annuals *Social trends*[15] and *Regional trends*[16]; monthlies such as *Economic trends*[17] and *Financial statistics*[18]; the 1991 *Census*[19]; *Household food consumption and expenditure*[20] (an annual sample survey by the National Food Survey Committee) and the relatively new *Share ownership*,[21] which provides information from the 1994 Share Register Survey.

In addition to hard copy publications the ONS has now launched several computer packages which will assist the user in analysing the vast quantities of data. The first of these, *Navidata*, allows the user to create tailor-made formats for data comparisons, to insert tables and graphs and to merge information from different data series. The second database is known as *Geostat regional database* and is aimed at local businesses and industries. Its many features include consumer expenditure by 32 sectors and a size analysis of UK business. There are also other ONS datasets available in a variety of electronic formats e.g. *Economic trends* and *Retail price index*. Also available on CD-ROM are *Social trends*, *Regional trends* and the *Guide to official statistics*.

2.1 Business monitors

The ONS produces a range of statistics that give information on the activity of business in the UK. Broadly they can be classified into three categories: primary production, the UK manufacturing industry and the UK service sector.

The Government has for many years collected data from industry, on the basis of which it compiled the former *Annual census of production* and also statistics on sales of products. Since 1994 the system has changed a little and there is now an ONS annual sample enquiry into production and construction known as PRODCOM. This is the name of the EU system for harmonizing the collection of production statistics throughout the EU countries. The system was agreed in the early 1990s and all EU member states are required to collect product statistics using the same list of questions to the same level of accuracy. The data covers approximately 5000 of the most commonly manufactured products in Europe. The data from the survey are mainly used by the Government to calculate the index of production, but the published information is also invaluable for marketing purposes. Also available is a product called PACSTAT (available on CD-ROM) which contains statistical data from PRODCOM.

As a result of the changes described, the collection and reporting of most of the data has been altered and the current range of publications is as follows:

Product Sales and Trade Data [22]

This relatively new series of reports is based on the results of the European Community Survey known as PRODCOM and replaces the old *Business monitors* and *PQ*. There are quarterly and annual publications available which include, for example, imports and exports both inside and outside the EU; average prices for all categories of manufactured products and trend data for recent years. Because of harmonization of definitions for manufacturer sales and trade data, accurate total market data in the form of *Net supply to the UK market* is now available. The reports are also available on CD-ROM and through The Stationery Office Intelligent Fax service known as Ifax.

There have been other changes such as the former *Business monitor P1007* which is now produced as *The directory of UK manufacturing business* [23] and is available in both hard copy and CD-ROM. Up-to-date information on which *Monitors* appear in which series can be obtained from the Library of the Office for National Statistics in Newport.

Business Monitor: service and distribution monitors[24]

The *SD* series may be monthly, quarterly or annual. They are based on the collection of data from banks, retailers and other service sectors, and include: *SDM 6 Credit business* (monthly); *SDQ 7 Assets and liabilities of finance houses* (quarterly); *SDQ 9 Computing services* (quarterly); SDA 25 *Retailing* (annual); *SDA 26 Wholesaling* (annual); *SDM 28 Retail sales* (monthly); and *SDA 29 Service trades* (annual). Data from 1995 onwards is presented in the Sector Review series.

Business Monitor: miscellaneous[25]

There is a variety of publications, including *MM 1 Motor vehicle registrations* (monthly); *MQ 6 Overseas travel and tourism* (quarterly); *MM 17 Price index numbers for current cost accounting* (monthly) plus the summary volume *MO 18* for 1983–87 (1988); and *MM 22 Producer price indices* (monthly).

2.2 Overseas trade statistics[26]

There are two main business monitor publications that deal with overseas trade statistics. The *Overseas trade statistics of the UK with countries outside the European Union (extra EU trade)* forms *MM20* in the *Business monitor* series. The other publication is the *Overseas trade statistics of the UK with countries within the European Union (intra EU Trade: intrastat)* which forms *MQ 20* in the *Business monitor* series. They are compiled from the customs declarations made to HM Customs and Excise and are published monthly and quarterly respectively. *MM 20* gives figures for the current month and from January to date, so that the December issue should be used for cumulative annual figures. *MQ 20* gives figures in a similar format for the relevant quarter. Data are given in both values and quantities. Products are classified by the UN Standard International Trade Classification (SITC). The classification is first by the SITC class numbers, and within these by detailed commodity codes, for example:

SITC – 666.13   Ceramic tableware etc.
        codes -   691200 10 0 common pottery
                691200 30 0 stoneware
                691200 50 0 earthenware or fine pottery
                691200 90 0 other

The main tables are in two parts, viz. imports and exports. Within each of these the data are presented twice, firstly by SITC class, showing country of origin (imports) or destination (exports); secondly by SITC class and within that by commodity codes. It is not possible to combine the two, so that from these tables one cannot extract, say, imports from a given country by specific commodities, only by the general SITC class. In addition, the tables show only the major countries in each case, with 'other countries' lumped into one group; however, totals for the EU are shown. More detailed searches can be done, for a fee, via the Customs and Excise computer. The C and E Bill of Entry Unit at Southend will supply data from computer records for the period up to and including 1986. From 1987, the service was transferred to what they call 'officially appointed marketing agents', in other words it was privatized. A list of agents is available from the Southend office.

In approaching the tables by commodity code, one should always start with the *Guide to the classification for overseas statistics, MA 21*,[27] which enables the exact code to be identified. There is an index in the monthly *Overseas trade statistics*,[28] but only to the level of SITC classes.

3 Unofficial statistics

Many non-governmental organizations collect and publish statistics, especially trade associations, which may collect from their members more detailed data than are available from official sources, or who rework and repackage official data. The Scotch Whisky Association is one such body. Another is the Society of Motor Manufacturers and Traders, whose annual *Motor industry of Great Britain*[29] assembles UK and world production figures, numbers of new registrations and vehicles in use in the UK and selected overseas countries, and overseas trade data. This annual is noteworthy in breaking down new registrations both by category of vehicle and by manufacturer.

Other organizations that issue statistics include local authorities – who often produce community profiles containing reworked census, health and education statistics as well as data of their own – professional associations and, of course, commercial publishers of business data. The *Public library statistics*[30] compiled and published by the Chartered Institute of Public Finance and Accountancy (CIPFA) from returns made by the public libraries themselves, are well known, and could be crucial for businesses wishing to market products and services to this sector.

Recent investigations of and guides to unofficial statistics have demonstrated that there is a surprising range of publications available at low cost. Two recent guides are the *European directory of non-official statistics*[31] and the third edition of the now standard work by Mort.[32] Finally, it should be remembered that the *Financial Times*[33] is a daily mine of information on data, commodity prices, and so on.

It should not be overlooked that much of the material of use to the market researcher appears in trade journals and newspapers, and the standard print and online periodical abstracts and indexes should therefore be considered as likely sources in appropriate cases.

4 International trade statistics

Most countries issue statistical publications similar to those outlined in this chapter, but international comparisons are often difficult to make because of differences in currencies and methods of compilation. There are three major publishers in this field.

4.1 The United Nations

The United Nations (UN) is an organization made up of many sovereign nations which aim to solve problems of concern to humanity. Due to this far-reaching aim the UN collectively has access to data from many different countries which is published as a range of different statistics. For example, the *International trade statistics yearbook*[34] is published annually in two volumes: trade by country and trade by commodity. Commodities are classified by SITC, using three or five digits. Values are in thousands of US dollars, enabling cross-country comparisons. There is also a *Handbook of international trade and development statistics*[35] which is produced by the United Nations Conference on Trade and Development (UNCTAD) and which contains comprehensive data on world trade. A list of publications can be found at the UN web site listed at the end of this chapter.

4.2 OECD statistics

The Organisation for Economic Co-operation and Development (OECD) produces statistics that cover not only OECD member countries but also trade with non-OECD countries. These are broken down into three separate series: A, B and C. Series A, *Monthly statistics of foreign trade*[36] gives summary tables for each OECD country by countries of origin and destination. Series B, *Foreign trade by country*,[37] gives statistics of trade for each OECD country, with full details of commodities. Series C, *Foreign trade by commodities*,[38] gives trade between OECD countries and others for commodity groups at one and two digit levels of the SITC.

Another set of statistics maintained by the OECD Statistics Directorate is *Foreign trade and globalization statistics*[39] which is composed of three main databases of statistics on foreign trade. OECD also publishes a wide range of other kinds of statistics, a list of which can be found on the web site given at the end of this chapter.

4.3 Eurostat

Eurostat is a department of the European Commission and is thus the general name for statistics issued by the European Union. Foreign trade is covered by numerous publications in various formats, and series. The main series are the *Statistical yearbook*[40] (time series), the *Monthly statistics*[41] which contains short term trends and the annual *Analytical tables*,[42] which gives export and import information.

The *Eurostat yearbook*[43] is an annual publication which compares significant features of each country of the EU and the US, Canada and Japan. A major attempt has been made to make comparisons easier, for example some of the statistics have been harmonized by Eurostat while others have been compiled in similar ways. The web site for Eurostat is given at the end of this chapter.

A final invaluable source of trade statistics is the TRADESTAT database available from the DIALOG Corporation.

5 Some problems with statistics

The use of statistical tables is fraught with traps for the unwary, and the following key points should be kept in mind.

5.1 Compatibility of purpose

Statistics may be collected for purposes that are at odds with the needs of the public user. Thus, as noted above, the ONS classifies its data by the SIC, whilst the Customs and Excise uses the SITC system. This makes collation and integration of the data from these series very difficult.

5.2 Units of measurement

Care should be taken to establish the precise units employed in a table. Values are often in thousands or even millions of pounds, thousands of kilograms, and so on, and in struggling with the tables it is all too easy to miss the units and so to understate the data by a large factor. In other cases, units may change over time, or metric and imperial measures may have to be reconciled. A classic example is the 'ton', three versions of which have been in use over the years. Currently British official sources, like others across the world, employ the metric ton or tonne. A tonne is 1000 kilograms, which is about 2205 lbs. In earlier British tables, in the old pre-metric days, the long ton was used, that is to say the old-fashioned British ton of 20 cwts or 2240 lbs. Finally, the Americans used to employ the short ton, 2000 lbs.

Obviously, if time-series data based on tonnage are being assembled, some recalculation may be necessary to avoid serious error. The more recent moves to ensure that all UK products are labelled in metric form is another fact to be considered when comparing statistics from earlier years.

5.3 Geographical scope

Geographical scope should be looked at in many cases. Some official UK tables cover the United Kingdom, others Great Britain, which excludes Northern Ireland.

5.4 Reworked material

Sometimes data are reworked in ways which may seem mysterious to the uninitiated. Much of the data in the *Monthly digest* is in the form of monthly averages, rather than actuals. This means that to obtain a yearly figure the number must be multiplied by 12. Some people have a problem with seasonal adjustment, which is used, for example, with unemployment statistics or balance of trade figures. This is not, as might be supposed, a trick to 'massage' the figures to make them look better: it is simply a mathematical calculation for producing a trend line, so that despite seasonal peaks and troughs the general trend may be observed. Doubters should consult any standard text on time series and moving averages such as that by Stephen and Hornby.[44]

6 Conclusion

This chapter has aimed to give the reader some insight into the world of statistics. It has dealt with the role which the UK Government plays in the compilation and publication of a wide variety of statistics and taken into account the first moves to harmonize the collection of statistics with other member countries of the EU. Increasingly we are witnessing the publication of more and more comparative European sources such the *Eurostat yearbook*[45] and no doubt these will increase with time. For a fuller idea of what European statistics are available the reader is recommended two works both published by Eurostat: *The Eurostat catalogue*[46] and the directory *European official statistics – a guide to databases*.[47]

References

1 *Government statistics: a brief guide to sources*, London, Office for National Statistics, annual.

2 Hibbert, J., 'Public confidence in the integrity and validity of official statistics (with discussion)', *Journal of the Royal Society*, Series A (part 2), 121–50.

3 'Better figures from fewer forms', *British business*, 19 May 1989, 7.

4 Norton, R., 'Statistics: less of a burden and better', *British business*, 14 July 1989, 16–17.

5 Norton, R., 'Statistics 2: the rationale behind the changes', *British business*, 21 July 1989,15–18.

6 'New government department', *British business*, 4 August 1989, 5.

7 See Reference 1.

8 *Statistical news*, London, The Stationery Office, quarterly.

9 See Reference 1.

10 *Guide to official statistics*, London, The Stationery Office, 1996.

11 *Retail price index*, London, The Stationery Office.

12 *Monthly digest of statistics*, London, The Stationery Office.

13 *Overseas trade statistics*, London, The Stationery Office, various frequencies.

14 *Business monitors*, London, The Stationery Office.

15 *Social trends*, London, The Stationery Office.

16 *Regional trends*, London, The Stationery Office.

17 *Economic trends*, London, The Stationery Office.

18 *Financial statistics*, London, The Stationery Office.

19 1991 *Census*, London, The Stationery Office.

20 *Household food consumption and expenditure*, London, The Stationery Office.

21 *Share ownership*, London, The Stationery Office.

22 *Product sales and trade data*, London, The Stationery Office, various frequencies.

23 *Directory of UK manufacturing business*, London, The Stationery Office, annual.

24 *Service and distribution monitors*, London, The Stationery Office, various frequencies.

25 *Miscellaneous monitors*, London, The Stationery Office, various frequencies.

26 *Overseas trade statistics*, London, The Stationery Office, various frequencies.

27 *Guide to the classification for overseas trade statistics*, MA 21, London, HMSO, 1996.

28 See Reference 13.

29 *Motor industry of Great Britain 1997: world automotive statistics*, London, Society of Motor Manufacturers and Traders Ltd, 1997.

30 *Public library statistics*, London, Chartered Institute of Public Finance and Accountancy, annual.

31 *The European directory of non-official statistics*, London, Euromonitor, 1997.

32 Mort, D. (ed.), *Sources of unofficial UK statistics*, 3rd edn, Aldershot, Gower, for the University of Warwick Business Information Service, 1997.

33 *Financial Times*, London, Financial Times Information, daily.

34 *International trade statistics yearbook*, New York, United Nations, annual.

35 *Handbook of international trade and development statistics*, New York, United Nations Conference on Trade and Development, irregular.

36 *Monthly statistics of foreign trade, series A*, Paris, OECD, monthly.

37 *Foreign trade by country: series B*, Paris, OECD, annual.

38 *Foreign trade by commodities: series C*, Paris, OECD, annual.

39 *Foreign trade and globalisation statistics*, Paris, OECD Statistics Directorate, OECD, database.

40 *External trade – statistical yearbook*, Luxembourg, Statistical Office of the EU, annual.
41 *External trade – monthly statistics (series B)*, Luxembourg, Statistical Office of the EU, monthly.
42 *External trade – analytical tables (series C)*, Luxembourg, Statistical Office of the EU, annual.
43 *The Eurostat yearbook*, Luxembourg, Statistical Office of the EU, annual.
44 Stephen, P. and Hornby, S., *Simple statistics for library and information professionals*, 2nd edn, London, Library Association Publishing, 1997.
45 *Eurostat yearbook '96*, Luxembourg, Eurostat, 1996.
46 *The Eurostat catalogue*, Luxembourg, Eurostat, annual.
47 *European official statistics – a guide to databases*, Luxembourg, Eurostat, 1996.

Web sites

Office for National Statistics	http://www.emap.co.uk/ons/
Government statistics in general	http://www.ons.gov.uk/pages/ links.htm
Eurostat	http://www.europa.eu.int/ eurostat.htm
OECD	http://www.oecd.org/ publications/catalogue
United Nations	http://www.un.org/

12 Advertising and distribution information sources

1 Introduction

The first part of this chapter deals with advertising and distribution and looks briefly at the 'green' environmental concerns of business. People tend to have strong opinions about advertising, which can be seen as entertainment, brightening our lives and enlivening the media. Certainly it seems at times that more skill is devoted by actors, directors and camera crew to television advertisements than to the programmes they interrupt: some advertisements, such as the 'will-they-won't-they?' mini-drama series of the Nescafé Gold Blend couple during the 1990s capture the public imagination. Advertising can, however, also be seen at times as an undesirable and unnecessary intrusion into our privacy, with accusations of brainwashing and such like. Whatever one's views, advertising is here to stay. A capitalist economy implies competition, and where there is competition there must be advertising by competitors.

The second part of this chapter examines the role of distribution in the market place – a product must not only be correctly promoted and priced, but also made available in the right places. To a great extent, the pattern of distribution will be determined by the nature of the product, thus cans of baked beans will reach customers by means that are poles apart from the routes appropriate for heavy goods vehicles. At the same time, the existence of certain types of outlet has encouraged the development of new products or packs. Thus, the enormous buying power of the superstores and hypermarkets has enabled them to induce manufacturers to supply the stores with own-label versions of branded products, usually at lower prices. Sometimes the large superstores attempt to imitate the packaging and presentation of a branded product, usually resulting in court proceedings, such as the case in the late 1990s involving ASDA and their 'Puffin' biscuit, which it was claimed could be confused with the well-established 'Penguin' chocolate biscuit. Of course each time cases such as these are brought to court there is much publicity, which in itself provides free advertising of the products in question.

2 Types of advertising

There are many different types of advertising, directed at different targets, and the techniques and media employed vary accordingly.

2.1 Consumer advertising

The most obvious type of advertising is concerned with fast-moving consumer goods, consumer durables and consumer services such as leisure and banking. Mass marketing uses media with a wide appeal such as television and women's magazines, but there are also many products and services for which specialist media such as special-interest magazines must be used.

2.2 Industrial or business-to-business advertising

This is directed at smaller audiences, consisting of the type of businesses likely to purchase the goods or services advertised. Appropriate media include trade journals and trade fairs.

2.3 Trade advertising

Trade advertising is aimed at retailers and other distributors. Trade campaigns are tied into and precede consumer advertising. Thus, a new chocolate product must first be promoted to the retailers to persuade them to stock it, so that when the subsequent consumer campaign creates a demand for the product it is already in the shops. Trade advertising is sometimes called *selling in,* consumer advertising *selling out.*

2.4 Retail advertising

Retail advertising is a term often used to mean selling the shop, rather than the goods sold, in other words, promoting the image of the retailer. Television advertisements of this kind are often produced by variety chains and department stores, sometimes in connection with January sales and similar events.

3 Agencies

Advertising agencies exist to advise clients on their advertising and promotion campaigns, to devise and produce suitable advertisements, and to arrange for their distribution in appropriate media. Agencies are of different kinds. Large *full-service* agencies are capable of conducting a complete advertising campaign. They include the agencies which handle the huge accounts of companies making consumer products with household names. Some agencies specialize in industrial and technical goods. There are many smaller companies which supply specialized services, sometimes to other agencies. These are often referred to as *à la carte* agencies, and include creative agencies (producing advertising copy, visuals or music), direct-response agencies (direct-mail campaigns or telephone selling), incentive scheme agencies, sponsorship agencies, and so on. Finally, there are the *media independents,* who concentrate on buying media space. They purchase their copy and visuals from creative agencies. Traditionally, advertising agencies have received an income in the form of commission paid by the media for placing advertisements with them. Thus, the advertiser paid a fee to the medium, which then paid a commission to the agency. This system has tended to break down in recent years, and agencies may obtain some commission from the media, but also charge a fee to the client.

4 Media

Media are often classified as either *above the line* or *below the line.* Originally, *above the line* meant the five types of media that paid commission to the agencies, i.e. press, radio, television, cinema and outdoor advertising. The rest of the media, which paid no commission, were referred to as *below the line.* The 'line' refers to the way in which the accounts of agencies were drawn up and presented to clients. The large agencies still obtain most of their income from above-the-line advertising. Until 1979 only an agency recognized by the media associations such as the Newspaper Publishers Association could claim commission in this way. But in that year the Office of Fair Trading decided that this was a restrictive practice, and nowadays any agency is entitled to buy space on commission.

Of the above-the-line media, press advertising still accounts for the largest share, despite the high public profile of television advertisements. It includes national and local newspapers, free sheets, and magazines and periodicals of all kinds. Outdoor advertising includes posters and transport (buses, tubes, etc).

Below-the-line methods are many and various. They include media such as sales and trade literature, point-of-sale displays, advertising bags and carrier bags, 'body' media (e.g. sweatshirts), stickers, and so on. Also included here are various types of sales promotion, such as in-store promotions and demonstrations, competitions, on-pack promotions, coupon and voucher offers, promotional games, multiple packs, and so on. Other below-the-line methods are sponsorship schemes, trade fairs and exhibitions, and direct mail advertising (direct response).

5 Direct response

Direct response deserves a little extra consideration, if only because it involves targeting specific groups and creating mailing lists and thus requires the use of information sources.

A fairly common use of directories is for the compilation of mailing lists. Thus, the UK *Kompass*[1] is arranged by county and town, and could therefore be used to draw up a mailing list of companies in a particular industry and located in specified places. In this connection, it should be noted that the online versions of directories such as *Kompass* and *Key British enterprises*[2] are more suitable for this purpose, in that it is much easier to search online for companies matching a combination of terms in this way. Indeed, *Key British enterprises* will supply a whole range of useful listings including mailing lists and addressed labels.

There exist specialist agencies (list brokers) who compile and sell mailing lists, both 'off the peg' and customized, and who may also manage the mail shot and service the whole operation. A typical example of a large computerized operation is the *Business decision-maker database*.[3] A similar service is offered by the specialist *Transport users database*[4] with details of vehicle usage in about 220,000 companies.

Professional and trade groups can be targeted by using appropriate directories and professional membership lists, such as the *Library Association yearbook*.[5]

6 Regulation of advertising

Advertisements are, of course, subject to the laws of libel, obscenity, trade descriptions, and so on. In addition, there are specific voluntary controls in operation.

According to the *British code of advertising and promotion*,[6] the Committee of Advertising Practice (CAP) has four main functions:

- It coordinates the activities of members to ensure that all advertising and sales promotions are within the law.

- It devises, reviews and amends the British Codes of Advertising and Sales Promotion.
- The Codes establish a standard against which advertisements can be assessed.
- It encourages any feedback or comment from all the members involved in the advertising industry.

The Advertising Standards Authority (ASA) was established in 1962 to provide 'independent scrutiny of the (then) newly created self-regulatory system set up by the industry'.[7] The ASA has two main functions:

- To promote and enforce the strictest of standards in advertisements.
- To investigate any complaints from sources in what is termed 'non-broadcast' media.

While the CAP states that advertisements should be 'legal, decent, honest and truthful', the code excludes TV and radio advertising, which is controlled by the Independent TV Commission or the Radio Authority. The ASA, on the other hand, exerts pressure on advertisers and agencies, and will investigate complaints from the public. There are also voluntary codes operating in the areas of sales promotion, direct mail, transport advertising, public relations and consultancy.

The Institute of Practitioners in Advertising (IPA) is the trade association for advertising agencies. The IPA has its own regulations relating to advertising practice, and rules for agencies' own house advertising. Members of the IPA must abide by the regulations and by the CAP and other codes sponsored by the Institute.

In the direct-response field, purchasers of off-the-page of goods advertised in certain newspapers and periodicals are protected by the National Newspaper Mail Order Protection Scheme Ltd (MOPS), which is operated under an agreement between the publishers, the IPA and the Incorporated Society of British Advertisers. Under the MOPS scheme, the publishers will reimburse any reader who loses money if an advertiser fails to deliver goods because of ceasing to trade through bankruptcy or other reasons. Approved advertisements covered by the scheme often include the MOPS logo, which provides the reader with some degree of assurance.

The EU member countries have similar bodies to enforce the strictest standard of advertising and the main body that looks after this is the European Advertising Standards Alliance which has its office in Brussels.

7 Media research

Advertisers, agencies and market researchers need various kinds of information about advertising. Companies need to know how much their competitors are spending on advertising; advertisers need to know who is viewing or hearing their advertisements, how often, and what impact they have on the recipient; agencies are interested in their position in the league table of agencies according to the value of billings, and so on. Some of the key information sources and research agencies in this field are outlined below.

7.1 *Advertising Statistics Yearbook* [8]

The *Advertising statistics yearbook*, the general data book for the industry, is based on an annual survey by the Advertising Association and on data supplied by other organizations. It carries detailed tables of advertising expenditure, both in aggregate and in specific categories such as direct mail, television, radio, poster, and newspaper advertising, together with tables showing statistics of the top agencies, the top advertisers, an analysis of complaints made to the ASA, and much else besides.

7.2 *The Quarterly Summary of Brands and Advertising* [9]

The quarterly summary of brands and advertising, published by Register-MEAL, gives expenditures on television (including satellite), cinema, posters, press and radio advertising for branded products. Each quarterly issue shows figures for the last quarter and a moving annual total. This data is widely quoted in other sources and reports. MEAL is also available in online form, hosted by the DIALOG Corporation, FT Profile and others.

Audience and readership research is carried out by various bodies, providing data on the numbers of people exposed to advertisements. The main research bodies are listed below.

7.3   Audit Bureau of Circulations

The Audit Bureau of Circulations certifies the number of copies of newspapers and magazines that are sold, using the publishers' own accounts data. ABC figures are quoted as averages over a six-month period, and are released twice a year. They are widely quoted in directories of media and elsewhere, and they are important because they tell an advertiser how many people are likely to see his or her advertisement. Clearly, the periodical with the highest ABC figure in its field could attract more advertising and charge higher prices. A subsidiary of ABC, Verified Free Distribution, performs a similar function for free sheets.

7.4 *National Readership Survey* [10]

The number of copies sold may grossly understate the actual readership of a publication, since one copy could be seen by many people. Consequently, readership surveys are important. The best known is the *National readership survey*, compiled by the Joint Industry Committee for National Readership Surveys (JICNARS). The survey is based on a sample of over 30,000 persons, and questions them about their reading habits. About 200 newspapers and periodicals are covered. Data are cross-tabulated by age, gender, socio-economic class, income, holiday-taking, car ownership, occupation, and so on. Statistics are also given on exposure to other media such as commercial television and radio, cinema-going and use of local directories. JICNARS data can be accessed online through Interactive Market Systems, with quarterly updating.

7.5 BARB

Television audience research is carried out by the Broadcasters Audience Research Board (BARB), which uses electronic meters attached to TV sets to monitor the viewing of ITV, BBC, Channel 4 and the Channel 5 programmes by a sample of more than 4500 homes. This monitoring takes place by three separate panels which examine homes with terrestrial TV stations only, homes that receive both terrestrial stations and satellite stations and homes that receive satellite stations only.

7.6 JICRAR

Radio listening is monitored by the Joint Industry Committee for Radio Audience Research (JICRAR), based on a changing sample over the course of the year of about 150,000 people.

7.7 *TGI* [11]

A general market-research survey, which also covers media habits, is the *Target group index*. TGI surveys 24,000 adults each year, using an extremely detailed questionnaire called *The national buying survey.* Questions are asked about purchases of foods, toiletries, DIY products, travel, pharmaceuticals, drinks, and other products and services, and about readership of newspapers and magazines and radio and TV usage. Data are analysed and cross-tabulated by social grades, income and the like, and by 'lifestyle' data on attitudes and opinions. The data are published annually in 34 volumes. Online access is also available.

7.8 TABS

The fact that someone has seen an advertisement does not say anything about its effect on that person. A technique for measuring the effect of advertising is the tracking study. The best-known organization in this field is Tracking Advertising and Brand Strength Ltd (TABS), who use a questionnaire to monitor the strength of reactions to advertisements and brands. This questionnaire is based on a sample of 13,000 adults each year, and TABS monitors about 160 brands. Weekly reports are provided.

8 Information about the advertising industry

The general directory for the industry is the *Advertisers annual.*[12] This is a single volume divided into a variety of sections that cover information about the advertising industry (e.g. agencies, sales promotion consultants, sponsorship agencies, public-relations companies and recruitment advertising agencies, together with national advertisers and their agencies); information about the media, and the final section comprises the very useful Marketing Handbook.

Many publications claim to be guides to the media. A sample of the main ones are listed below.

8.1 *Benns Media Directory*[13]

Benns is a well-known publication in its 145th edition at the time of writing. Its three volumes cover the United Kingdom, Europe and the rest of the World. The UK volume covers press and broadcasting media, directories, advertising agencies and services, and media organizations. Entries for newspapers and periodicals include ABC audited circulation figures. The European and World volumes are arranged by continent and country, with a classified list for each country, showing broadcast media, newspapers, and periodicals (by subject).

8.2 *Willings Press Guide* 14

Another long-established directory is *Willings press guide*. It contains a guide to 30,000 UK publications in more than 150 countries and appears in two volumes which cover the UK and the overseas market. The guide includes publisher details, contact names and circulation and a summary of the content of the periodical or newspaper and the target audience.

8.3 *BRAD: Media Facts at your Fingertips* 15

BRAD is a monthly publication noteworthy in providing considerable detail on publications, especially national newspapers, for which detailed advertising rates and printing-copy requirements are given. BRAD (British Rate and Data), concentrates on press media, but has shorter sections on outdoor and broadcast media. BRAD issues a number of other publications, including *BRAD agencies and advertisers; BRAD media ownership; BRAD inserts and guides* and *BRAD direct marketing.*

8.4 *Hollis UK Press and PR Annual* 16

This is divided into sections and includes information on sources such as news contacts, official and public information sources, PR consultancies, regional and world PR and sponsorship information.

8.5 *Building and Maintaining a European Direct Marketing Database* 17

Building and maintaining a European marketing database is a comprehensive manual published by Gower on European direct marketing divided into two sections. The first section looks at the stages of database management and the second looks at individual European countries.

Details of forthcoming trade exhibitions can be found in the appropriate trade journals, but a useful general list is the *Promotions guide* issued as a supplement to *Overseas trade: the DTI/FCO magazine for exporters,*18 which covers both UK and overseas trade fairs.

9 Distribution

Once the product has been duly advertised and the consumer has made the decision to purchase, the next marketing task is the decision of where to place the products – this is the area covered by all aspects of distribution. Products may be sold direct to the customer or through intermediaries, depending on the situation. The distribution method must be appropriate to the product and the manufacturer, but also convenient for purchasers – and their families.

9.1 Channels of distribution

Part of the price paid by the buyer is for the convenience of having the product delivered at a convenient location. Possible channels include:

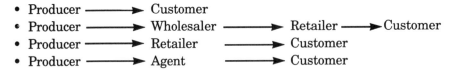

- Producer ⟶ Customer
- Producer ⟶ Wholesaler ⟶ Retailer ⟶ Customer
- Producer ⟶ Retailer ⟶ Customer
- Producer ⟶ Agent ⟶ Customer

Patterns are constantly changing. Thus, the logic of mass-produced branded foods demands intermediaries. Manufacturers of baked beans cannot deal with individual buyers, even if they wanted to, and must distribute the product through many outlets. The traditional corner shop independent grocer obtains supplies from a wholesaler, perhaps a cash-and-carry warehouse, but large retail chains, which sell vast quantities, can require the manufacturer to deal direct with them, cutting out the wholesaler. Thus, the pattern of grocery distribution has been affected by the development of superstores and hypermarkets. Agents, such as brokers and factors, operate in some sectors offering, for example, specialist export forwarding and freight services or advice to the customer, as in the case of insurance brokers, who advise the client on the choice of policy and arrange the deal with the insurance company.

Some organizations perform dual or multiple functions; thus many builders' merchants sell direct to the consumer but also operate trade counters, selling goods wholesale to approved retailers or small builders.

Wholesalers and retailers are sometimes referred to as 'middlemen' who perform essential functions for many products, although the term is one of abuse in some quarters. They concentrate and assemble the products of many firms into one place convenient for the buyer, thus enabling customers to compare competitive products and their prices. They break down bulk quantities of materials into the smaller quantities that customers wish to buy. They sometimes provide a local delivery service and may offer other services such as advice on purchase, installation and after-sales service and repairs.

Some large manufacturers have set up their own wholesale and/or retail channels, that is to say they are vertically integrated. A well-known example is that of Boots PLC, which makes drugs and toiletries, but also has its own retail shops.

In general, the wholesale trade has had to find new ways of working, in order to counteract trends in trades that they have traditionally serviced. The change to cash-and-carry operation is one such development, which cuts the cost of wholesaling and is cheaper for the retailers, since they collect their own goods instead of paying someone else to deliver them. Chains such as Spar (see below) have also come into being partly as a result of initiatives by wholesalers, as a way of preserving their business in the face of bulk delivery from manufacturers to large retailers.

10 Retailing

Key Note[19] forecasted that by the end of 1998 retail sales in the UK would reach £190.5 billion. However, it should also be noted that the same report states that 'since the start of the 1990s it is estimated that 13.8% of total retail outlets in the UK have closed down'. Most of these were the small independent retailers that had not been able to compete with the market caused by the expansion of the larger chains and superstores, which are presently competing for customer loyalty.

There is a great variety of retail modes, and new ones are being invented all the time. Some of the main ones are:

10.1 Direct marketing

This can cover a number of variants, such as:

- door-to-door selling;
- the party plan (e.g. Tupperware)
- mail order through catalogues (e.g. GUS, Littlewoods) or book clubs such as Readers Digest
- 'off-the-page' selling through newspaper or magazine advertisements
- telephone selling

It should be noted that member firms of the Association of Mail Order Publishers are bound by the Mail Order Publishers Authority Code of practice, which has been in existence since 1970.

10.2 Independent retailers

These exist in large numbers and tend to be relatively small, often one-shop family businesses. They often charge relatively high prices, but justify this by claiming to provide friendly personal service and advice. Independents have lost ground in recent years to chain stores, supermarkets and the like, and have responded, for example, by forming voluntary chains (see below).

10.3 Multiples

A multiple is a chain of shops owned by one firm, such as Sainsburys. Some multiples specialize in one type of merchandise, such as clothing, e.g. Principles; others are variety chains, e.g. Marks & Spencer, British Home Stores. The existence of many competing chains demonstrates that there are individual niches in the market that can be occupied; firms such as Marks & Spencer have established their own niche, clientele, marketing policy and customer loyalty.

10.4 Department stores

A collection of departments or 'shops' under one roof, each with its own buyer and range of goods is known as a department store. Examples are Harrods, Lewis's and Debenhams. Department stores are struggling with an old-fashioned image, and often with inconvenient city centre locations. Some, like Lewis's, have resorted to *concessions,* whereby space is rented out to other firms, which in effect operate shops within a shop. In some such cases only a tenth of the space may be operated by the store itself.

10.5 Co-operative stores

The co-operative movement is a special case, with local co-operative societies' shops and Co-operative Retail Services being supplied by the Co-operative Wholesale Society. Traditionally, the Co-ops were owned by the 'members', who were paid a dividend on their purchases. Although this system has long been abandoned there are presently moves to reintroduce the 'Co-op dividend' in response to superstore 'smart cards' such as those introduced by Tesco and Sainsburys. The Co-op shops have had to update their image and compete with other food and variety chains.

10.6 Discount stores

Stores such as Comet Warehouses save on costs by providing minimum service and display. The customer is expected to know what he or she wants and can sometimes select from a catalogue and price list. Discount stores may also use cheap out-of-town locations, which provide further cost reductions. Increasingly 'outlet' stores and villages are springing up around the UK, following the American style of discount retailing.

10.7 Supermarkets and hypermarkets

A supermarket is conventionally defined as a self-service shop with a sales area of over 4000 sq.ft. but less than 25,000 sq.ft. A hypermarket is a self-service shop with at least 25,000 sq.ft. of selling space. These stores are invariably in drive-in locations, and offer one-stop shopping, mostly at keen prices, and have proved to be extremely successful. For example, a typical venture of Tesco's into the hypermarket scene was the purchase of a 90,000 sq.ft. unit in Pitsea, Essex. ASDA and the other main supermarkets also have plans for massive hypermarkets set to change the habits of the high street shopper. The Internet and the creation of the 'Net Shopper' is also changing the habits of a lifetime – all of the main superstores now have advertising on the Net and most offer some form of Internet shopping. The best-known guide to these stores is the *The hypermarkets and superstores database*,[20] produced by the Unit for Retail Planning Information (URPI). This gives details of over 500 stores, listed by county, showing the gross and the trading-floor space and the number of car-parking spaces.

10.8 Voluntary chains

The development of chains such as Spar was a joint response by some wholesalers and groups of independent retailers to protect themselves against competition from the multiples. A small retailer who joins a voluntary chain enjoys advantages such as joint advertising and promotion (e.g. Spar shops as a group have advertised on television, something that one small independent could not afford) and bulk purchasing by the wholesaler at lower cost, a common established image, and access to central advice and management expertise.

10.9 Franchise

In this system, the franchiser supplies the technology, the brand name and image, and advice and technical help; the franchisee supplies the capital and agrees to buy supplies from the franchiser. In this way, the small entrepreneur maintains a degree of independence but enjoys support from a large company. Franchising was initially common in the catering field, e.g. Kentucky Fried Chicken and Wimpy Bars, but it is becoming increasingly common in a wide range of industries – from make-up and cosmetics such as The Body Shop to American cleaning services such as Merry Maids, which is part of the Service Master group of companies.

The above classifications are something of a crude simplification. For example, many large stores belonging to variety chains may constitute self-service shops easily meeting the definition of a supermarket, and the boundaries between some of these categories are diffuse. Retailing is also very dynamic and new styles and methods are constantly appearing.

11 Sources of information on retailing

The retail sector has seen tremendous growth and diversification in the last decade, though there were some casualties in the late 1980s. Nevertheless, the retail sector is very active and has generated a considerable body of information and research. The following indicates the major sources of information on retailing.

11.1 *Retail Directory of the UK* [21]

This lists retailers in the UK and Ireland, and includes a survey of major shopping streets by town, showing which retailers are located on each street.

Euromonitor is very active in this field, publishing a number of reports on UK trends in retailing, sector reports, and several journals. Major titles include the following:

11.2 *Retail Trade International* 22

Retail trade international includes information on the latest retail developments, information on retail sales and structure in 50 countries. It also contains analysis and global overview.

11.3 *European Own Brands Directory* 23

This directory includes an industry overview and sources of marketing information, which are useful for identifying many suppliers of own brands.

11.4 *Hypermarkets and Superstores – the International Market* 24

This is one of a number of sector reports on a variety of markets including convenience stores, specialist food retailing, food multiples, garden retailing, fashion retailing, off-licences, booksellers and stationers, co-operative retailing and others.

11.5 *Retail Monitor International*

Each issue of this monthly journal includes an analysis of one sector, a discussion of current trends such as franchising, profiles of two major retailers and a section on world retailing.

Details of all current Euromonitor retailing reports for both UK and Europe can be found in the catalogue *The Euromonitor index.* 25

11.6 The Unit for Retail Planning Information

An important organization in the field, whose *The hypermarkets and superstores database* 26 was described earlier, is the Unit for Retail Planning Information. URPI provides information and advice to help with store planning and location. It achieves this in two ways: first, subscribing members have free use of the enquiry and advice services and the URPI library; second, URPI runs the very successful 'Data Consultancy' which deals with software, data and datasets concerned with retail information. URPI also issues a number of publications that can be bought by the public, including individual reports on specific sectors or geographical locations, papers and monographs, bibliographies, information briefs and others.

11.7 Key Notes

Key Notes is also well represented in the retail sector by a variety of reports such as *Retailing in the UK*,[27] *Mixed retail business*[28] and other specific areas such as horticultural retailing, reports on own brands, bookselling, convenience retailing and supermarkets and superstores.

11.8 *The Nielson Retail Index* [29]

Worth mentioning as the standard index is the Nielson retail index. It can provide the key to all aspects of retailing such as company profiles, new product development, brand data, marketing and advertising.

11.9 *The Directory of European Retailers* [30]

The directory of European retailers is a useful work in this area and lists over 5000 retailers in 16 countries.

11.10 *Retail Trade International* [31]

Retail trade international gives statistics and market analysis covering 52 countries in both western and eastern Europe, and the major markets throughout the rest of the world.

11.11 *MTI Countryfiles* [32]

Information on market analysis, trade, politics and retailing and advertising is available in *MTI countryfiles*.

12 The Green Movement

The consumer lobby has a long history. For example, Ralph Nader[33] was a thorn in the side of the US car industry as long ago as 1965, castigating car designs on grounds of safety. In Britain, the Consumers Association, properly called the Association for Consumer Research, was founded in 1956. CA is best known as the publisher of *Which?* Magazine (monthly), together with its companions *Holiday Which?*, *Gardening Which?*, *Which? wine monthly* and *Which? way to health. Which?* publishes independent reports on consumer goods and services, and is not constrained by commercial considerations since it carries no advertising at all. CA purchases specimen products anonymously for testing, and also conducts surveys of their subscribers. The association has over 1,000,000 members, which is an indication of its strength as a proportion of the UK population. Similar associations exist in overseas countries.

Governments and political parties have a mixed record on consumerism. In 1963 the then Board of Trade established the Consumer Council to promote consumer interests and to encourage action by government and other bodies. Its present-day successor, the National Consumer Council, was set up in 1975 and is funded by a grant from the DTI. All major political parties claim to have environmentally friendly policies, but whether these are wholly genuine or merely cosmetic is for the individual to assess. Various agencies have been set up in recent years, such as OFWAT (Office of Water Services) in 1989 and OFTEL (Office of Telecommunications) in 1994, to ensure among other things that the consumer is actually getting value for money. Various Green Parties exist in the UK and abroad, claiming to represent more fully whole-earth and environmental concerns. In June 1992 a world conference was held in Rio known as 'The UN conference on environment and development', popularly called the Rio Summit. This conference proposed a variety of measures and actions in the report *Programme for action*[34] to be taken by all countries to ensure that government's promote 'environmentally friendly' policies and strategies to ensure the 'safe' future of the planet.

In the late 1990s the main issues of concern seem to have been the building of new roads and motorways and the building of the second runway at Manchester Airport. Although the early 1980s saw the green movement as a separate business issue, many businesses now perhaps take the view that this is no longer new, but a part of their everyday strategy. Because of this, many of the green handbooks and directories are no longer in print. However, a good overall introduction to green business is the book by Wheatley.[35]

13 Conclusion

This chapter has covered both advertising and distribution in some detail.

The advertising section has included the different types of advertising, the regulation of advertising and identified sources of information about the media and the advertising industry. There are many general textbooks on advertising which can be consulted for further detail. A good introductory text on advertising by a British author is the third edition of White's *Advertising: what it is and how to do it*,[36] which is 'endorsed by the Advertising Association, the CAM Foundation and the Institute of Practitioners in Advertising'. Butterfield's *Excellence in advertising*[37] offers a broad viewpoint on the advertising industry and this book is endorsed by the IPA and the Chartered Institute of Marketing (CIM). News of the advertising industry can be followed in the weekly magazine *Campaign*,[38] which also includes frequent insert reports on topics such as the top agencies and the major advertisers.

The distribution section covered channels of distribution, types of retailing, listed the main sources of information and concluded with a brief discussion on environmental issues. As marketing is a constantly changing area, many new ideas, products and sources of information are created in response to demands – and so it is likely that the Internet will increasingly be used as one of the key sources of marketing information. Much information is already available either freely or on a subscription basis and some of the main web sites are listed below.

References

1 *Kompass,* East Grinstead, Reed Information Services, 1997.
2 *Key British enterprises,* High Wycombe, Dun and Bradstreet Ltd, 1997.
3 *Business decision-maker database,* London, TDS Marketing Group Ltd, 1997.
4 *Transport users database,* London, Market Location Ltd, 1997.
5 *Library Association yearbook,* London, Library Association Publishing, annual.
6 *British code of advertising and promotion*, London, Committee of Advertising Practice, 1995.
7 See Reference 6.
8 *Advertising statistics yearbook,* Henley-on-Thames, NTC Publications Ltd, for the Advertising Association, annual.
9 *The quarterly summary of brands and advertising,* London, Register-MEAL, quarterly.
10 *National readership survey,* London, JICNARS, six-monthly plus monthly estimates and other supplements.
11 *Target group index,* London, British Market Research Bureau International, annual.
12 *Advertisers annual,* Teddington, Hollis Directories, annual.

13 *Benns media directory,* Tonbridge, MG Information Services, annual.

14 *Willings press guide,* Teddington, Hollis Directories, annual.

15 *BRAD: media facts at your fingertips,* London, Emap Publications, monthly.

16 *Hollis UK press and PR annual,* Teddington, Hollis Directories, annual.

17 *Building and maintaining a European direct marketing database,* Aldershot, Ashgate, 1994.

18 *Overseas trade,* London, Overseas Trade Services, monthly.

19 *Retailing in the UK: market review,* London, Key Note, 1997.

20 *The hypermarkets and superstores database,* Reading, Unit for Retail Planning Information.

21 *Retail directory of the UK,* London, Newman Books Ltd, annual.

22 *Retail trade international,* 4th edn, London, Euromonitor, 1995.

23 *European own brands,* London, Euromonitor, 1996.

24 *Hypermarkets and superstores: the international markets,* London, Euromonitor, 1997.

25 *The Euromonitor index,* London, Euromonitor, annual.

26 See Reference 20.

27 *Retailing in the UK,* Hampton, Key Note Publications, 1997.

28 *Mixed retail business,* Hampton, Key Note Publications, 1997.

29 *Nielson retail index,* London, Hadleigh Marketing Services, quarterly.

30 *The directory of European retailers,* London, Newman Ltd, bi-annual.

31 *Retail trade international,* London, Euromonitor, 1995.

32 *MTI countryfiles,* Essex, MTI UK Ltd, 1996.

33 Nader, R., *Unsafe at any speed: the designed-in dangers of the American automobile,* New York, Grossman, 1965.

34 *Agenda 21 – programme of action for sustainable development. Rio declaration on environment and development.* The final text of agreement negotiated by governments at the UN Conference on Environmental Development, June 1992, New York, UN, 1993.

35 Wheatley, M., *Green business: making it work for your company,* London, Institute of Management, 1993.

36 White, R., *Advertising: what it is and how to do it,* 3rd edn, Maidenhead, McGraw-Hill, 1993.

37 Butterfield, L., *Excellence in advertising,* Oxford, Butterworth-Heinemann, 1997.

38 *Campaign,* London, Haymarket, weekly.

Web sites

Corporate Intelligence on Retailing   http://worldwide.cior.com.
Key Note   http://www.keynote.co.uk
Market Tracking International   http://www.market file.co.uk
Hollis   http://www.hollis.pr.co.uk

Part 4

Identifying business regulations and control

13 Patents

1 Introduction

This chapter is concerned with the nature of patents and the patent system, patents as sources of information, and the bibliographical apparatus used for patent searching. In general, this chapter is confined to the UK system, together with some consideration of developments in Europe and world patents.

Patent specifications are technical documents, but they are included in this book because of their commercial implications. As a form of monopoly, a patent is a restraint on trade; moreover, patents themselves are commercial property, which can be bought and sold, and the owner of a patent can license others to use it, in return for the payment of royalties. All in all, the commercial and legal nature of patents is as important as their technical aspects, a fact which, as we shall see, has implications for the usefulness of patents as sources of technical information.

Patent protection is a serious business, of enormous commercial importance in cases where being first in the field means the difference between success and failure. Patent protection over a longish period is vital, for example, in the pharmaceutical industry, where a lead-time of ten years from the beginnings of research into a new drug to its commercial launch is quite common. Such a long period of development and testing means that it may be many years before a drug begins to earn a profit; in these circumstances, the 20 years of protection afforded by the British system is quite reasonable, and some would argue that it should be longer.

Patents do however have their lighter side, and the business of invention has attracted more than its share of eccentrics, not to put too fine a point on it. The Victorians, for example, were very fond of gadgetry, and the 19th century produced a crop of comical and curious patents, such as the device for raising one's hat to a lady without taking one's hands out of one's pockets. Even in modern times, there are some unusual inventions to be found, such as those produced by the fertile mind of Arthur Paul Pedrick, who has proposed, amongst other things, irrigating the Australian desert by propelling giant balls of ice at speed from the Antarctic along specially designed tubes (see for example BP 1,047,735 and others). Another curious modern patent is BP 1,387,598, issued to a Jeremiah Quinlan and published in 1975. This patent concerns a cure for sciatica, comprising a mixture of a minor proportion of tincture of guaiacum and a major proportion of whisky. Whatever the prospect of a cure, no doubt the whisky would provide substantial relief from the symptoms! For further enlightenment, the reader is referred to the writings of Hope[1] and Jones.[2]

2 The nature of patents

A patent may be defined as a temporary monopoly granted by the state in respect of an invention, in return for publication of the invention. This concise definition covers all the essentials, but requires further explanation.

All developed countries have patent systems and laws empowering the state to grant patent monopolies. The system is in effect a bargain between the state and the applicant. The applicant gains a commercial advantage and the state gains by the encouragement of technical development to the benefit of the public at large. It is to be noted that publication of the invention is a condition of the grant, since publication is essential to establish the scope of the monopoly: in order to avoid trespass, one must know where the boundaries lie. But in addition, it is the intention of the system that laying inventions open to public inspection will encourage others to build on what is already known. It is argued that, if there were no patent system, inventors and companies would have to resort to close secrecy and this would stultify technical development. The monopoly granted is the exclusive right to use an invention, but the right can be sold to others or transferred under licence. In the UK, 'temporary' means 20 years, after which anyone may use the invention.

The word 'invention' has still to be defined, and for this purpose we have recourse to the Patents Act 1977.[3] In addition the Copyright, Designs and Patents Act 1988,[4] (which enables any person to act for others for the purpose of applying for patents), the latest edition of the Patent Rules and any relevant statutory instruments that may be subsequently issued all serve to regulate the present UK system in all its aspects. According to the Act, an invention must be new, be capable of industrial application and involve an inventive step.[5] Each of these terms requires elaboration.

2.1 Newness

Newness, or novelty, depends on prior use, prior publication, or both. Thus, a published patent might be invalidated by demonstrating that the invention has already been used. Generally speaking, commercial-scale use would be required, and laboratory experimentation or similar small-scale use would not suffice. Or a patent could be opposed by showing that its substance has previously been disclosed in a published document. In this context, publication refers not to the date of publication of a document as commonly understood, but to the date on which it became available to the public. It will readily be understood that these are two different things, for example a journal published in the USA might take two weeks to get on to the shelves of a British public library or to go on sale in this country. For this purpose, availability in any library open to the public would satisfy the requirement (private libraries such as industrial libraries would not). If for no other reason, all material received in a public technical library should therefore be date-stamped as proof of availability. Note that prior publication can also take place orally, e.g. by presenting a paper at a conference. Prior publication and use also raise the question of priority. For an opposition to succeed on these grounds, use or publication must normally be demonstrated to be prior to the earliest application date (priority date) of the patent opposed, although another patent published later than the priority date, but itself having an earlier priority date, could be taken into account. Searching for prior publications (novelty searches) is a frequent concern of many industrial librarians and information scientists, either to assist in opposing a patent issued to a competitor perhaps, or to try to establish the novelty or otherwise of an invention produced in one's own firm.

2.2 Industrial application

Industrial application refers to the fact that an invention must relate to some useful object or process – the word 'industrial' is perhaps slightly misleading. In other words, patents cannot be obtained for theories or concepts, though their practical embodiment in some physical form may be patentable. At this point, it is convenient to refer to the excluded categories which are set out in the Act.[6] Thus the following are not inventions:

- a discovery, scientific theory or mathematical method
- a literary, dramatic, or artistic work

- a scheme, rule or method for performing a mental act, playing a game or doing business, or a program for a computer
- the presentation of information.

Items covered by 'a discovery, scientific theory or mathematical method' are, of course, public knowledge, though the form in which they are expressed would be *copyright*. The other three items are also covered by copyright. The Act also states that a patent will not be granted for an invention, the publication or exploitation of which would be expected to encourage offensive, immoral or antisocial behaviour; nor for any variety of animal or plant or any biological process for the production of animals or plants, though microbiological processes and their products are permitted. Some plant varieties are protected in the UK under the Plant Varieties and Seeds Act 1964[7] although these are not dealt with at the Patent Office but are registered at the Plants Variety Rights Office. (Note that some countries do grant patents for biological varieties, e.g. the USA, which issues plant patents.) Finally, methods of 'treatment of the human or animal body by surgery or therapy or of diagnosis . . . shall not be taken to be capable of industrial application'. Thus, one could obtain a patent for a new drug as such, but not for its use – obviously it would be quite unreasonable to grant monopolies for the treatment of disease or injury.[8]

2.3 Inventive step

The concept of the inventive step was introduced in the 1977 Act, and was not present under the 1949 procedure (see 4.1). Many disputes have arisen because of the difficulty of deciding whether a specification is sufficiently different from an earlier one. The inventive step provides a label for this difference and specifies it as a legal requirement, but what constitutes an inventive step will of course be established gradually by case law.

3 Difficulties of the patent system

The rationale underlying the patent system and its undoubted advantages are set out above, but there are several problems with it.

In the first place, a system will be effective only if applicants have confidence in it, and this will depend on a number of things, such as whether the courts can enforce the monopoly, and whether the owner of a patent can actually detect an infringement. The fact that many firms still maintain closely guarded trade secrets that are not patented indicates that confidence in the system is not universal.

Secondly, in a global economy, worldwide patent protection is increasingly desirable, and firms may have to apply for patents in many different countries in order to obtain such protection. The procedures are very expensive and elaborate, despite a number of developments over the years. For example, under the International Convention for the Protection of Industrial Property, signed in Paris in 1883, one may file an application in the home country, and then in a signatory country not more than 12 months later, and still retain the original priority date. Other developments, such as the Patent Co-operation Treaty and the European Patent, are considered below.

Under the 1949 procedure, many patents accepted by the British Office were subsequently found to be invalid, or were at any rate subsequently opposed on grounds of prior publication. This occurred very largely because at that time the Patent Office search was essentially confined to previous British patents, and then only to those of the previous 50 years. Other types of document, such as scientific and technical journals and foreign patents, were not searched, although the Office would always accept evidence of such prior publication, if presented by a third party. Many patents were therefore later found to have been anticipated by documents not originally examined by the Office. This situation has improved under current procedures, as will be seen below.

The Quinlan patent, cited above, also emphasizes an important fact about the system. It is not part of the Patent Office's job to test whether an invention actually works. If the form of words in the specification meets the legal requirements, does not infringe any of the stated exclusions, and is not obviously contrary to the presently understood laws of nature, then the Office has no reason to reject it. Provided, therefore, that Mr Quinlan's mixture does not claim to render the drinker invisible or to confer immortality, for example, it will be accepted at face value. Of course, an interested third party might wish to oppose the patent. He could do so by showing prior use or prior publication, but also by demonstrating that the cure does not work. According to the rules, a specification must give sufficient information so that someone 'skilled in the art' (i.e. familiar with the relevant technology) can reproduce the process or the product from the specification. If one were able to show that the mixture did not effect the cure claimed, then the patent might be held invalid.

The system also facilitates what is sometimes called 'obstructive patenting'. Some companies will identify gaps in the patent coverage of a technology and deliberately fill them with applications that may have little substance but which serve to clutter the field and make it difficult for competitors to enter. In this context, mention should be made of disclosure journals. These give abstracts and drawings of patentable inventions and can be cited as prior publications, though of course they afford no patent protection. A company could, for example, disclose a patentable idea which it did not think worth the cost of patent protection. Unless action were taken, another company could patent the invention and perhaps compel the first company to pay for its use. Disclosure would prevent this. Some companies, such as IBM, publish their own disclosure journals, but there are also a few commercially published ones, such as *Research disclosure*,[9] which publish disclosures for a fee.

Finally, it can easily be imagined that it is in the interests of an applicant to delay publication of a specification as long as possible, and also to reveal in the document only as much as is necessary in order to meet the legal requirements and to specify the matter for which protection is claimed. This means that a patent specification may be only as informative as it needs to be – it is written primarily for legal purposes, not as a vehicle for technical information. This point will be developed below.

4 The application process

The great divide in British patent procedure was on 1 June 1978. Prior to this date, applications were processed under the 1949 Act, after it under the 1977 Act: as with much other legislation from this time onwards, the 1977 Act was passed partly to bring the UK into line with European practice. Patent searches commonly go back several decades and it is therefore still essential to understand how the pre-1977 system operated.

4.1 Application under the 1949 Act

The applicant first filed a provisional application in order to establish priority. At this stage the Patent Office would take no action other than to file it with an application number in the form P1234/72 (provisional application number 1234 of 1972).

Within 12 months, if the applicant wished to proceed, a complete application would be filed. This was a full-scale specification, complete with claims and any necessary drawings. Applicants commonly waited until the last moment to file, so as to delay the eventual publication as long as possible. Applications originally made abroad would also be filed in the UK at this stage, under the International Convention. Such applications would be in the complete format and would be given an application number in the form C5678/73.

From this point on, the Office examined the application for novelty and so on, based partly on a search of previous British patents over a 50-year period. If there were no obstacles, the patent was published with a number in the form BP (British Patent), 1,234,567, following which there was a three-month period during which interested parties could mount an opposition. During this time, a librarian or information scientist might well have been involved in searching for prior publications as part of the opposition process. Assuming there were no successful opposition, the patent would be granted and sealed, after which it was much more difficult to oppose.

It should be noted that a British company seeking protection abroad might also have applied under the International Convention, in several other countries, towards the end of the initial 12 months. Some countries, such as Belgium and the Netherlands, operated a cheaper and faster system, simply publishing the application and leaving interested parties to fight it out among themselves as it were. The effect of this can be seen in the following table, taking Belgium as an example.

Table 13.1 *A patent application in the UK and Belgium*

	Application by a British company	
	UK	Belgium
Provisional	1 Jan 1972	–
Complete	1 Jan 1973	1 Jan 1973 (under Convention)
Publication	Jun 1974	Sept 1973

For this imaginary application, the priority date is 1 January 1972. Under the Convention, the company has also applied in Belgium within 12 months, but obtained the original priority date in that country also. Under this system it took about two-and-a-half years to get a UK patent through to publication, whereas the application would typically be published after about nine months following the Belgian application. The result was that foreign equivalents of British applications often appeared in certain countries long before publication in the UK. This situation applied in Belgium, France and the Netherlands, for example; the consequence was that at that time there was considerable interest in monitoring the patent publications of such countries, since they often gave early indication of the activities of one's UK competitors.

4.2 Application under the 1977 Act

Initial application

The initial application must be made on the official forms available from the Patent Office. The application must contain the following four items:

* a straightforward request for a patent
* the applicant's personal details
* a description of the invention and any necessary drawings
* the required filing fee.

The application may include claims at this stage, or they may be filed later. The Patent Office assigns an application number in the form 9812345 (application number 12345 of 1998).

Preliminary application and search

Within 12 months of the application date, the applicant, in order to keep the application in being, must file a request for a *preliminary examination and search*. If not filed earlier, one or more claims must be filed at this stage, together with an abstract. (Note that the old-style *abridgements* used to be written by the Patent Office examiners; the *abstract* is written by the applicant, though it may be amended by the Office if the examiner thinks it is not adequate.)

The search

The examiner will now check that the application meets the formal requirements, and will carry out a search of the literature to try to establish novelty. Current policy is to search about 60 years of British patents, European applications, and applications under the Patent Co-operation Treaty (PCT). Foreign patents, especially those of the USA, Japan, Germany and the USSR, will also be searched, if the examiner knows that any of these countries has produced a lot of patents in the appropriate field. Journal literature may also be searched. In general, the search is much more wide-ranging than under the 1949 procedure, and this should help to ensure that fewer applications lacking novelty get through the net.

Publication

If the preliminary examination and search are successfully passed, the application will be published as soon as possible after the end of an 18-month period from the earliest priority date. It should be stressed that the specification represents at this stage a published *application*, not a granted patent. The specification is given a number in the form GB 2,345,678 A. 'GB' denotes Great Britain of course, and 'A' denotes a published application. If the patent is subsequently granted, the suffix is changed from A to B. British published applications under the 1977 procedure commenced with number 2,000,001. This new procedure ensures that specifications are laid open to public inspection much more quickly than the old BPs. In the case of a Convention application originally filed abroad, the specification could well be published only six months after application in the UK.

Granting the patent

If the applicant wishes to proceed further, a request must be filed, within six months of the publication date, for a *substantive examination*. The examiner will then consider the application for novelty, inventiveness etc. on the basis of the literature search, the substantive criteria, and any observations made by interested parties since publication. If this process is successfully negotiated, the patent is granted.

Details of the procedures, fees, forms and so on can be found in a booklet issued by the Patent Office.[10]

In summary, it can be seen that the current procedure has two clear advantages over the old one: it ensures much earlier publication, which is beneficial for technical development in general; and the literature search is more comprehensive, which gives greater confidence in the novelty or otherwise of an application.

4.3 The specification

The change of procedure introduced by the 1978 Act brought with it a new form of patent specification. Figure 13.1 shows the first page of a pre-1978 British patent specification: Figure 13.2 shows the front page of a new-style published application.

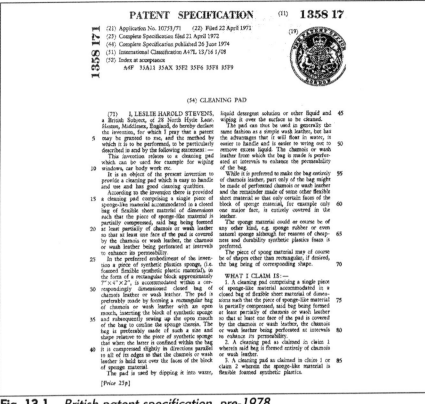

Fig. 13.1   *British patent specification, pre-1978*

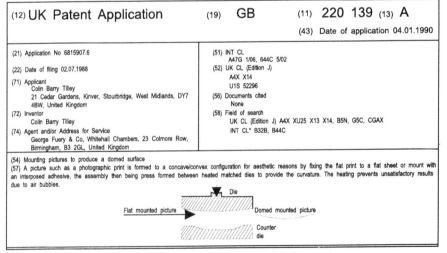

Fig. 13.2   *GB published patent application, 1978 onwards*

It will be noted that key dates and other data in Figure 13.2 are listed at the head of the document, using standard code numbers which are in use throughout Convention countries. Thus (51) is always the International Classification number, (71) the name of the applicant, and so on. The use of these codes means that data can be recognized even when patents are in an unfamiliar language. Index at acceptance (52) refers to the class number(s) assigned by the British office. The archaic form of words in the opening paragraph of the old style patent has now been abandoned. The numbered claims set out precisely the scope of the protection that is being claimed. The first claim is the main one, all others being dependent on it; consequently the first claim is often used as an abstract of the specification. The earlier abridgements have been replaced by the abstract (57), written by the applicant. An important difference between the two styles is that in the new specifications any documents found and cited as a result of the preliminary examination and search are listed (56). This list can often be a useful starting point for subsequent literature searches in the same field.

5 Patents as technical information

There have been some studies which show that patents are underused as sources of information. See for example a report by Stephenson and Riley.[11] This is no doubt due in part to ignorance and lack of awareness. The quarterly newsletter of the Patents Information Network, *Patents information news*[12] (formerly *PIN bulletin*), has recorded several cases showing that some people have gone to extraordinary lengths to discover technical details of an invention, when a full description already existed in a patent specification freely available to the public. For example, the Australian yacht contending for the America's Cup race in 1983 was reported to have a novel keel design. Journalists tried all manner of tricks to obtain information about it, including hiring frogmen to take underwater photographs. They might have saved themselves a lot of trouble by a visit to the Science Reference and Information Service Library, where a copy of GB2,1 14,5 ISA disclosed full details and drawings of the keel.[13] It is also undoubtedly the case that the legal format and language used in specifications, particularly in the claims, tends to make them unattractive and difficult to read.

However, there may be yet another reason for the low use of patents. It was suggested above that a patent may be designed to reveal as little as possible, and the following example may be used to show what is meant. The form of words chosen could be used to reveal less than the full information available. US patent 3,227,665 claims a resinous composition with particular moulding properties. According to the first claim, it is made by 'dissolving a cross-linkable . . . resin in a . . . solvent . . . the said solvent comprising from about 10% to about 60% of the total weight of the solution, adding thereto from about 1% to about 2% by weight of benzoyl peroxide, from about 0.05% to about 0.3% by weight of stannous chloride, and from about 0.025% to about 1 % by weight of 4-methyl-2, 6-di-tertiary butyl-phenol, [and] admixing said ingredients while maintaining the temperature from about 10 degrees C to about 80 degrees C . . .'. A moment's thought is enough to establish that, even in steps of one degree Celsius and one percentage point, there are hundreds of possible combinations covered by this claim. The claim is designed to set out the widest possible scope for protection, without of course infringing some other patent. Admittedly, the specification also contains 29 different examples of the invention, offering some more practical information. Obviously, all these examples must work, otherwise the patent would be open to invalidation by demonstrating that the invention is unworkable; however, it is quite possible that the preferred formulations which give the best results are not included in the examples, though they will naturally be covered by the claim. In this way, the specification might well have been written to obtain legal protection without actually revealing the most valuable information.

Whatever the reasons, it is clear that patents do not receive the use they deserve. At the end of the first stage of their research, Stephenson and Riley report:

> Patent information is not exploited as a source of technical information by either the librarian or his user, but it is used by technical and commercial staff for *commercial* intelligence. Other sources, such as journals and books, are the first, and sometimes the only, source of reference for technical information, and there is no evidence that patent information is regarded in the same light or even as a complementary source.[14]

6 Searching British patents

This section describes and discusses the official published bibliographical apparatus for use with British patents, and indicates some of the other unofficial sources that may be used.

6.1 Patent Office publications

Obviously, searches will be mainly by name or subject; accordingly the two major annual publications are the name index, *Names of applicants*[15] and the *Abridgements and abstracts*.[16]

6.1.1 Names of applicants

The index appears annually and is a single alphabetical list showing the titles and published numbers of specifications. The main entry is by the applicant or assignee, with cross-references from inventors. In earlier years, British patents were collected in blocks of 25,000, so that the name index volumes and the abridgements covered that number, which represented about eight months' output at the time. Recently, the rate of publication of British specifications has fallen considerably, partly because of the greater use made of the European patent (see below), and so annual publication of the indexes has been adopted.

6.1.2 Abridgements of patent specifications, abstracts of patent applications

These represent the official subject approach to British patents, but in order to use them one must first understand the classification system. This system, which is constantly being updated and modified, is perhaps the ultimate enumerative hierarchical classification.

The whole relevant field of knowledge is first divided into Sections, each with a letter code, thus:

A   Human necessities
B   Performing operations
C   Chemistry, metallurgy
D   Textiles, paper
E   Civil engineering, building accessories
F   Mechanics, lighting, heating
G   Instrumentation
H   Electricity.

Sections are divided into Divisions by numbers, so that a Division has a two-digit code, e.g. A2 Food, tobacco; H2 Electric power. Divisions are further broken down into Headings by letters, so that a Heading has a three-digit code, such as: A2A Bakery apparatus, H2C Electric cable installation.

There are 40 Divisions in the system, ranging from Al to HS, and the Abstracts are issued in annual sets, one or more Divisions per volume, for example: A1-A3 Agriculture, food, tobacco, apparel; D1-D2 Textiles, sewing, ropes, paper. A full list of the Sections and Divisions will be found at the front of every volume of Abstracts.

Each volume is self-contained, with its own bit of the classification, name index and abstracts for the specifications falling within its Division(s). Volumes can be purchased separately, conveniently for information managers interested in only certain technologies. Note that a patent may be classified at several different numbers; and also in different Divisions, in which case an abstract will appear in more than one Divisional volume.

For any subject classification an alphabetical subject index is essential. In this case, it takes the form of the *Catchwords index to the classification key*,[17] which is revised at intervals. However, this volume indexes only to the level of Headings. Having located the desired Heading, the searcher must then examine the detailed classification and indexing schedules in the appropriate volume, in order to find the precise class number, which will be in alphanumeric form. Once the class number has been established, the next step is to locate it in the Subject-matter index of the volume, which lists the seven-figure numbers of patents classified at that class number. The abstracts for these specifications can then be found in number order within the volume.

There is no disguising the fact that the schedules are difficult to use, even for the experienced searcher. This is not the place for a detailed examination of the system, which deserves a book to itself. For further explanation and guidance, the reader is referred to works such as that by Eisenschitz.[18] Technical knowledge is, of course, essential and users of the system will claim to understand only those parts relating to technologies with which they are familiar. Every heading is provided with scope notes and cross-references, and these should always be read carefully before tackling any part of the schedules. It must be remembered that the Patent Office is concerned only with patentable features of inventions; therefore some scientific or technical matters may not be classified or indexed.

Minor revisions of the schedules are frequent, and the same subject may be classified at different numbers over a period of time. There was one major change, effective from BP940,001; at this point the new system of

Divisions replaced an earlier one of Classes. A two-way concordance was published to help the searcher in moving from one to the other.

Before 1978, the Patent Office examiners wrote their own abridgements of specifications. These were highly regarded in their day as models of the abstractor's art. They were often so detailed that the searcher did not need to consult the original specifications. Under the new system, the applicant is required to write his or her own abstract, and these are by no means as helpful, being often just a summary of the first claim. For the early years after the 1978 changeover while both old- and new-style patents were going through the system together, both abridgements and abstracts will be found in the same volumes, in two sequences. For a time, the new abstracts were arranged, not by patent number, but by the class Heading and then by number (see for example the 1980 set of volumes), but this was very confusing and was soon abandoned in favour of a straight numerical sequence.

A minor published index is the *Divisional allotment index*,[19] which cross-refers from the published number to the appropriate Division or Heading, to enable one to locate the abridgement or abstract.

The name-index and abstracts volumes naturally take time to complete and publish and are inevitably months out of date. To a limited extent, searches can be brought up to date by using the *Official journal (patents)*.[20] This weekly journal contains official notices and announcements, but from the point of view of the information manager its main purpose is to list the week's new applications and published applications. The latter are arranged both by class Heading and by a seven-figure published number in one sequence. The *OJ* is mainly intended as a current-awareness device and many working in special libraries face the weekly chore of scanning it to select new specifications for ordering. It is feasible to use the weekly name indexes to update a name search of the volume indexes, but to do the same with subjects would usually be extremely tedious, because only the three-digit Headings are used to classify the entries.

A convenient way of searching British patents by subject up to date is to use the Patent Office File-list service, which provides on request lists of specifications classified at a class mark specified by the purchaser. Series C and D file-lists are computer-generated to order and cover specifications from BP 1,000,001 to date. The client specifies the class mark for the subject required and the computer prints a list of the specifications at that class. Series C lists are available for a single class mark, while series D lists allow for combinations of two or more class marks, using Boolean search.

In general, the Patent Office Search and Advisory Service should be considered when worldwide patent searches are being planned. The service offers manual, online and chemical-structure searches covering British, European and other international patents. The service is quite independent of formal filing of applications, but the search is as extensive as that carried out under filing procedures.

7 International developments

If a UK resident wishes to apply for a patent elsewhere than the UK, then permission must be obtained from the UK Patent Office. The reason for this is on grounds of national security: 'If the Patent Office considers that an application contains information the publication of which might be prejudicial to the defence of the realm or the safety of the public, it may prohibit or restrict its publication or communication'.[21]

7.1 European patents

The number of British applications has fallen significantly in recent years, due largely to the existence of the European patent. The European patent system started in 1978. Eighteen countries, including the UK, Germany, France and the Netherlands, are parties to the agreement as specified in the European Patent Convention (EPC). The aim of the EPC is to allow rights to be obtained in countries recognized as EPC contracting states, in order that a single European patent application is now feasible. The European Patent Offices (EPO) Headquarters are in Munich with a branch office at The Hague and sub-offices in Berlin and Vienna. A single application is normally made to the European Patent Office in Munich, designating the member countries in which protection is sought. The process is generally faster and cheaper than applying separately to each national office. Like the new-style GB specifications, the European specifications are published applications. When granted, the result is a number of separate national patents, one for each country designated. Full details of the procedure can be found in a pamphlet issued by the EPO.[22]

The situation regarding the creation of a community patent remains undecided. In 1997 there was a Green Paper[23] issued by the European Commission based around the central question of whether the patent system in Europe was in need of improvement and modernization. The Paper covered issues such as the implementation of a single EU-wide patent application, implications of such a system for fees and charges of patents, employee inventions and, in general, further harmonization between countries. The Commission will take decisions on how the issues are to be taken forward during late 1998. However, the issue of community patents has been around for a long time and it is unlikely to be sorted out quickly.

7.2 World patents

Another important development in recent years was the Patent Co-operation Treaty (PCT), signed in 1970. This system produces a separate national patent for each designated country, but simplifies the procedure at the application stage, largely by utilizing a standard search. An agreed minimum of documentation is searched by an International Searching Authority, including The Hague branch of the EPO, and the results of the search are accepted by all participating countries. This reduces the costs for the applicant and the workload of the national offices. The number of applications made in this way are presently increasing. Details of the scheme can be found in a publication of the World Intellectual Property Organisation.[24]

The WIPO is a United Nations body responsible for dealing with international procedures on intellectual property. All national patent offices must send their various reports, which are then published on a yearly basis. WIPO also oversees the updating of the international system of patent classification.

8 Access to patents and patent literature

The Patent Office, an agency of the DTI, is located at Newport, Gwent in South Wales and keeps all the original documents relating to the application and restoration of documents. Although the Patent Office runs a reasonably priced Search and Advisory Service, the largest and most important collection of British and foreign patent literature in the UK is the Science Reference and Information Service (SRIS) of the British Library, which was formerly the Patent Office Library and receives specifications and other literature from all over the world. The SRIS is based at the new British Library building at St Pancras from 1999 onwards. Its many services are described in a work by Van Dulken,[25] and includes a limited range of free enquiry services on the status of British patents and applications, and on patent equivalents. The library maintains a unique card index of applicants for British patents, which is kept in cumulative annual sequences, in effect cumulating the lists in the *Official journal (patents)* and used to trace recent applications. The *Currentscan* service is provided by Patent Express, the delivery group of the Service. *Currentscan* provides a regular watch on British, European and PCT applications against a customer's profile (subject or name). Copies of the complete specifications of patents matching the profile are delivered within 48 hours of publication. The SRIS also offers a *Patents on-line* service which will deal with enquires of a technical and commercial nature and *Transcript*, which gives English language translations of patent specifications.

Since the last century, copies of British patents and official literature have traditionally been deposited in a number of provincial libraries which undertook to make them available to the public. By the late 1970s the cost, which was being met by the British Library, had risen to over £¼m. In 1980, following consultations with interested parties, the Patents Information Network (PIN) came into being. The continued existence of the PIN recognizes the fact that access to patent literature outside London is essential if the system is to be fully exploited. Originally there were 25 libraries in the network, located at public reference libraries. Six of these (Birmingham, Glasgow, Leeds, Liverpool, Manchester and Newcastle) received UK, US, European and PCT patents, together with other literature. The others received journals, abstracts and indexes but not specifications. More recently the network has been reduced still further to 13 libraries: seven Patent Information Libraries with substantial holdings of British, European and PCT documents, and six Patent Information Centres with limited holdings of British patent documentation. The future of some of these seems to be in doubt. Reduced funding of local authorities, following government policy on the community charge, may mean that some libraries cannot continue to provide the professional staff and other resources needed to ensure the exploitation of the documents which is a condition of continued supply. Developments in the network are reported in *Patents information news*.[26]

Much information about Patents is now available on CD-ROM, online or increasingly via the Internet. The Patent Office has a home page at http://www.ukpats.org.uk.

Many commercially produced abstracting services, whether in hard copy, online, in CD-ROM format or available via the World Wide Web, include British and foreign patents in their coverage, for example *Chemical abstracts*[27] and *RAPRA abstracts*.[28] Such services are often preferred, because the terminology is more familiar, patents are listed alongside other materials and the indexing system is not constrained by the peculiar requirements of legality. Of course, complete coverage is not guaranteed, whereas in the official British sources every patent is there somewhere. Other important ways of approaching patents include the following.

8.1 INPADOC

The International Patent Documentation Centre was founded by the Austrian government in 1972, following an agreement with the World Intellectual Property Organisation. It is a microfiche service indexing subjects, applicants, inventors and patent numbers and covering countries from all over the world. The subject series is arranged by the International Patent Classification. In addition INPADOC offer various searching services such as INPADOC patent application service, INPADOC patent inventor service and INPADOC watch.

8.2 Derwent Information Ltd

This company has specialized in patent information for over 40 years. Its services cover many countries and employ a combination of printed bulletins, microfiche, online searching, CD-ROM and Internet access to worldwide patent specifications, with detailed indexing systems for chemical and electrical patents.

As well as providing the well established Derwent World Patent Index (WPI) database plus related databases Derwent also offers customized search services which provide users with customized information to meet specific requirements. Finally Derwent is the developer of the first database of patented gene sequences called 'Geneseq'.

8.3 Micropatent

The company Micropatent was founded in the late 1980s and is now becoming one of the best-known providers of Patent and Trademark information on CD-ROM and related World Wide Web sites. Micropatent covers European, US, Japanese and World Patents. Of particular interest is the family of CD-ROMs called 'Patent Images' which uses MIMOSA (Mixed Mode Software) to allow complete patent searching including technical drawings and images.

8.4 EPIDOS

The European Patent Office runs the 'European Patent Register On-line Service' (EPIDOS) – a database which contains all published European applications and international applications that have mentioned member states of the European Convention. The aim of EPIDOS is to ensure that

Patent Information is available in the public domain. The MIMOSA software mentioned above is also presently being applied to a range of the EPI-DOS products.

8.5 ESPACE

The European Patent Office also produce a series of CD-ROMs known as the ESPACE series. These include:

- *ESPACE EP*, a weekly disc containing all European patent applications
- *ESPACE WORLD*, a weekly disc containing complete PCT patent applications
- *ESPACE FIRST*, containing images of the first pages of EPO and PCT patents (bi-monthly)
- *ESPACE UK*, produced by the UK Patent Office and containing all UK patent application (monthly)
- *ESPACE LEGAL*, containing decisions of the Board of Appeal of the EPO, useful for specialist patent solicitors (two per year).

9 Recent developments in patents

9.1 Life forms and genes

The developments in biotechnology have 'raised issues about the patenting of genes and life forms'.[29] This is a subject that is presently causing heated debate in some areas. During 1995 a Directive was proposed to the European Commission on the legal protection of biotechnological inventions. However the proposal was not accepted and the matter was still under discussion at the time of writing.

9.2 Computer software

Section 1 of the Patent Act specifically excludes computer programmes from being patented. However, it has also been found that there are circumstances in which a patent for a computer programmes that may make a technical improvement might be accepted. For full advice on this matter, it is wise to seek advice from the Patent Office.

10 Conclusion

This chapter has covered the nature of patents, explained the difficulties of the patent system, outlined the application process under both the 1949 Act and the 1977 Act and discussed various ways of searching patents. In addition the chapter has briefly described the situation regarding European and World Patents, access to the patent literature and closed with a tentative look at some of the recent and ongoing developments in the exciting world of patents.

The literature of patents is vast, and this chapter is no more than an introduction to a complex subject in which rapid developments are taking place. For example, in the US Manning and Napier Information Services have launched improved software tools to assist with searching patents known as MAPIT. This system makes searching much easier and has been applied to the US Patent and Trademark Office. For further guidance the reader is referred to the books by Williams[30] and and others previously mentioned.[31] There is now an increasing amount of information available via the Internet and the main sites are listed below.

References

1 Hope, A., *Why didn't I think of it first?: a light look at patents*, Newton Abbot, David and Charles, 1972.
2 Jones, S. V., *Inventions necessity is not the mother of: patents ridiculous and sublime*, London, Allen and Unwin, 1975.
3 Patents Act 1977, London, HMSO, 1977.
4 Copyright, Designs and Patents Act 1988, London, HMSO, 1988.
5 Patents Act 1977, Part I, para. 1(1). London, HMSO, 1977.
6 Patents Act 1977, Part I, paras. 1(2) and 1(3).
7 Plants Varieties and Seeds Act 1964, London, HMSO, 1964.
8 Patents Act 1977, Part I, paras. 4(2) and 4(3). London, HMSO, 1977.
9 *Research disclosure*, Emsworth, Kenneth Mason Publishers Ltd, monthly.
10 *How to prepare a UK patent application and then apply for a patent*, London, Patent Office, 1986.
11 Stephenson, J. and Riley, N. W., *The use of patent information in industry*, Boston Spa, British Library Lending Division, 1982 (Library and Information Research Report no.4).
12 *Patents information news*, London, British Library, quarterly.
13 *PIN bulletin*, **8**, November 1983, 1.
14 See Reference 11, page 30.
15 *Names of applicants*, London, Patent Office, annual.
16 *Abridgements of patent specifications: abstracts of patent applications,*

17   *Catchwords index to the classification key*, London, Patent Office, irregular.
18   Eisenschitz, T. S., *Patents, trade marks and designs in information work*, London, Croom Helm, 1987, 96–102.
19   *Divisional allotment index to abridgements, heading allotment index to abstracts*, London, Patent Office, annual.
20   *Official journal (patents)*, London, Patent Office, weekly.
21   *How to get a European patent – guide for applicants*, Munich, European Patent Office, no date.
22   See Reference 21.
23   *European Commission Green Paper on the Community patent and the patent system in Europe*, Brussels, EC, 1997.
24   *PCT applicants guide*, Geneva, World Intellectual Property Organisation, looseleaf, 1978–.
25   Van Dulken, S. (ed.), *Introduction to patents information*, London, British Library, Science Reference and Information Service, 1990.
26   See Reference 12.
27   *Chemical abstracts*, Columbus (Ohio), American Chemical Society, weekly.
28   *RAPRA abstracts*, Shawbury, RAPRA Technology Ltd, monthly.
29   *The Patent Office: annual report and accounts 1995–1996*, London, HMSO, 1996.
30   Williams, J.F., *A manager's guide to patents, trade marks and copyright*, London, Kogan Page, 1986.
31   See Reference 25.

Web sites

British Library	http://www.portico.bl.uk
Derwent	http://www.derwent.com/
European Patent Office	http://www.epo.co.at/epo
Micropatent	http://www.micropat.com
Patent Information Users' Group	http://www.piug.org/
UK Patent Office	http://www.ukpats.org.uk
UK Patent Information Libraries	http://www.sunsite.unc-edu/ patents/ptodoc/uklib.txt
World Intellectual Property Organisation	http://www.uspto.gov/wipo-html

14 Trade marks and related issues

1 Introduction

A trade mark is applied by a producer to goods or services to distinguish them from similar ones supplied by other producers. For many years, registered trade marks could be obtained in Britain only for products, but since 1986 service marks have also been registrable. A trade mark may consist only of a word or words; or it may be a picture or device; or the actual shape of the goods. In addition, since the 1994 Trade Mark Act there is now potential to register a colour, a sound or a smell. This chapter covers brands, an explanation of the registration of trade marks, briefly mentions the European situation and then lists the major sources of information in this area.

A few words about terminology are desirable at this point, since the terms 'trade mark', 'brand' and 'trade name' are frequently used interchangeably. The correct legal term, in the context of registration under the Acts, is 'trade mark', and marks may be divided into 'word marks', 'devices' or combinations. The term 'trade name' is often used by the compilers of directories, who may include lists of 'trade names' in their publications. In official language, these would be 'word marks'. Finally, marketing people tend to use the term 'brand', which covers all kinds of trade marks, and they talk of branding and brand image, which are important commercial concepts.

A related class of marks, which should not be confused with trade marks proper, are certification trade marks, which are usually intended to certify quality or standard. Registration of a certification trade mark is made under the Trade Marks Act, but has a different effect in that it gives rights in the use of the mark to the proprietor, who may authorize others to use it, but might not personally carry on a trade in the goods concerned.

2 Brands

Brands are of tremendous commercial significance and value. Advertisers spend enormous sums of money to promote a brand image and to create brand loyalty among their customers. A good brand is a valuable piece of commercial property, and companies may take over other businesses partly in order to gain possession of a brand. The fact that unscrupulous firms will copy or imitate a well-known brand on their own counterfeit goods is itself a tribute to the power of that brand. Counterfeiting is in fact a very serious problem nowadays, with millions of pounds worth of counterfeit goods being produced in certain parts of the world, notably the Far East. For some discussion of the problem see the book by Murphy,[1] and other articles in business periodicals.

The power of brands may be demonstrated by the fact that some have come into common use as generic terms, that is to say the brand is used as the common name for the class of product. A good example is 'cellophane', which is commonly used to denote any kind of cellulosic film even though it is or was the trade mark of the French company La Cellophane that introduced it. Another example is 'hoover'; not only do some people refer to their 'hoover' even though they own some other make, but the term is even used as a verb – to 'hoover' the carpet. Yet another interesting example is 'sellotape', which tends to be used to refer to any kind of contact adhesive transparent tape. It seems that this fate of 'genericism' is likely to overtake the brand name of the first product in the field, which thereby suffers from being the innovator. If the product is new and the descriptive generic term for it is long or cumbersome, people may come to use the brand because it is snappier and easier to say. A good example is 'biro'; because Mr Biro invented the first ball-point pen, all such pens were for a long time referred to as biros, although the generic term 'ball-point' seems now to have superseded the earlier term. A final example may be that of the name 'Elastoplast' which seems to be undergoing the same process; after all, it is much easier to say than 'self-adhesive surgical plaster'.

Another fact illustrating the force of brand names is that quite often the purchaser and viewer of the advertisement is aware only of the brand and may not know who the manufacturer is. Detergents and washing powders seem to be especially prone to this phenomenon and it is noticeable that in television advertisements for them the maker's name is rarely mentioned. The fact is that the manufacturer does not want us to remember its name, only that of the brand, which is all-important. The corollary of this is that two brands of washing powder advertised on TV in competition with each other, sometimes even on the same night, may well both be made by the same company. It is in the interests of the firm to do this, because by maintaining loyalty to two brands instead of one it may be able to hold on to a bigger share of the market.

Brands are a fascinating phenomenon, both in business and in society in general, and they have many interesting facets – technical, commercial and legal. For an interesting, entertaining and often amusing account of all aspects of branding, the reader is referred to the book by Murphy.[2]

Given the enormous commercial value of brands, it is in the interest of owners to protect them. In Britain there is a right of ownership of brands under common law and it is not strictly necessary to protect a brand by registering it, though it is strongly advisable to do so, especially in the case of a new trade mark. Old-established brands are perhaps less vulnerable and it is easier to establish ownership, but new brands certainly need protection. Common law rights in brands do not exist abroad, for example in Europe, so it is essential to seek legal protection in such cases.

3 Registration

Registration used to be made in the UK under the Trade Marks Act 1938. Originally, only products were registrable, but since the Trade Marks (Amendment) Act 1984 came into force in October 1986, marks have also been registrable for services. The system is operated by the Trade Marks Registry, which is a branch of the Patent Office. However, in 1994 the new Trade Marks Act replaced the 1938 Act. The 1994 Act has in essence brought the 1938 Act up to date with current issues. For example, it prepares much of the groundwork for UK industry and commerce to have protection of trade marks overseas by making application more straightforward. The Act also helped to prepare the transition to the adoption of the Community Trade Mark. Most notably however, the 1994 Act does not exclude that a colour, a sound or a fragrance may be registered as a trade mark – providing it is distinct and can be represented graphically. In addition the 1994 Act also allows for the registration of Collective Marks. These are marks used by members of associations and displayed on goods to be purchased. The collective marks thus serve to indicate a business connection with the association that owns the mark.

The requirements and limitations that apply to registration are set out in pamphlets available from the Patent Office.[3] In order for a mark to be registrable, it must be characterized by at least one of the following:

- the name of a company or individual represented in a particular manner; this would include typographical styles, colours and the like
- the signature of the applicant, or some predecessor in the business; a good example is W. K. Kellogg, whose signature used to appear on corn-flake packets
- an invented word or words, e.g. 'Wispa', 'Daz'
- a common word that has no reference to the nature of the goods or services in question, e.g. 'Swan' (pans), 'Fairy' (soap).

In general, a trade mark must be distinctive in itself, independently of the goods; and must not be deceptive, that is in implying that the goods possess characteristics they do not possess.

Certain words and devices cannot be registered, notably the royal arms and crowns; the royal and national flags; military insignia such as the anchor devices of the Admiralty; representations of members of the royal family; and words such as 'Anzac', 'Royal', 'Imperial', 'Empire', 'Dominion' and 'Crown'. In addition, the Act prohibits the registration of any matter that would be 'contrary to law or morality or any scandalous design'.[4]

Registrations are classified into 34 classes of goods and 8 of services, and application for registration must be made separately under each class. It is possible to register the same mark under several or all classes, but the rules explain why the same mark may be used by different owners, i.e. providing they are for different classes of goods. Thus we have 'Swan' pans and also 'Swan' matches (and formerly also 'Swan' pens and ink).

It should be remembered that many trade marks are in use without being registered, and in some cases they may constitute prohibited categories. Hence 'Crown' paints: presumably 'Crown' is not registered as a trade mark and/or there is nothing to prevent a company from calling itself 'Crown', in which case it can refer to its products accordingly. It is common practice to denote a registered mark by a small encircled superscript 'R' after the mark, while the letters 'TM' are sometimes used after marks that are not registered.

Application for registration results in a search by the examiners among registered and pending marks. If none is found and the mark meets all the requirements, full details, including devices if any, are published in the weekly *Trade marks journal*.[5] A period of one month is allowed for any opposition to be made. If there is none, the mark is registered and again advertised in the *Trade marks journal,* showing the registered number, the journal reference at which originally advertised, and the owner's name. The initial registration is for ten years, after which the mark may be renewed for periods of ten years at a time. Unlike patents and designs, trade mark monopolies last for ever, provided the renewal fees are paid.

A new problem concerning legislation of trade marks is that of the trade mark or domain name used by people or organizatons as part of their 'address' on the Internet. Some problems have arisen where trade marks have been unlawfully used as a domain name, and this has led to some confusion over (a) what is actually being advertised/offered through the Internet, and (b) the legal owners of the trade mark having the ability to protect their rights. At the time of writing this is an ongoing debate, and concrete legislation may appear in the future which covers the domain name situation. For further information see the web site at http://www.ntia.doc.gov/ntiahome/domainname/dnsdrft.htm.

4 European trade marks

Parallel with the development of European patents and standards, the European Commission has introduced regulations for implementing Community-wide trade marks. Since 1 April 1996 there has been a European Trade Mark Office, officially called OHIM (Office of the Harmonisation of the Internal Market) and informally known as CTMO (The European Community Trade Mark Office). The CTMO is located in Alicante, Spain. The Community Trade Mark system enables trade marks to be registered in all member states of the European Union by one single application. In addition, under the Madrid Protocol and the Paris Convention for the Protection of Industrial Property, registration of a trade mark can be made in another country, claiming the original priority, provided that the application is made within six months of the original application date.

5 Sources of information

The most common enquiry in this area is for the owner of a named mark. So far as British trade marks are concerned, the Patent Office Trade Marks Registry runs an excellent Search and Advisory Service. The services offered include:

- OPTICS Computer Word Search, accessible by appointment to the public at the British Library or details can be requested by post or fax. The database contains details of all registered UK trade marks.
- Searches using manual indexes and online searches.

- Consultation with a Hearing Officer.

There are several commercial organizations that maintain a watching service on new marks on behalf of clients and provide search services. One such firm is Computer Patent Annuities of Jersey, C.I., whose activities are described in an article by Tagg.[6] Commercial sources of information include the following.

5.1 *UK Kompass Industrial Trade Names* [7]

This Kompass directory, which makes up volume 5 of the Kompass volumes, now contains over 100,000 trade names. The alphabetical list of trade marks is supplemented by a list of companies' names and addresses, showing the marks they own. The information can also be accessed online using the 'Kompass Online' database. At the time of writing there were plans to release the trade names volume on CD-ROM.

5.2 *A–Z of UK Brands* [8]

This directory is no longer published, having been replaced by the *European directory of consumer brands and their owners* (see below). However, it is included here as it is a useful book to be found in the reference collection of most academic and public libraries. Brands are listed by product groups, and there is an index of names. Other sections include: a list of 600 brand owners; a list of brand leaders by product sector, showing the percentage market share held by each brand; and a list of major brands ranked in order of sales value.

5.3 Trade Directories (UK)

Many specialist directories include lists of brand names in their fields, for example *Sell's building and construction index*[9] published by Reed Information Services. To find which directories contain such lists, the enquirer should consult the index to *Current British directories*,[10] (published every three years) under the heading 'trademarks and names', where directories are listed by subject.

5.4 *The European Directory of Consumer Brands and their Owners* 11

This directory, published by Euromonitor, contains an index of brand names and lists the owners and their brands by country and product sector.

There are several trade-mark information services with international coverage. Online access to US, German, French, Italian and other marks is provided by the Science Reference and Information Service, which uses the IMSMARQ host and other sources.

Other international sources follow.

5.5 *Répertoire Alphabétique* 12

A well-known source with international scope is Compu-Mark's *Répertoire alphabétique*. This is a directory of word marks and verbal elements of composite marks registered at the International Bureau of the World Intellectual Property Organization in Geneva and published in the journal *Les marques internationales* from 1968 to date. Marks are grouped into five classes and then listed alphabetically. They are listed as spelt and also according to phonetic equivalents, so that for example the mark 'Ceral' would also be listed at 'Seral'. This is helpful to the searcher trying to establish the novelty of a mark, since applications for new marks can be rejected on grounds of phonetic as well as orthographical similarity with existing marks.

5.6 *The International Directory of Consumer Brands and their Owners* 13

This Euromonitor publication is arranged as the European Directory and lists over 100,000 brands. With the European directory on CD-ROM, it is issued as *The world database of consumer brands and their owners.*

5.7 *International Companies and their Brands* 14

This directory published by Gale Research Inc contains details on 25 importers and distributors of nearly 80,000 consumer products. It excludes the USA.

5.8 Trademarkscan [15]

For US trade marks, the Trademarkscan database should be considered. It includes about one million records representing all registrations filed in the US Patent and Trademark Office. Trademarkscan uses string searches and other sophisticated techniques, including searches for phonetic equivalents of a name. The database is supplied by Thomson and Thomson and is hosted by the DIALOG Corporation. Thomson and Thomson also provide a variety of trademark searching and watching services covering US, Canadian and foreign trade marks.

6 Other sources of information

Brand names are sometimes mentioned in technical abstracts and may therefore appear in the indexes. Thus, the index to *Chemical abstracts* [16] (weekly) contains many brand names of commercial chemicals. Likewise the monthly RAPRA *abstracts* [17] (The Rubber and Plastics Research Association) is a fruitful source for trade marks in rubber and plastics. The RAPRA Library collects large quantities of trade literature and indexes trade marks in its annual *New trade names in the rubber and plastics industries*, [18] which dates back to the 1930s. Trade marks and other names may be mentioned in articles indexed in both in the hard copy and CD-ROM version of Bowker-Saur's *Current technology index*. [19] Such names are collected and indexed in a quarterly supplementary publication called *CATNI (Catchword and trade name index)*. [20]

7 Chemical synonyms

One final pitfall that may be encountered in the chemical field is that of chemical synonyms. Chemical compounds, especially if they have long and cumbersome systematic names, may be referred to more commonly by trivial names, which could be mistaken for trade marks. For example the compound normally called propyl alcohol is sometimes called propanol, which sounds like a trade mark but is not. A useful guide to such names, which also includes some trade names, is *Gardner's chemical synonyms and trade names*. [21]

It should also not be overlooked that current price lists such as the monthly *Chemist and druggist monthly price list* [22] which is arranged in alphabetical order by brand name, can often be used to identify brand owners.

8 Conclusion

Finally, in searching for trade marks, it should be remembered that only *registered* marks are retrievable from some sources, especially the UK Trade Marks Registry files. As we have seen, many marks in use, especially in the UK, are not registered but may appear in other lists such as directories. There are an increasing number of sources of information that combine UK and European sources and the next few years will no doubt see these sources streamlined into international products available both on CD-ROM and via the Internet.

For further guidance on trade marks, the reader is referred to the works by Williams[23] and Eisenschitz.[24] Readers interested in pursuing the role of the brand in more depth are recommended to consult the book by Watkins,[25] which is an economic analysis of brand development and management in the context of the marketing process.

References

1 Murphy, J.M., *Branding: a key marketing tool,* London, Macmillan, 1986.
2 See Reference 1.
3 *Registering for a trade mark*, London, Patent Office, 1994.
4 *Applying for a trade mark*, London, Patent Office, 1994.
5 *Trade marks journal*, London, Patent Office, 1994.
6 Tagg, L., 'Online access to trade marks', *Business information review,* **2** (2), 1985, 37.
7 *UK Kompass industrial trade names*, East Grinstead, Kompass, 1996.
8 *A–Z of UK brands,* 2nd edn, London, Euromonitor, 1990.
9 *Sell's building and construction index,* 70th edn, Epsom, Sell's Publications Ltd, 1992.
10 Henderson, C.A.P. (ed.), *Current British directories: a guide to directories published in the British Isles,* 12th edn, Beckenham, CBD Research Ltd, 1993.
11 *European directory of consumer brands and their owners*, London, Euromonitor, 1996.
12 *Repertoire alphabétique phonétique des marques internationales,* Antwerp, Compu-Mark, 1996, plus quarterly supplements. 6 vols, 29 parts.
13 *International directory of consumer brands and their owners*, London, Euromonitor, 1996.

14 *International companies and their brands*, Detroit, Gale Inc, 1995.

15 Trademarkscan database, Thomson and Thomson, USA.

16 *Chemical abstracts*, Columbis (Ohio), American Chemical Society, weekly.

17 *RAPRA abstracts*, Shawbury, RAPRA Technology Ltd, monthly.

18 *New trade names in the rubber and plastics industries*, Shawbury, RAPRA Technology Ltd, annual.

19 *Current technology index*, London, Bowker-Saur, monthly, with annual cumulations.

20 *CATNI – Catchword and trade name index*, London, Bowker-Saur, quarterly.

21 *Gardner's chemical synonyms and trade names*, 9th edn, Aldershot, Gower, 1987.

22 *Chemist and druggist monthly price list*, Tonbridge, Benn Retail Publications Ltd, monthly.

23 Williams, J.F., *A manager's guide to patents, trade marks and copyright*, London, Kogan Page, 1986.

24 Eisenschitz, T.S., *Patents, trade marks and designs in information work*, London, Croom Helm, 1987.

25 Watkins, T., *The economics of the brand*, London, McGraw-Hill, 1986.

Web sites

There are also an increasing number of useful Internet sites (including those already mentioned in the patent section which are not repeated here):

Institute of Trade Mark Agents	http://itma.org.uk
National Telecommunications and Information Administration	http://www.ntia.doc.gov/ntiahome/domainname/dnsdrft/htm
Thomson and Thomson	http://www.thomson-thomson.com
Trademark Research (US)	http://warrior.com/tmsearch

15 Standards and regulations

1 Introduction

This chapter looks at standards and regulations as they affect business, with reference to the key sources of information. Our daily lives at work and in private are governed by law, regulation and standardization at every turn. Private and public safety, business economy and social control necessitate conformity to rule, whether statutory or voluntary. The Highway Code, the Consumer Protection Act and the Health and Safety Act are just three examples of regulation in our lives. At one end of the scale, consider for a moment the humble watercress. A packet of cress bought from the greengrocer will usually be found to contain a tag stating that the cress was grown in accordance with the appropriate Code of Practice, together with the name of the firm and its registered number under the Code. At the other end of the scale we have massive investment by firms in quality control systems to the quality standard BS EN ISO 9000, entailing approval of every step in the manufacturing process and the maintenance of rigorous standards.

The best-known standards are those published by national bodies such as the British Standards Institution (BSI), but standards are also issued by trade associations, government departments and companies. A technical standard specifies quality of materials, performance requirements, method of construction, or other characteristics appropriate to the article in question. Logically, if a standard is specified, then there must also be a test method by which any given sample can be tested against the standard.

Another type of standard is the code of practice. Such codes specify not a standard for an article but a standardized way of doing something, for example approved methods of installing domestic electric wiring. Codes of practice are common in building and construction and in service industries. In Britain, the major technical standards, test methods and codes of practice are issued by BSI, of which more below.

Yet another important area of standardization is that of scientific measurement. There must be internationally agreed definitions and measurement methods for scientific units such as the joule and the micron, and scientific instruments must be accurately constructed and calibrated so as to give acceptable uniform measurements. An important British organization in this field is the National Physical Laboratory (NPL), which researches methods of measurement, helps to standardize units and administers a service for testing and calibrating instruments. In addition NPL closely measures and standardizes the accuracy of time, including responsibility for the grand Millennium countdown on New Year's Eve 1999.

2 Reasons for standardization

There are several benefits offered by standards, as follows.

2.1 Safety

Firstly, there is the matter of safety. This is particularly important in cases like domestic electrical equipment, such as electric irons, blankets and plugs. If such articles are made to an approved standard, they should be safe for all to use. In many cases such as these, the use of the appropriate standard is mandatory in law, so that the relevant Statutory Instrument may specify the British Standard that is to be applied. For detailed consideration of Statutory Instruments, see below.

2.2 Economy

Standards also lead to economies in business. The existence of a standard will tend to reduce the number of variations in which an article is made, thereby simplifying manufacturing processes and reducing costs. By specifying a minimum level of performance, a standard also tends to ensure that products are not made to a much higher standard than they need be in order to qualify. This also tends to cut costs.

2.3 Simplification of procedure

Standards help to streamline and simplify procedures. Thus, when ordering a product, a customer needs only to quote the appropriate standard, instead of having to specify the details individually. Moreover the suppliers of a product are geared up to make an article that they know will be demanded to a given standard. In this way, both the supply side and the demand side operate to a common standard which oils the wheels of their trade.

It follows from all this that both buyers and sellers must operate internally in accordance with the relevant standards. The manufacturer must have a quality-control system that ensures that its goods are produced to the specified standard. Testing of random samples from the production line and continuous inspection of woven fabrics are two examples of such quality-control processes. But equally the buyer must ensure that the goods bought are up to standard. A plastics processor, for example, who purchases bags of raw materials such as pigments and polymers, will take samples at random from the bags on receipt and test them in the laboratory. It may easily be imagined from the above how important standards are in the daily work of many businesses, and why standards are among the most heavily used types of documents in industrial libraries.

There are three levels of standards: national standards emanating from individual countries; European standards which are recognized in the European Union countries; and international standards which are used all over the world. However it should be noted that the drive to harmonize standards blurs the distinction between each of these levels. Each of these types of standards will be examined in turn.

3 National standards

Most developed countries have national standardizing agencies. This section looks in some detail at the British and US systems, and gives brief examples from other countries, namely Japan, Germany and France.

3.1 National standards: United Kingdom

The national body in the UK is the British Standards Institution. The BSI has a long history dating from the 1920s. It is an autonomous body that receives some government funding, but depends largely on member subscriptions and on sales of publications and services.

The BSI operates in a collaborative way, by bringing interested parties together to discuss and set standards. It functions through a series of standing committees, each dealing with a given subject area. Sub-committees are set up *ad hoc* to generate particular standards. A sub-committee will have on it representatives of suppliers and customers and any other interested parties; for example, a standard for the title leaves of books was produced by a sub-committee on which sat representatives of the Publishers Association, the Booksellers Association, The Library Association, the Society of Authors, and other bodies. Sub-committees produce draft British standards, which are circulated to interested parties and are notified in *Business standards*,[1] so that copies may be requested. Comments are invited and taken into account in further discussions. If all goes well, in due course the standard will be approved and published, with a number in the form BS1234 (for the General Series, that is; other series such as the Automobile, Aerospace and Marine Series have their own numbering systems). BSI is a large organization with interests in many different areas. New developments are constantly in the professional literature. One of the more recent developments has been the formation of the Construction Sector Publications Unit (CSPU) which aims to help understanding and the use of Standards within the construction industry.

Apart from the standards themselves, the chief publications of BSI are:

Business standards [2]

This was formerly known as *BSI news* but changed title in November 1996. This monthly periodical contains technical articles and news, but the item of chief interest to information managers is the regular listing of new and revised British standards, drafts circulated for comment, amendment slips, and the like.

BSI standards catalogue [3]

The catalogue is revised annually. It is complete to 30 September of the year preceding the publication year: e.g. the 1998 volume is complete to 30 September 1997. Subsequent issues of *Business standards* can be checked to bring a search more or less up to date. The catalogue lists standards in numerical order, with brief annotations. The longest list is that of the General Series, followed by shorter lists for the various special series. The *BSI catalogue* is also available on CD-ROM. Other ways of searching British standards is to use the CD-ROM *The British Standards service*[4] produced by Technical Indexes Ltd.

BSI electronic books [5]

There are electronic versions of British, European and International standards which cover three main areas: quality management systems; information security management; and environment management systems.

3.1.1 The Quality Standard – BS EN ISO 9000

An important development in Britain has been the National Quality Campaign initiated by the DTI in 1983. The overall aim is to enhance the quality and competitiveness of British firms both at home and abroad and to encourage the adoption of the original quality standard then known as BS 5750 and the use of other British standards as appropriate.

However, BS 5750 was revised during the summer of 1994 and relaunched as BS EN ISO 9000 to better reflect the importance of quality on an international scale. The standard, entitled *Quality systems*[6] is issued in various parts and covers quality systems that can be used for internal quality control and as a guarantee of quality to offer to customers. Included in the related BS EN ISO 9001 standard is a long list of items and factors, all of which must be taken into account in the quest for registration as a 'quality organization'. These factors include management responsibility, quality policies, quality systems, contract review, inspection and testing and so on. The list is exhaustive and detailed to ensure that all aspects of an organization are thoroughly checked before receiving the quality mark.

Firms can also be approved by certain other large purchasing bodies, such as the Ministry of Defence. Lists of firms approved by these other organizations, as well as by BSI, will be found in the *DTI QA register*.[7] BSI also runs a BSI Quality Assurance customer services helpline which will deal with queries relating to aspects of relevant standards.

3.1.2 BSI Standards: information sources

The BSI Standards Information Centre offers the following services:

- Standards quick search – a quick free service on up to five documents.
- Standards research – a charged service for more in depth research
- Consultancy – for detailed work on specific projects.
- Technical Help to Exports (THE), which gives advice to exporting firms on foreign standards, regulations and technical requirements. Its services include an enquiry service and a research and consultancy service.

The BSI Library is a first-class, comprehensive collection of standards and regulations from all over the world. Other services available from BSI include Language Services for translation of foreign documents and PLUS which is a Private List Updating Service.

One way of maintaining a collection of British and other standards is to subscribe to the Technical Indexes service. Technical Indexes Ltd has long been in the business of providing 'packaged libraries' of trade literature, in various formats including CD-ROM. Its service includes the full text, with regular updating, of several standards series including British standards, defence standards such as those of NATO, international standards, and the national standards of France, Germany and Japan.

3.2 National standards: USA

The national body in the USA is the American National Standards Institute (ANSI). Unlike the BSI, this body does not write standards itself, apart from a very small minority of specifications. Instead, it adopts standards produced by other bodies and issues them as national standards. ANSI standards are listed in their annual *Catalog.*[8] New ANSI standards are announced in their periodical *Standards action.*[9]

The main bodies producing standards in the USA are the influential societies such as the American Society for Testing and Materials (ASTM) and the Society of Automotive Engineers (SAE). A list of such bodies can be found in the ANSI *Catalog,* and includes such diverse organizations as the American Petroleum Institute, the Health Physics Society Standards Committee and the National Fire Protection Association.

The ASTM is roughly equivalent to BSI, in that it is the main American standardizing organization though its influence extends all over the world, ASTM standards being cited in many other countries. Its subject coverage is slightly narrower than that of BSI, since it does not deal with areas that are fully covered by other bodies such as the SAE. ASTM standards are separately published, but are also collected into a large set called the *Annual book of ASTM standards.*[10] The set is revised and reissued annually, and is divided into more than 60 subject volumes such as non-ferrous metals, textiles and plastics. Each subject volume is complete with its own indexes and can be bought separately, conveniently for information managers working in specialist information units. There is an index volume for the whole set. ASTM also publishes the monthly journal *ASTM standardization news,*[11] which contains, amongst other things, lists of new ASTM standards and other publications.

The SAE, already mentioned above, issues standards covering all aspects of motor vehicles. SAE numbers may frequently be observed on cans of engine oil or brake fluid bought in Britain, since SAE standards are often used here.

3.3 National standards: other countries

3.3.1 Germany

The German national body is called Deutsches Institut für Normung (DIN) – the German Institute for Standardization. Its initials are familiar in this country to the photographer, who will recognize, for example, DIN 21 as the film speed equivalent to ISO 100. (It is worth noting that some years ago films were labelled, say, ASA 100 – ASA being the initials of the American Standards Association, an earlier name for ANSI.) The annual catalogue of DIN standards is the *DIN Katalog*.[12]

3.3.2 France

The French national body is called the Association Française de Normalisation (AFNOR). Details of its standards are listed in the *AFNOR catalogue*.[13]

3.3.3 Japan

In Japan industrial standardization is promoted at national, industry and company levels. Japanese industrial standards (JIS) are voluntary national standards mainly for industrial and mineral products. In addition some companies have their own standards which have been adopted from JIS. The aims of JIS are to improve quality of products, rationalize production and ensure fair and simplified trade. The JIS mark on products therefore has a similar meaning to the BSI mark in the UK.

Similar national standardizing bodies exist in more than 70 countries.

4 European standards

There are two European standards bodies: the European Committee for Standardization (CEN) and the European Committee for Electrotechnical Standardization (CENELEC). International standards naturally take a long time to be approved, but developments in world trade increase the need for international agreement. This is especially the case now in Europe.

In order to ease the flow of goods in and around the EU the European Commission publishes 'New approach directives' which are 'mandatory on all member countries to enact through national legislation'. In the UK these take the form of '*Regulations*'.[14]

5 International standards

International standards are identifiable by the prefix ISO followed by the relevant number. There are several important international bodies generating standards. Some, like the International Organisation for Standardisation (IOS), founded in 1947, and the International Electrotechnical Commission (IEC), founded in 1906, have been operating for many years. The ISO in conjunction with the European Commission is slowly succeeding in harmonizing national, European and international standards.

6 Harmonization of national, European and international standards

EC directives set out essential requirements that products must meet before they can be sold anywhere in the Community, whether across national boundaries or not. The essential requirements refer to standards that have been approved by member countries through the European standards bodies (e.g. CEN). In some cases, existing ISO or other international standards are adopted: in others, the directives refer to the new European Standards (ENs), which are being generated by CEN and CENELEC. It is important to understand that when an EN has been agreed by all members it supersedes any conflicting national standard. In Britain, ENs are issued as British standards in identical texts. In the very long term, no doubt, most – if not all – national standards in the EU countries will be replaced by ENs. A list of ENs in force can be found in the *BSI standards catalogue*.[15] New ISO, EN and other international standards are listed in *Business Standards*.[16]

A recent development that deserves mention at this point is PERINORM, a multinational database of standards on CD-ROM (PERINORM Europe and PERINORM international). BSI, AFNOR and DIN combined in 1989 to produce this disc, which gives full bibliographical details and descriptors for all British, French and German standards, plus European and international standards, including those produced by ISO, IEC and CEN/CENELEC.

7 Other forms of regulation

In addition to technical standards, there are many other kinds of regulations affecting trade and industry. This account cannot hope to be exhaustive, but aims to indicate the chief types that are likely to be encountered and to give some specific examples by way of illustration.

7.1 Legislation

In the first place, virtually all trades and industries are affected by general legislation on weights and measures, trade descriptions, consumer protection, health and safety and many others. Perhaps the most important recent development in this field has been that of product liability and consumer protection. The EC Directive on product liability (85/374/EEC) was adopted in 1985 after some nine years of debate. The text of the Directive and the British Government's commentary will be found in a consultative document issued by the DTI.[17] In due course, the directive was implemented in the UK by the Consumer Protection Act 1987, which improves protection in the following way. Prior to the Act an injured person had to prove that the manufacturer of a defective product had been negligent. Under the Act, there is no need to prove negligence. Anyone injured by a defective product can sue the supplier, whether or not the product was sold to that person. Not only manufacturers, but also importers and own-branders can be sued; wholesalers and retailers are not liable unless they fail to identify the producer when asked, i.e. if the manufacturer cannot be identified, the retailer could be sued. It is also now a criminal offence to supply unsafe consumer goods.

The Institute of Trading Standards Administration also has a role to play in enforcing these types of standards. The chief enforcers on a day-to-day basis are the Trading Standards Officers employed by local authorities. They are responsible for the enforcement of a wide range of national legislation such as consumer safety, animal controls, trade description and many others.

7.2 Statutory instruments

When Parliament passes an Act, the appropriate minister is in effect empowered or instructed to implement it. This is done by means of Statutory Instruments (SI), a form of secondary legislation drawn up by government departments and laid before Parliament. An SI is the instrument used to implement the law from a given date, and frequently specifies the details that arise from the general principles set out in the Act. From a business point of view, SIs can affect many products and services directly, and there are many bearing on such areas as food and drink, road vehicles, labelling of goods, and so on.

Hundreds of SIs are issued each year and are collected and published in annual volumes in number order within each year. They are referred to by year and number e.g. SI 1990/1234. SIs are listed in the *The Stationery Office daily list*,[18] but not in the monthly or annual catalogues. However, separate monthly and annual lists of SIs are available on subscription from The Stationery Office. The annual *Table of government orders*[19] lists SIs in force by year and number, and the annual subject index is the *Index to government orders in force*.[20]

Another way of approaching SIs is via *Halsbury's laws of England*,[21] which not only gives the substance of an SI but also sets it in the legal context, cites case law, and so on. Using *Halsbury's*, the SI is quickly found from an index entry under 'seat belt', referring to the appropriate part of the text. Butterworth's are generally prominent amongst the publishers of legal commentary. Two of their other publications, *Butterworth's law of food and drugs*[22] and the *Product liability and safety encyclopaedia*[23] will be found helpful in giving the complete text of relevant SIs, with commentary, and they are generally well indexed and easy to use.

8 Conclusion

This chapter has covered reasons for standardization; national, European and international standards including the UK quality standard; harmonization issues, and other forms of legislation.

No doubt the next few years will see some major changes in the world of standards and regulations. Most significantly there will be greater availability of electronic delivery of standards and an increase in the speed of writing and drafting the standards. Every trade or industry has its own particular structure of standardization and regulation, and the current scene is dominated by rapid developments in Europe. It is hoped that this chapter has at least succeeded in enabling the reader to see the main issues, institutions and lines of enquiry regarding standards and regulations.

References

1   *Business standards*, Premier magazines, London, monthly.
2   See Reference 1.
3   *BSI standards catalogue*, London, British Standards Institution,

annual.

4 *The British Standards Service*, Bracknell, Technical Indexes Ltd, 1997.

5 *BSI electronic books*, London, BSI.

6 *Quality systems: BS EN ISO 9000I*, London, BSI, 1994.

7 *DTI QA register: the United Kingdom register of quality assessed companies, 5* vols. and supplements, London, The Stationery Office, 1996.

8 *Catalog of American national standards,* New York, American National Standards Institute, annual.

9 *Standards action,* New York, American National Standards Institute, bi-weekly.

10 *Annual book of ASTM standards,* Philadelphia, American Society for Testing and Materials, annual.

11 *ASTM standardization news*, Philadelphia, American Society for Testing and Materials, monthly.

12 *DIN Katalog für technische Regeln (DIN catalogue of technical rules),* 2 vols, Berlin, Beuth-Vettrieb, annual.

13 *AFNOR catalogue,* Paris, Association Francaise de Normalisation, annual.

14 *BSI – an introduction to CE marketing regulations*, London, BSI 1997.

15 See Reference 3.

16 See Reference 1.

17 *Implementation of EC directive on product liability: an explanatory and evaluative note,* London, Department of Trade and Industry, 1985.

18 The Stationery Office daily list, London, The Stationery Office, daily.

19 *Table of government orders,* London, The Stationery Office, annual.

20 *Index to government orders in force on . . .* [e.g. 31 December 1998], London, The Stationery Office, annual.

21 *Halsbury's laws of England,* 4th edn, London, Butterworth, 1983.

22 *Butterworth's law of food and drugs,* London, Butterworth, loose-leaf.

23 *Product liability and safety encyclopaedia,* London, Butterworth, loose-leaf.

Web sites

British Standards Institute   http://www.bsi.org.uk/bsi/standards/
National Physical Laboratory   http://www.npl.co.uk/

Index

Accounting Standards Board 47
Accounting Standards Committee
59
accounts 47–61
balance sheet 51–8
creative accounting 60
problems 58
profit and loss 48–51
Advertisers annual 196
advertising information sources
189–97
agencies 190–1
direct response 192
media 191–2
media research 194
regulation of 192–3
types of 190
Advertising Standards Authority
193
Advertising statistics yearbook 194
annual reports 128
Audit Bureau of Circulations
194–5
auditor 47

balance sheet 47, 51–8
Banking and Financial Services
Act 25
BC-NET (Business Co-operation
Network) 169
Benns media directory 196
Big Bang 74
BIS strategic decisions 156
BRAD 197
brands 233–5
*Britain's top privately owned com-
panies* 137

British Chamber of Commerce 8
British Library patents literature
227–8
British Standards Institution
(BSI) 243, 245–8
Broadcasters Audience Research
Board (BARB) 195
*Building and maintaining a
European direct marketing
database* 197
Building Societies Commission 25
Business Co-operation Centres
169
Business in Europe 168
Business information basics 127
Business Link Network 94
Business monitors 6–8, 180–1
Business Names Act 36
Business point 8
Business ratio reports 64
business *see also* companies and
firms
growth 3–23
information needs 87–95
legal status 24–38
names 34–7
organization 24–9
structure 3–23
statistics 5–6
Business Shops 94
Business Statistics Office (BO)
178

capital funds 39
capital structure 39–46
cash flow statement 47
Central Statistical Office 4, 178

City Information Group 112
classification of industrial activity
    3–12
  geographical 10
  industry sector 4–8
  institutional 9
  size of firm 11–12
Committee of Advertising Practice
    (CAP) 192
companies *see also* business and
    firms
companies 26–37
  accounts 47–61
  advertisements 130
  annual reports 129
  contacts 134–5
  credit information 143
  debts 33
  directories 135–40
  disclosure 30
  finance 39–65
  information agencies 131
  information sources 125–46
  names 34–7
  news sources 141–2
  patents 130
  press releases 129
  registration 30–2
  reporting 30, 33
  trade literature 129
  web sites 131, 145
Companies Act 24–29
  accounts 48
  balance sheets 51
  company names 37
Companies House
  company information 131
  company names 37
  deposit of accounts 47
  new shares 76
  role of 30–4
  subscription services 30
Company guide 137

Competition Act 20
consumer groups 150
Copyright, Design and Patents
    Act 212
credit information 143
Current british directories 135
Customs and Excise 6

data interpretation 6
data, definition of 87
decision support systems 90
Department of Trade and
    Industry 24
  Business Link network 94
  Business Shops 94
  Companies House 30
  statistics 176
Deregulation and Contracting Out
    Act 20
Directory of directors 128, 140
Directory of European retailers
    204
disclosure of information 24
discussion lists 115
distribution information sources
    197–9
Dun and Bradstreet 136

e-mail 115
*European companies: guide to
    sources of information* 127
*European directory of consumer
    brands and their owners* 239
European Documentation Centres
    (EDC) 171
European Information Centres
    (EIC) 171
European own brands directory
    203
European Patents Convention
    (EPC) 226
European Patents Office (EPO)
    226

European Union 162
Eurostat statistics 184
Export intelligence 167
exporting 165–76
    Asia-Pacific 172–4
    Central and Eastern Europe
        172
    information sources 167–74
    North America 174
    opportunities 167
    procedures 165
    sources of assistance and advice
        166–7
    web sites 176

Fair Trading Act 20
finance 39–65
financial indicators 61–4
Financial Reporting Council (FRC)
    47
Financial Services Act 82
financial services regulation 82–3
Financial surveys 137
firms *see also* business and compa-
    nies
    diversification 18
    environment 90–3
    families 29
    growth 16–17
    information systems 89–90
    location 14–16
    mergers and takeovers 20, 29
    size 11–14
FT Extel 131–2
FTSE 77–8

GATT 164–5
gearing 45
gearing ratios 63–4
Government Office for the Regions
    10
Government Statistical Service
    178–9

*Government statistics: a brief
    guide to sources* 177
green movement 150, 204–5

*Headland business information
    reports* 155
Hollis UK press and PR annual
    197
*Hypermarkets and superstores –
    the international market*
    203

ICC British company information
    136
industrial activity classification
    see classification
Industrial and Commercial
    Libraries Group 112
industrial espionage 135
industry structure 3
information
    as a resource 97–105
    audit 101–2
    brokers 133
    definition of 87
    formats 106–18
    management 87–90
    needs of businesses 89–95, 106,
        126
    overload 98–101
    professionals 94–116
    sources *see* sources of informa-
        tion
    strategy 101–2
    systems 89–90
    users 93, 126–7
    value 97–102
Inland Revenue 24
Institute of Information Scientists
    112
*International companies and their
    brands* 237
International directory of

consumer brands and their owners 239
international trade information sources 162–76
Internet *see* web sites
intranets 102–3
investments 66–71
    banks and building societies 66–9
    government schemes 69
    insurance funds and pension schemes 69–70
    stock markets 70–1
    web sites 84

Joint Industry Committee for Radio Audience Research (JICRAR) 195

Kelly's directories 128, 137
Key British enterprises 138
Key note reports 157, 204
knowledge management 87–8
Kompass UK 128, 138, 238

legal status of businesses 24–38
Library Association 112
limited companies 28
limited liability 26
Limited Partnership Act 25
limited partnerships 25
liquidity ratios 60–2
loan capital 44
London gazette 131

Macmillan's stock exchange year-book 139
Macmillan's unquoted companies 138
Market direction reports 155
market research 152–4
Market research Europe 157
Market research Great Britain 157

marketing 147–62
    bibliographies 158–9
    databases 157–8
    periodicals 156–7
    reports 154–6, 158–9
    web sites 161
Marketing in Europe 156
marketing information sources 147–62
Marketing surveys index 159
markets
    alternative investment 73
    British Government Securities 73
    definitions 148–50
    deregulation 75
    factors affecting 150–2
    financial 71–8
    trading 74–7
    web sites 84
Marketsearch 159
mergers 20–2, 29
Mintel international 156–7
Monopolies and Mergers Commissions (MMC) 20–2
Monthly digest of statistics 12
MTI countryfiles 204
multinational companies 164

National readership survey 195
Nielson retail index 204

OECD statistics 184
off balance sheet finance 59
Office for National Statistics (ONS) 6, 9, 20, 178
Office of Population Census and Surveys (OPCS) 178
Online company information 128
online information sources 113–18
    markets 116–7
Overseas Trade Service 169–70
    statistics 181

ownership 29

Partnership Act 25
partnerships 25
Patent Office 219, 227, 235–6
    publications 223–5
patents 211–32
    application process 216–21
    difficulties of patents system
        214–16
    definition of 212–14
    specification 219–21
    technical information 221–2
Patents Act 212
Patents Information Network 221
    European 226–7
    information sources 227–30
    recent developments 230–1
    searching British patents 222
    web sites 232
    world 227
Patents information news 221
performance ratios 62–3
*Price Waterhouse corporate regis-
    ter* 139
PRODCOM 6, 180
product life-cycle 90
profit-and-loss account 47, 48–51

*Quarterly summary of brands and
    advertising* 194

ratios 61–4
    gearing 63–4
    liquidity 60–2
    performance 62–3
Regional trends 10
Répertoire alphabétique 239
Reports index 159
reserves 43
Retail business 156
Retail directory of the UK 202
Retail monitor international 203

Retail trade international 203–4
retailing 199–204
    information sources 202–4
rights issues 42

scrip issues 43
secondary information sources
    107–11
*Sector classification for the nation-
    al accounts* 9
service life-cycle 90
share capital 40
shareholders 26, 40–4
shares 40–4, 70–1
sole traders 24
sources of information 106–18
    advertising 189–97
    company 125–46
    distribution 197–205
    electronic 110–11
    evaluation criteria 117–8
    international trade 162–76
    investments and markets 78–82
    online 113–17
    patents 227–30
    statistical 177–88
    web sites 120
Soviet bloc 163
Special Libraries Association
    112
Standard industrial classification
    (SIC) 4–7
standards 243–50
    BS EN ISO 9000 243, 247
    codes of practice 243
    European 249–50
    harmonization 250
    international 250
    national 245–9
    reasons for 244–5
    scientific measurement 243–4
    United Kingdom 245–8
    web sites 253

statistical information sources
177–88
British official 177–82
international trade 183
unofficial 182–3
overseas trade 181–2
problems 184
web sites 188
Statistical Office of the European
Communities (Eurostat) 4
*Statistics and market research
bulletin* 159
Statutory Instruments 251–2
Stock exchange, London 47, 71–8
stock market crash 45, 75
stock market indices 77
Strategic management overviews
158
Strategy 2000 reports 158

takeovers 20–2, 29
Target group index 195–6
Technical Help for Exporters
(THE) 170
Tenders electronic daily 168
tertiary information sources
107–11
Times 1000 11, 129, 139
Top markets 155
Trade Mark Act 233, 235
Trade Mark Registry 235, 237,
241
trade marks 233–42
chemical synonyms 240
European 237
information sources 237–40
registration 235–7
websites 242

trade tariffs 150
Tracking Advertising and Brand
Strength Ltd (TABS) 196
Trading Standards 251

UK business finance directory 39
UK Online User Group
(UKOLUG) 112
United Kingdom national accounts
9
United Nations statistics 183
World Intellectual Property
Organisation 227
unlimited companies 28

VAT 7, 24

web sites
business information 115, 120
companies 38
company information 145–6
exporting 176
investments and markets 84
marketing 161
patents 232
retailing 207–8
standards 253
statistics 188
trade marks 242
US Census Bureau 23
Who's who in the city 140
Willings press guide 197
winding up 46
World databases in company information 128
World Intellectual Property
Organisation 227
World Trade Organisation 164–5